YOUR GARDEN
WEEK BY WEEK

A. G. L. Hellyer, a gardening writer and plantsman of the very first rank, is particularly well qualified to advise on the practical side of the gardener's work. His life-long experience of gardening and his close contact with amateur gardeners have given him a special awareness of their problems and interests.

This book tells the reader just what to do in the garden during each week of the year. Every operation is described in detail so that the volume as a whole has become a manual of garden craft as well as a calendar of seasonal operations. Food crops are considered with as much care as ornamental plants, and the management of greenhouses, frames and cloches receives due attention. Successful planning of the garden is made easy by unusually comprehensive lists of flowers, vegetables and fruit in season from January to December. The arrangement of the matter as a whole and the comprehensive index make it easy for the reader to find any information required without delay or fuss. This is of vital importance in a book that is intended not merely to be read once but to be referred to time and again, year after year. There are many line drawings to supplement the text.

YOUR GARDEN
WEEK *by* WEEK

Arthur Hellyer

CHANCELLOR
PRESS

First published in 1936 by W.H. & L. Collingridge Ltd.
4th edition published in 1977 by The Hamlyn Publishing Group Limited
part of Reed International Books

This 1992 edition published by
Chancellor Press
Michelin House
81 Fulham Road
London SW3 6RB

ISBN 1 85152 159 3

Printed in Great Britain by Collins, Glasgow

Line drawing by Patricia Capon

Contents

Introduction

In this book I have set out to provide something more than a mere calendar of operations. Week by week I have tried to show not only *what must be done* but also *the best way in which to do it*. The volume is intended primarily for beginners, and so I have not included hot-house plants and orchids, nor the more uncommon vegetables usually grown only by connoisseurs.

The plan of the book demands a few words of explanation. It is divided into twelve monthly sections each of which is further split into five sub-sections under the headings General Work, First Week, Second Week, Third Week and Fourth Week. The first of these sub-sections contains all those tasks which cannot be referred to any particular week but must be spread more or less continuously throughout the month. In the other four sections the remaining work is more precisely allocated. The expert may feel that this is too arbitrary a scheme, contending that most garden tasks can be done over a longer period than I have indicated, but I would remind such that the book is intended for beginners and that these invariably desire precise guidance. As they gain in experience they will learn just what liberties they can take, but at first they will be more likely to get good results by following rather rigidly a definite calendar of operations than by trying to sort out a mass of vague information. The formalized scheme of four weeks per month will, I hope, simplify and not complicate the application of the information to each and every year. The odd days in the month must be tacked on at the end, or the beginning of the next as common sense suggests.

The calendar is based mainly upon experience around London and may need a little adaptation for certain parts of the country. Differences, however, are likely to be most apparent in late winter and early spring and are of little account at other seasons. From February to April the extreme south-west may be anything from a fortnight to a month ahead, while very cold north-eastern districts may be almost as much behind London and the Midlands, but, of course, these big differences are only applicable to outdoor work.

The lists of flowers, vegetables and fruits in season are intended for reference when planning the garden in all its branches. They have been made as complete as possible and I make no apology for the strings of botanical names which they contain, for these provide the beginner with the only certain means of turning up further information and of explaining to the nurseryman exactly what he needs.

There are certain tasks which are 'in season' from January to December, and to avoid monotony and save space I have not repeated them month by month. Here is a list of them:

Planting from Containers. The planting dates given in this book are, unless otherwise stated, for plants lifted from beds of soil. Nowadays many nurserymen grow most or all their plants in containers. Provided the plants are sufficiently well established in these for their roots to have bound the soil together, but have not been growing so long in the containers that they have rooted through into the gravel below, they can be planted at any time when the soil is in reasonable working condition. Broadly speaking this means that it must not be baked hard, nor be frozen, nor be waterlogged. The essential thing with container planting is that it must be possible to remove the container, or peel it off if it is thin polythene, without disturbing or damaging the roots. Provided the plants are then put in firmly, are well watered in if the soil is at all dry, and are securely staked if they are big enough to run the risk of being rocked by wind, they should scarcely suffer any check and should grow away steadily.

Dutch Hoeing. This can be done whenever the surface of the soil is dry enough not to stick to the blade of the hoe. Its object is twofold: first to destroy weeds, and second to break up the surface soil and so prevent loss of water by evaporation. Always keep the blade of the hoe sharp, and work it backwards and forwards just beneath the surface so that weeds are severed from their roots, not pulled up and left lying on the surface to grow again.

Weed and Moss Killing. Another method of killing weeds is by means of plant poisons, which are known as herbicides, but it must be remembered that few of these are very selective in action, and so it is not safe to apply many of them to ground in which garden plants are growing. Simazine is one of the best herbicides, in that when watered on to the soil it will stay exactly where it has been applied, and will not 'creep' sideways. Weedkilling may be slow but it will clear the ground completely and keep it clean for at least twelve months.

Another herbicide called paraquat is useful in the garden as a kind of chemical substitute for hoeing since it kills almost every plant if it reaches their leaves in sufficient quantity. It has little or no effect on hard woody stems and is actually inactivated by contact with the soil. The method of application is to use a watering can with a short (about 8 cm, 3 in) dribble bar, taking great care not to splash the fluid about accidentally. The fluid will be delivered fairly slowly and you can move between the garden plants with the dribble bar about 2·5 cm (1 in) above the weed leaves so that they, and nothing else, are wetted.

Another method of killing weeds is by giving excessive doses of certain plant hormones. These are frequently referred to as selective weed killers because they are extremely potent to some plants and almost harmless to others. The ones in most common use, 2,4-D and MCPA, can be purchased in proprietary brands either as a liquid to be further diluted according to manufacturer's instructions and then applied from a watering can fitted with a fine rose, or else in powder form already mixed with a carrier for immediate application. These two selective herbicides and some others such as mecoprop and dicamba are particularly valuable for the treatment of lawns because they affect grass very little indeed but are deadly to most lawn weeds.

Several excellent proprietary preparations are made for killing moss on lawns, and these can be used at any season, so long as manufacturer's instructions regarding strength are not exceeded. Raking vigorously with a spring-toothed grass rake will remove a lot of the moss, but you must not overlook the possibility that the cause of the growth is poverty of the soil or bad drainage – two conditions that must be rectified if you wish to effect a permanent cure.

Lawn Mowing and Rolling. There is a widespread but mistaken notion that the lawn mower and roller should be put away for the winter. Really good lawns cannot be produced in this way, for though it is true that winter mowing will be infrequent and that the roller must never be used on waterlogged soil, it is equally certain that complete neglect from October to April will result in coarse grasses ousting those of a finer nature. I have referred to this in the notes for April, General Work.

Soil Mixtures. John Innes seed and potting composts are referred to frequently in the text. These are standard mixes of soil, peat, sand and fertilizers perfected at the John Innes Horticultural Institution and widely used by both commercial and private gardeners. There is no patent on the mixes and beyond publishing the correct formulae the John Innes Horticultural Institution takes no responsibility for their preparation and sale. Many of the commercial seed and potting composts marketed as 'John Innes' do not conform accurately to the John Innes formulae, though this does not necessarily mean that they are inferior in performance as there is room for wide divergence in composts for use in garden and greenhouse.

One difficulty with all composts embodying soil (usually described as loam, which may be defined as a mixture of clay, sand and humus) is that this cannot be precisely defined and samples of loam differ widely in their composition. In an effort to avoid such inconsistencies many gardeners, particularly in America, use mixtures based solely on peat and fertilizers often with the addition of sand. These, when properly made and used, are excellent for seed germination, rearing seedlings and growing on young plants. They tend to break down in texture and lose their fertility more rapidly than soil-based composts and so are often less satisfactory for older or more permanently grown plants.

The standard John Innes seed compost, usually described as J.I.S., is composed of 2 parts by bulk medium loam, 1 part granulated peat and 1 part coarse sand. To each litre of this mixture is added 1·2 g of superphosphate of lime and 0·6 g of either ground limestone or chalk. (In imperial measure, 1½ oz of superphosphate of lime and ¾ oz of ground limestone or chalk are added to each bushel of the soil mix.)

John Innes standard potting compost, usually referred to as J.I.P.1, is composed of 7 parts by bulk medium loam, 3 parts granulated peat and 2 parts coarse sand. To each litre of this

INTRODUCTION

mixture is added 0·6 g of either ground limestone or chalk and 3 g of John Innes base fertilizer. The latter can be purchased ready for use and the ingredients, by weight, are 2 parts hoof and horn meal, 2 parts superphosphate of lime and one part sulphate of potash. John Innes potting compost No. 2, usually called J.I.P.2, has the same amount of loam, peat and sand but 1·2 g per litre of ground chalk or limestone and 6 g per litre of John Innes base fertilizer, while J.I.P.3 has 1·8 g of ground limestone or chalk and 9 g of base fertilizer. (In imperial measure 4 oz of John Innes base fertilizer and ¾ oz of ground chalk are added to J.I.P.1, and double and treble this amount for J.I.P.2 and J.I.P.3 respectively.)

It is recommended that the loam used in all John Innes composts should be steam sterilized. When the composts are made at home this is usually impracticable but provided good clean loam or garden soil is used good results are generally obtained.

Peat composts can be purchased ready for use and manufacturers never divulge the precise formulae they use. One formula that has been devised at the University of California and gives good results with a wide range of plants is prepared with equal parts by bulk of medium grade sphagnum peat and fine sand (particle size 0·05 to 0·5 mm). To each 20 litres of this mixture is added 3·5 g of nitrate of potash, 3·5 g of sulphate of potash, 35 g of superphosphate, 90 g of finely powdered magnesium limestone and 35 g of chalk or limestone.

One difference when using peat-based composts is that they are not firmed anything like so much as soil composts. Usually it is sufficient to give the container several sharp raps on a wooden bench to settle the compost around the roots. At most, fingers are used to press the compost in lightly. A good watering completes the operation.

Irrigation. Plants that are in growth require water and if there is insufficient of this they will grow at a reduced rate, or stop growing altogether; they may even die. It is impossible to say

11

when water will be required outdoors as this will depend on the weather, the soil (some dry out much more rapidly than others) and the plants being grown. However, in most parts of the British Isles it is probable that at some time from May to September extra water will give beneficial results since natural rainfall will be inadequate to maintain growth at full capacity.

Water outdoors can be applied in many ways from the simple watering can to sophisticated automatic irrigation installations. The ideal is to apply water slowly so that it has time to soak in and does not run uselessly off the surface, or spoil the texture of the soil, or knock down soft-stemmed plants. Sprinklers that give a rain-like shower and apply 1 cm ($\frac{1}{2}$ in) water per hour are ideal.

Under glass plants are entirely dependant on the gardener for their water supply and much of the art of growing greenhouse plants well is to know when to water and how much to apply. The ideal to aim for is to keep the soil moist right through but never allow it to become waterlogged.

Numerous automatic watering systems are available, some of which convey an individual supply of water by fine bore plastic pipes to each plant. Less elaborate, and quite satisfactory for most pot plants is the capillary bench. This is a bed, an inch or so deep, of sand or pea gravel or a mixture of both which is kept constantly moist by various systems of water supply. Plants, preferably in plastic pots, are stood on this moist bed and draw water from it through the drainage holes. If clay pots are used it will be necessary to put a wick of glass wool or some other absorbent material through the drainage hole to draw the water up as these pots are usually too thick to allow soil and sand to come into contact and this is essential if the capillary action, which takes the water upwards, is to operate.

BHC. This useful insecticide has recently had its name changed and is now known as HCH. It is referred to as HCH in the text.

January

GENERAL WORK

Dig All Available Ground. When the ground is frozen so hard that it cannot be dug it is an ideal time for wheeling out manure and placing it about in handy heaps for spreading and digging in as soon as conditions improve. It is not wise to dig soil immediately after a thaw nor during or immediately after a heavy fall of snow, for it is then too wet on the surface to break up properly. The clods will lie in the bottom of the trenches and gradually harden into brickbats, especially if the ground is of a clayey nature. But whenever the soil is soft enough to be dug, and yet not so wet that it sticks to the spade badly, digging can proceed – and it is an axiom of gardening that the early digger gets the crops.

Prick over Bulb Beds. During the month tulips, daffodils and hyacinths will appear through the soil. As soon as the green

13

sprouts can be seen clearly, go over the beds carefully with a small border fork, pricking up the soil between the bulbs, but only to a depth of about an inch. This will improve aeration and kill moss, green scummy growth and weeds. At the same time give the soil a dusting of some good and properly blended chemical fertilizer. If you wish to make your own mixture, do so with seven parts of superphosphate of lime, five parts of sulphate of ammonia, two parts of either sulphate or muriate of potash and one part of bonemeal (all parts by weight). Use this at 110 g per square metre (4 oz per square yard). Of course, you must choose a fine day for this work and one when the soil is neither very wet nor frozen.

Prune Roses. Continue to prune bush and standard roses (see November, General Work).

Take Chrysanthemum and Carnation Cuttings. A task which can be carried on as opportunity permits throughout January is that of taking late-flowering chrysanthemum cuttings. It is rather early yet to start on the outdoor flowering chrysanthemums, though even with these I would not hesitate to have a few cuttings, if there are any good ones showing, of any variety that is known to be shy in producing them. Later on, when the proper time arrives, there may be no suitable shoots to be had – and a cutting in the pot is certainly worth two in the bush.

Nevertheless in the main it is the late-flowering kinds that are to be propagated in January and particularly the incurves and exhibition Japanese kinds. Full particulars are given in the notes for December, Third Week.

You should also propagate perpetual-flowering carnations as opportunity occurs. This task I have described in detail in the General Work notes for December.

Pot Rooted Carnation and Chrysanthemum Cuttings. During the month keep a careful watch on carnation cuttings taken during December, and if these are in pure sand get them potted up singly in 5-cm (2-in) pots as soon as they are well rooted

14

(which means that roots 1 cm ($\frac{1}{2}$ in) long have been formed). It is quite easy to tell when a cutting is rooted, because it will start to grow at once. Until then it will remain quite at a standstill. There is not the same urgency with carnation cuttings that are in soil and sand, nor with chrysanthemum cuttings, which are almost always rooted in soil and sand, but even with these it is a good plan to get them singly into pots before the roots get tangled together. Use 8-cm (3-in) pots for the chrysanthemums, for these grow more rapidly. Propagating cases must be ventilated freely as soon as cuttings start to grow. Use a compost such as John Innes potting compost No. 1 or a soilless equivalent for both carnations and chrysanthemums at this early stage. Shade the plants from direct sunlight for a few days and then start to harden them off by placing on a shelf near the glass and ventilating more freely.

General Greenhouse Management. The well-managed greenhouse should be full of plants during January, many of them in flower and all wanting careful watering. Greenhouse calceolarias are particularly susceptible to bad watering and may collapse quite suddenly if given too much; yet dryness is equally bad. Winter-flowering primulas, greenhouse calceolarias and some other plants are apt to suffer severely if water is allowed to collect at the base of the leaves and in the heart of the plant. Do not forget the golden rule of all watering – namely, that when water is given it must be supplied in sufficient quantity to moisten the soil in pot or box right through. There is nothing worse than keeping the surface wet and letting the lower soil remain dry.

Ventilation is also bound to be a tricky matter, especially in a small house or one that is not too well heated. The ideal is a constant circulation of air without draughts or sudden variations of temperature. Only the top ventilators will be needed during January, and even these must be closed at night. Open them a little during the day provided it is not freezing or foggy, but, if there is any choice in the matter, be sure to open them on the side away from the wind – and be equally sure to get them closed well before the sun goes down, for a little sun heat trapped late in the afternoon will go a long way towards keeping up the night temperature. Watch carefully for decaying leaves – a sure sign of a stuffy atmosphere (see November, General Work).

The ideal average temperature to be aimed at for the common winter-flowering plants such as primulas, cinerarias, calceolarias and cyclamen is 13 to 16°C (55 to 60°F) by day and 7 to 10°C (45 to 50°F) at night. If winter-flowering begonias are grown, it will be all to the good to have 2 or 3°C more, but most plants are able to stand quite a wide variation in temperature. A good deal of nonsense is talked upon this subject, and one is sometimes left with the impression that there are many plants which cannot be grown in anything but a thermostatically controlled atmosphere. A thermostat is certainly an immense help, but it is by no means a necessity. The great thing to avoid is any very sudden fluctuations, especially in the early morning or evening.

Bring Bulbs into the Greenhouse. Successive small batches of tulips, narcissi of all types, including trumpet daffodils, hyacinths and *Iris tingitana*, should be brought into the greenhouse from plunge bed or frame to maintain a continuity of flowers later on (see November, First Week).

Force Seakale and Rhubarb. You should also bring in at least two batches of seakale and rhubarb to force in heat if you wish to maintain an unbroken succession. These, of course, are forced in complete darkness (see November, Second Week).

Lift and Blanch Chicory. Roots can be lifted as required from the open ground and blanched in a warm place (see November, General Work).

Pot and Plant Lilies. There is no doubt that early autumn is the best time to pot and plant most lilies, but it is sometimes impossible to get certain varieties then, especially if they have to be imported from America or Japan. Such should be dealt with as soon as they are available, and this often adds quite appreciably to the extent of one's January tasks. Bulbs that have travelled a long distance may have become rather soft or shrivelled and it is wise to plump them up before potting or planting them. This is done by placing them in seed trays, partly surrounding them with moist moss peat, and keeping this damp by daily spraying with water. As soon as the bulbs get plump and firm, plant or pot without further delay.

Ventilate Violets and other Plants in Frames. Violets and other hardy or nearly hardy plants in frames, such as violas, pansies, anemones, penstemons, bedding calceolarias, antirrhinums from late summer seeds and cuttings, sweet peas, cauliflowers and bulbs, and alpines in pots, etc., must be ventilated just as freely as the weather permits. On all mild, sunny days remove the lights altogether for a few hours. If there is a cold wind blowing, tilt the lights with blocks of wood placed on the leeward side. At night the frames should be closed, and if the weather is very cold

Taking Root Cuttings. Plants such as anchusa and oriental poppies can be readily propagated by root cuttings at this time of year. Cut the roots into 2·5- to 5-cm (1- to 2-in) lengths and insert them, right way up, in boxes or pots of a sandy compost

it is advisable to throw a few sacks over them into the bargain. An occasional stirring of the soil between the plants with a pointed stick does a lot of good.

Take Root Cuttings. Many plants can be raised more readily from root cuttings taken during January than in any other way. Well-known examples are oriental poppies, perennial statices, anchusas, perennial verbascums, *Romneya coulteri*, *Phlox decussata* and gaillardias. The roots are cut up into pieces about 2·5 cm to 5 cm (1 to 2 in) in length. In all except the last three these cuttings are pushed vertically, right end up, into a sandy compost in well-drained pots or boxes. The tops of the cuttings should be just level with the soil. Romneya, phlox and gaillardia cuttings are simply strewn thinly over the surface of the soil and covered with a further 0·5 cm ($\frac{1}{4}$ in) of compost. Place in a frame or greenhouse (slightly heated or unheated) and water moderately. Shoots will form slowly, and in late spring, after proper hardening off, the small plants can be established outdoors.

Protect Cauliflowers. The curds of cauliflowers will require protection as they start to form (see November, General Work).

Sow Small Salads under Glass. Various small salads may be sown during the month in a slightly heated greenhouse or a frame with soil-warming cables. Mustard and cress can be grown very readily in this manner or in shallow boxes in a warm greenhouse. Sow the mustard every week and the cress about once a fortnight, as it lasts longer. A couple of small sowings of radishes and lettuces made at fortnightly intervals under similar conditions in a frame or in deeper boxes or beds in the greenhouse will provide useful saladings later on.

Spray Fruit Trees with Tar Oil. When the weather is favourable spray all outdoor fruit trees and bushes with tar oil wash. The object of this is to kill any insect eggs which may be left in the crevices of the bark and to clean the trees of green, scummy growth and pests such as scale insects. It is at this season of the year that really powerful insecticides can be used without fear of damaging the trees, and the gardener who neglects this opportunity must not be surprised if his trees in the summer are more freely attacked by pests and diseases than those of his more alert neighbour.

Tar oil washes are sold under many different trade names and can be purchased from any dealer in horticultural sundries. They are prepared by diluting with water, the usual strength being six parts of the neat tar oil to a hundred parts of water, for instance 6 litres in 100 litres (or 6 pints in 100 pints, 12½ gallons). Instructions are always given on the tin, and you should consult these in case the purchased brand is not of standard strength.

The important thing in tar oil spraying is to employ a machine that will give a fine but driving spray capable of penetrating well down into the crevices of the bark. A powerful coarse spray is efficient but wasteful. It is also wasteful to attempt to spray trees when the weather is windy, and it is not effective to spray while it is freezing; so choose a calm and comparatively mild day for the work, and not one when it is raining, or the dilution will be upset.

Complete Fruit Tree Pruning. Fruit tree pruning should really be done in November and December but, if it is delayed then for one reason or another, it can be completed in January – the sooner the better. Work on the peaches, nectarines and apricots first, then do the plums, gooseberries and red and white currants, and leave the pears and apples till the last. Very soon sap will be on the move once more and the wise gardener will always get his trees pruned while they are quite dormant.

Collect Scions for Grafting. This is a good time to collect suitable shoots for grafting if you intend to do any later on. Ordinary prunings do quite well. Select strong, well-ripened shoots formed the previous summer. Label them carefully and then heel them in in a trench about 10 cm (4 in) deep prepared in a cool, shady place, preferably under a north wall or fence.

The object is to keep them dormant until grafting time (see March, Fourth Week). Old trees that are to be reworked should also be headed back now; that is the main branches should be sawn off about a couple of feet from the trunk. Apples and pears stand this treatment best. Plums, cherries and other stone fruits resent the hard cutting back.

Fruit Trees and Vines under Glass. Glasshouses in which vines or fruit trees are grown should still be ventilated as freely as possible (see November, General Work), except early houses (see later). No heat must be used, and ventilators should be opened widely whenever it is not actually freezing hard. Light frost will do no harm, but rather good, preparing the trees for very rapid growth when the house is closed later on.

FIRST WEEK

Order Seeds and Seed Potatoes. The very first task for January should be to compile a complete list of all seeds that will be required during the following two or three months, and to get these ordered without delay. It is true that a good many of the seeds cannot be sown before March or even April, but later on seedsmen become inundated with orders and even with the best of organizations there may be delay in execution. There is no sense in risking that, because the seeds can be kept quite as well at home as in the seedsmen's store, and they will then be at hand the very moment that the most favourable opportunity arrives. Order seed potatoes at the same time, and as soon as they arrive set them up in shallow trays, eyed ends uppermost, and place them in a light but frost-proof room, shed or greenhouse to form sprouts. This is particularly important with early varieties, but is worth doing with all kinds.

Bring Shrubs and Roses in Pots into Greenhouse. The first week in January is a good time to bring into the greenhouse the first batch of bush roses well established in pots. Give them a light, airy place preferably on the staging, not too far from the glass. Water the soil moderately and spray with slightly warm water every morning. Maintain a temperature of about 13 to 16°C (55 to 60°F). All the roses must be pruned, previous year's growth being shortened to within an inch or so of the older wood. It is also a good plan to bring in a few deutzias, Indian azaleas, lilacs and viburnums to provide a succession to earlier batches (see November, First Week). A start may also be made with hydrangeas and astilbes, both of which require rather liberal watering once they have started into growth.

Prune Climbers in the Greenhouse. Several of the permanent climbers commonly grown in greenhouses should be pruned now. These include *Plumbago capensis* and the passion flower. The plumbago is pruned by cutting each of last year's growths back to 23 cm (9 in) or thereabouts. This applies to fully developed specimens. With young plants which have not yet filled their space, some shoots may be left unpruned. The passion flower is pruned by cutting out weak shoots altogether and reducing the remainder of the previous year's growths to about two buds each.

Sow Onions for Exhibition. If you aspire to great successes on the vegetable show bench later in the year, you must make a sowing of exhibition onions in a heated greenhouse. It is no use to sow onion seed as yet outdoors or in an unheated frame. But if sown thinly in John Innes seed compost in well-drained seed trays and placed in a greenhouse with an average temperature of from 13 to 16°C (55 to 60°F) the seed will soon germinate and provide sturdy seedlings for transferring to the open ground in the spring. The best method is to sow the seeds singly 2·5 cm (1 in) apart; then the seedlings need not be pricked off.

Sow Shorthorn Carrots in a Frame. If a frame with soil-warming cables is available, you can make a first sowing of shorthorn carrots. Sow these directly in the soil in the frame and not in boxes. The rows should be about 15 cm (6 in) apart. If the seedlings are thinned to a couple of inches apart later on, there will be a nice supply of tender young roots in the early spring.

Start Early Peaches, Nectarines and Apricots. With the aid of a heated glasshouse it is possible to have ripe peaches, nectarines and apricots at any time during the summer. If you wish to eat ripe fruits in June, this is the time to start the trees into growth. Close doors and ventilators and maintain an average temperature of 8°C (45°F) at night, rising to 13°C (55°F) by day. Spray the trees every morning with slightly warm water, and damp the floor of the house to maintain the moisture in the atmosphere.

Start Early Vines into Growth. You may also start early vines such as Black Hamburgh, Foster's Seedling and Buckland's Sweetwater into growth, provided you have a heating apparatus installed in the vinery adequate to maintain a temperature of 13°C (55°F) at night during February and March. A temperature rising to 16°C (60°F) by day, will do for the present. The higher temperature is only necessary when growth actually starts. Spray the vines several times daily to keep the atmosphere moist, and give a little top ventilation by day whenever outside conditions permit this without lowering the temperature or causing cold draughts. Soak the border thoroughly with clear water and fill any evaporating trays over the pipes. Spread a 5-cm (2-in) thick layer of well-rotted manure or compost all over the border to feed the roots.

Prune Late Vines. Late-fruiting vines such as Alicante and Gros Colmar should be pruned. Details of this are the same as for the pruning of early vines (see November, Fourth Week).

SECOND WEEK

Sow Exhibition Sweet Peas. This is the time for the exhibition grower to sow sweet peas in pots if this was not done in a frame in September. A warm greenhouse will be needed for germination, but a great amount of heat is not desirable; 10 to 13°C

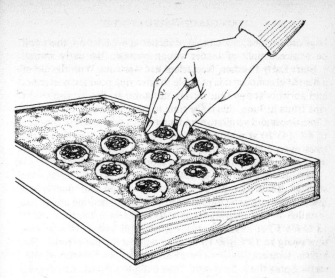

Starting Begonia and Gloxinia Tubers. These are now started into growth by placing them in trays of moist peat – just cover the tubers

(50 to 55°F) will be ample. Sow four or five seeds in each 8-cm (3-in) pot of John Innes seed compost or an equivalent mixture.

Start Begonia and Gloxinia Tubers. If you own a well-heated greenhouse, you may start tuberous-rooted begonias and gloxinias into growth. The begonias can be managed quite satisfactorily in a temperature of 13°C (55°F), but a little more is advisable for the gloxinias. If the two have to be grown in the same house, the extra warmth will not do the begonias any harm. Prepare some rather deep seed trays with good drainage in the bottom and then a layer of moss peat. Set the tubers almost shoulder to shoulder in this and just cover them with more peat. Be careful to moisten the peat thoroughly some while before it is actually required. When peat is quite dry it is very difficult to make it take up water, which runs off the granules instead of soaking into them, but once they have become moistened they go on soaking up water like a sponge. If the peat is well wetted a few days before the begonia and gloxinia tubers are to be boxed, no further watering will be needed at first, but do not let it dry out. Keep it just nicely moist until growth appears, and then give more water.

Sow Tomatoes for an Early Crop. Sow tomatoes now if you want a crop in June, but do not forget that this means plants 1 to 1·25 m (3 to 4 ft) high by the beginning of May. They will take some accommodation, and the June crop may not be worth it if it means ruining your bedding plants. If you sow now, do so very thinly in well-drained seed boxes, using John Innes seed compost. Germinate in a temperature of 16 to 18°C (60 to 65°F). Tomatoes love warmth, and will get hard and blue in the cold, obstinately refusing to grow and becoming more miserable every week. Germination will be more rapid if each box is covered with a sheet of glass and brown paper. Keep the soil well moistened, but not sodden.

THIRD WEEK

Sow Begonias, Gloxinias and other Plants. Sowings should be made now in the warm greenhouse of begonia, gloxinia, streptocarpus, canna, verbena, antirrhinium and scarlet salvia. With the exception of cannas, all can be managed in an average temperature of 18°C (65°F). The antirrhinums will even do with rather less, but for preference the gloxinias should have a little more, for they will then germinate more rapidly and grow more sturdily. Cannas need 24°C (75°F), and even then germinate very irregularly. Do not forget that plants from these early sowings will be quite big by May, the time when many plants accommodated in the greenhouse during the winter can be put out in the open once more. If your greenhouse is already rather full and you plan to sow half-hardy annuals later on (see February, Third Week) and take a lot of cuttings, it may be wise to omit these first sowings and be satisfied with smaller plants. But if space is not pinched you can take advantage of an early start. It will be reflected in the abundance and quality of the flowers.

Plant Potatoes in Frames and Pots. Potatoes in frames and pots are not difficult to grow, but they do take up a good deal of valuable space. However, if you want them, this is the time to start, with one well-sprouted tuber in each 20-cm (8-in) pot of John Innes potting compost No. 2 or with tubers planted 20 cm (8 in) apart in rows 30 cm (1 ft) apart directly in a bed of good soil with which some manure or garden compost and a sprinkling of general fertilizer have been mixed.

Mulch Asparagus Beds. If possible, get some well-rotted manure (farmyard manure is best, though stable manure will serve), break it up well, and spread it a couple of inches thick over the asparagus beds. This will have a marked effect upon the quality of the shoots later on, and the only condition under which this is inadvisable occurs when the soil is of a heavy, cold nature and is already inclined to be waterlogged. In these circumstances a light dressing of hop manure will be more suitable.

Protect Fruit Trees from Birds. From now onwards birds are very liable to attack the buds of fruit trees, particularly pears, plums and gooseberries. The best protection for small bush fruits is obviously a properly constructed fruit cage covering the whole plantation. Pear and plum trees can be protected by passing black thread from twig to twig, but it is a laborious and troublesome proceeding. A good protection against birds is Scaraweb, which consists of strands of nylon fibre stretched over bushes or trees. This disintegrates gradually within about six to eight weeks. Various other chemical deterrents are available and these should be used in accordance with the manufacturers' instructions.

FOURTH WEEK

Start Early Hippeastrums. You can start hippeastrums by bringing the bulbs in the pots in which they flowered the previous year into a temperature of 16°C (60°F) or thereabouts and giving them a gradually increasing quantity of water. If any of the bulbs that have been resting since October (see October, General Work) show signs of starting, select these in preference to those that are still dormant.

Pot on Greenhouse Calceolarias. It is time to give greenhouse calceolarias their final move into the pots in which they will flower. These should be 18 to 20 cm (7 to 8 in) in diameter. Use John Innes potting compost No. 1. Stand the plants in a light, airy place on the staging, water very carefully, and maintain an average temperature of 13°C (55°F).

Force Rhubarb and Seakale Out of Doors. This is a good time to start forcing rhubarb outdoors. There is not much point in starting earlier, as it will be well-nigh impossible to generate sufficient heat to start any growth. The essentials for successful forcing are complete darkness and a mild, even temperature. First of all, the roots must be covered with something: either special earthenware forcing pots, these are not unlike chimney pots with a lid on the top, but are not easy to obtain nowadays, or with old barrels, large boxes or plastic drums or buckets. It is convenient, but not essential, to have a removable lid on top so that the sticks of rhubarb can be gathered without having to move the whole contraption. Place the cover in position either before or after heaping up dead leaves around the crowns, the more the better so long as the containers are not completely full. The leaves will keep the rhubarb crowns at a nice even temperature and encourage steady and early growth. Never attempt to force newly planted or semi-established crowns. Only really strong roots should be covered, preferably those three or four years old.

Forcing Rhubarb. Work some dry leaves around the crown, cover with a box, then more leaves and sacking to keep the crowns warm and dark

Seakale can also be forced outdoors where it is growing by covering each strong crown with a large plant pot inverted and placing a piece of turf to block up the drainage hole in the bottom of the pot. Complete darkness is essential.

Sow Leeks. This is a good time to make a first sowing of leeks if large stems are required. Sow the seeds singly 5 cm (1 in) apart in well-drained seed boxes, using ordinary John Innes seed compost. Germinate in a greenhouse or frame with an average temperature of 13°C (55°F).

Sow French Beans for Forcing. You can obtain a May crop of french beans by sowing now – five or six in each 20-cm (8-in) pot filled to within a couple of inches of the rim with John Innes potting compost No. 1 or an equivalent mixture. Cover with a further inch of soil, water freely, and place in the greenhouse in a temperature of from 16 to 21°C (60 to 70°F).

FLOWERS, VEGETABLES AND FRUITS
IN SEASON DURING JANUARY

Herbaceous Plants: *Adonis amurensis, Helleborus abchasicus* vars., *H. corsicus, H. foetidus, H. maximus, H. niger, H. orientalis* vars., *Iris unguicularis, Petasites fragrans, Pulmonaria angustifolia, P. rubra, P. saccharata.*

Hardy Bulbs, Corms and Tubers: *Colchicum decaisnei, Crocus aureus, C. imperati, C. laevigatus, C. tomasinianus, Cyclamen coum, Eranthis cilicica, E. hyemalis, E. tubergeniana, Galanthus byzantinus, G. caucasicus, G. nivalis* and vars., *G. plicatus, Iris histrio, I. histrioides, I. reticulata* and vars.

Rock Plants: *Primula edgeworthii, Saxifraga kellereri.*

Evergreen Shrubs: *Azara integrifolia, A. microphylla, Camellia sasanqua* vars., *Daphne bholua, D. laureola, D. odora, Erica carnea* and vars., *E. darleyensis, E. lusitanica, Garrya elliptica, Mahonia acanthifolia, M. bealei, M. japonica, M. lomariifolia, M. media, Sarcococca confusa, S. hookeriana, S. humilis, S. ruscifolia, Viburnum burkwoodii, V. tinus* and vars.

Deciduous Shrubs: *Chimonanthus fragrans, Corylus avellana* and vars., *Daphne mezereum grandiflora, Hamamelis intermedia, H. japonica, H. mollis, Lonicera fragrantissima, L. purpusii, L. standishii, Osmaronia cerasiformis, Rhododendron mucronulatum, R. nobleanum, Viburnum bodnantense, V. foetens, V. fragrans* (*farreri*).

Deciduous Trees: *Crataegus monogyna biflora, Prunus davidiana, P. subhirtella autumnalis.*

Hardy Climbing Plants: *Clematis cirrhosa, Jasminum nudiflorum.*

Greenhouse Plants: *Acacia dealbata*, arum lilies, azaleas (Indian in var.), *Begonia fuchsioides, B. manicata, B. socotrana*, hybrid begonias of the Optima and Gloire de Lorraine types, *Boronia heterophylla, B. megastigma*, bouvardias, *Browallia speciosa major*, camellias, carnations (perpetual flowering), cinerarias (hybrids), *Coleus thyrsoideus*, *Columnea gloriosa*, cyclamen (Persian), *Daphne indica*, epacris (all), *Erica gracilis*, *E. melanthera*, *Euphorbia fulgens*, freesias, gardenias, hyacinths (Roman and large flowered), *Iris reticulata*, *I. tingitana*, *Jacobinia pauciflora*, *Jasminum gracillimum*, *J. mesnyi*, *Kalanchoe blossfeldiana*, lachenalias, narcissi (Paper White, Soleil d'Or, Christmas Cheer and other early flowering varieties), *Pachystachys lutea*, poinsettias, *Primula kewensis*, *P. malacoides*, *P. obconica*, *P. sinensis* and vars., *Reinwardtia trigyna*, *Schlumbergera buckleyi*, *Sparmannia africana*, tulips (Duc van Thol), veltheimias.

Vegetables in Store. Jerusalem artichokes, beetroot, carrots, onions, parsnips, potatoes, shallots, turnips.

Vegetables in the Garden: Jerusalem artichoke, broccoli (sprouting), Brussels sprouts, cauliflower (winter vars.), celery, coleworts, endive, kale, leeks, parsnips, savoys, spinach (August sown), turnips.

Vegetables under Glass: Chicory, endive, lettuce, mushrooms, mustard and cress, radish, rhubarb, seakale.

Fruits in Store: *Apples:* Adams' Pearmain (D), Allington Pippin (CD), Annie Elizabeth (C), Barnack Beauty (CD), Baumann's Red Winter Reinette (CD), Beauty of Kent (C), Beauty of Stoke (CD), Belle de Boskoop (CD), Bismarck (C), Blenheim Orange (D), Bramley's Seedling (C), Brownlees' Russet (D), Christmas Pearmain (D), Claygate Pearmain (D), Cornish Gillyflower (D), Court Pendu Plat (D), Cox's Orange Pippin (D), Crawley Beauty (C), Crimson Bramley (C), Crimson Cox (D), Cutler Grieve (D), Delicious (D), Edward VII (C), Encore (C), Gascoyne's Scarlet (D), Golden Delicious (D), Howgate Wonder (C), John Standish (D), King of Tompkin's County (D), King's Acre Pippin (D), Lane's Prince Albert (C), Laxton's Pearmain (D), Lord Hindlip (D), Madresfield Court (D), Margil (D), Monarch (C), Newton Wonder (C), Norfolk Royal (D), Orlean's Reinette (D), Reinette du Canada (D),

Ribston Pippin (D), Rosemary Russet (D), Roundway Magnum Bonum (D), Saltcote Pippin (D), St Cecilia (D), Superb (D), Triumph (D), Wagener (D), Warner's King (C), Wellington (C), Winston (D), Wyken Pippin (D). *Grapes:* Alicante, Canon Hall Muscat, Gros Colmar, Lady Downe's Seedling, Muscat of Alexandria and Prince of Wales. *Pears:* Bellissime d'Hiver (C), Beurré Easter (D), Catillac (C), Glou Morceau (D), Joséphine de Malines (D), Uvedale's St Germain (C), Vicar of Winkfield (CD), Winter Nelis (D).

Nuts in Store: Cobnuts, filberts, walnuts.

February

GENERAL WORK

Finish Planting Trees and Shrubs. There is still just time to plant fruit trees, and also deciduous ornamental trees and shrubs, including roses, but the earlier this can be done in February the better, provided soil conditions are good. There is considerable controversy about the pruning of fruit trees transplanted as late as this, some experts urging that it is unwise to give the tree two shocks at once, root disturbance and a curtailment of branches. This group argues that it is better to leave the late-planted trees unpruned until the following November and then, if they have not made much new growth, to cut them hard back into the older wood; in other words, to prune them to just about the point where they would have been cut had the work been done at planting time. My own view is that this is a waste of time, and that in any case the idea that proper pruning is a shock is a fallacy. I would not hesitate to prune late-planted fruit trees immediately before planting. Ornamental shrubs and trees should certainly be cut back fairly drastically to encourage vigorous growth later on. February-planted roses are better left unpruned until the end of March.

Complete Digging and Break Down Soil. The good gardener should have completed all his digging and trenching by this time, but if not, the quicker it is finished the better. Ground that was turned over earlier in the winter and left rough should be broken down to a fine surface some time during February. It is essential to choose a day when the surface is fairly dry; you will do more harm than good if you walk about on beds that are soaking wet. Still, the right day often turns up several times during this month, and may be looked for after a period of steady east winds. Lawn sites that are to be sown or turfed later should also be prepared now.

Prune Roses. Continue to prune bush and standard roses (see November, General Work).

Complete Planting of Lilies. There is still time to plant lilies outdoors and also to transplant established lilies from one part of the garden to another. The latter will be in growth and must be handled in the same way as herbaceous plants – that is to say, they must be lifted carefully and with a good ball of soil, which should be kept around the roots while replanting.

Continue to Pot Rooted Cuttings. Throughout the month you must keep a sharp eye on chrysanthemum and perpetual-flowering carnation cuttings, and pot them singly as soon as they start to grow freely (see January, General Work).

Take Chrysanthemum and Carnation Cuttings. As opportunity occurs during the month continue to take chrysanthemum and perpetual carnation cuttings. It is getting late for exhibition Japanese chrysanthemums in full-size pots, but decorative varieties can still be propagated with advantage, and February is the ideal month to start on the hardy border varieties.

General Greenhouse Management. Plants in flower or coming into flower in the greenhouse are very much the same as those for January, and for general management I refer you to notes in that month (see January, General Work). If there are any bright, warm days, seize the opportunity to give more top ventilation, but beware of cold winds. An occasional thorough airing, so long as it does not involve a drop in temperature or the admission of cold draughts, does the greenhouse a lot of good. Most plants will require rather more water, but begonias of the Optima type should have less.

Seedlings from January sowings of begonias, tomatoes, leeks, onions, etc., should now be appearing. At any rate, it is essential to examine the seed trays and boxes very carefully every day so that covering materials can be removed before seedlings get thin and drawn. Give water if the soil appears to be dry. The best method is to hold each receptacle almost to its rim in a pail of water for a few moments and let the water soak up from below, but if there are a number to be done and this method takes too long, water from an ordinary watering can fitted with a very fine rose. Be sure to go over the surface several times, because the fine spray of water tends to collect on the top and not soak in immediately.

Ventilate Frames According to the Weather. There is little to add to my remarks on this subject in the General Work for January. As the days get a little longer you will be able to ventilate more freely, but run no unnecessary risks with frost.

Continue to Protect Cauliflowers. The curds are still liable to be damaged by frost, and must be protected as they form (see November, General Work).

Sow Small Salads for Succession. To maintain a supply of mustard and cress and radishes, make further small sowings as advised in the notes for January, General Work.

Harden Off Autumn-sown Cauliflowers. Cauliflower seedlings growing in frames from late summer sowings must be gradually

33

hardened off during February in readiness for planting out next month. Take the lights right off during the daytime if the weather is not frosty and the wind is not very cold. Even at night a little ventilation can be given on the leeward side if weather conditions are at all reasonable.

Continue to Force Seakale. Continue to pot and force seakale roots for succession (see November, General Work). There is not much point in bringing in any further supplies of rhubarb, however, as successional supplies will be obtained from the roots covered outdoors (see January, Fourth Week).

Pollinate and Disbud Early Peaches, Nectarines and Apricots. Peaches, nectarines and apricots in heated glasshouses may be in flower during the month, and as there will certainly not be enough insects about to effect pollination it is necessary to do this by hand. The best method is to have a camel-hair brush and scatter the dry pollen from bloom to bloom with this, the most favourable time being towards midday when the sun is shining. While the fruit trees are in bloom it is necessary to discontinue spraying with water and to raise the temperature by about 5°C (10°F) night and day and keep the atmosphere dry by judicious ventilation (see January, First Week). When the fruit is set spray the trees freely again once every morning.

As shoots grow you must, on peaches and nectarines, start the process known as disbudding. The small side shoots that form on the fruiting laterals are gradually pinched off, a few at a time, until only two are left to each lateral, one at its base and the other at its extremity. Then in the winter the old fruiting lateral is cut right out and the young basal shoot is trained in its place. The object of leaving the terminal shoot is simply to encourage the flow of sap through the branch and so help the fruits to swell. This method of disbudding is only fully practised on established trees that have filled their space. Small young trees may be allowed to form new laterals wherever there is room for these to be trained in as branches. Apricots bear on old as well as new wood, and with these only shoots that are awkwardly placed are removed. Other side growths are cut back to four or five well-developed leaves each as soon as they start to get hard and woody at the base.

Pollinate and Train Early Vines. Vines started into growth last month (see January, First Week) will also come into flower during February and will need hand pollination just like the peaches. The young laterals must be pulled down little by little until they lie along the training wires. If more than one lateral forms at each spur, pinch out the growing point of the weaker at the earliest opportunity. The points of the flower-bearing laterals must also be pinched just beyond the second leaf formed after the truss. If any secondary laterals form, pinch these just beyond the first leaf. While the vines are in flower, raise the temperature to 18°C (65°F) at night, rising to about 24°C (75°F) by day. From this stage onwards you should soak the border

Pollinating Peaches. Using a soft camel-hair brush or a rabbit's tail scatter pollen from flower to flower to assist fruit setting

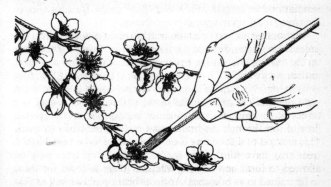

occasionally with very weak liquid manure. Give sufficient to wet the soil to a depth of a couple of feet, and repeat the application as soon as the soil looks at all dry an inch or two below the surface.

FIRST WEEK

Prune Flowering Shrubs and Clematis. Flowering shrubs which should be pruned now include *Hydrangea paniculata*, *Spiraea japonica* (and varieties or hybrids such as Anthony Waterer), *SS. douglasii, menziesii, salicifolia, Holodiscus discolor ariaefolius, Sorbaria aitchisonii* and *SS. arborea, sorbifolia* and *tomentosa, Tamarix pentandra, Hypericum moserianum*, all kinds of willows, unless grown principally for bark effects (see April, First Week), also varieties of *Cornus alba* grown for leaf but not those grown primarily for bark colour. In all these, stems made last year should be cut hard back to within one or two joints of the older wood. With the bigger shrubs you can, if you wish, allow some strong branches to remain at three-quarter length to build up a main framework of growth and so lay the foundation of larger specimens than could be obtained by constant hard pruning.

Pot Annuals for the Greenhouse. If you were able to sow various annuals in September (see September, First Week) for flowering in the greenhouse during the spring, you should get the plants potted singly into 13- to 15-cm (5- to 6-in) pots, according to the growth they have made. Use John Innes potting compost No. 1 or an equivalent mixture. Stand the plants on the staging or a shelf quite close to the glass to encourage sturdy growth. Schizanthus sown in August (see August, Third Week) must also be potted on in the same way. If you want very bushy plants pinch out the tips of the shoots.

Force Roses and Flowering Shrubs. Bring further batches of bush roses, azaleas, deutzias, lilacs, astilbes, etc., well established in pots, into the greenhouse to provide a succession of flowers after those introduced in January (see January, First Week).

Start Achimenes. Place achimenes tubers thinly in shallow boxes half-filled with a light sandy compost and just cover them with the same mixture. Water very moderately and place on the staging in a temperature of about 16°C (60°F). Very soon shoots will appear, and when these are a couple of inches in length the plants should be transferred to pots or pans. Five or six roots can be grown in a pot 13 cm (5 in) in diameter. An alternative method is to grow them in hanging baskets, but in any case the initial starting process is the same. Do not start all the tubers at once. Successional starting will give a longer display.

Sow Broad Beans under Glass. You can make a sowing of broad beans in boxes or pots during this week. Do not scatter the seeds haphazard, but set them out at regular intervals 5 cm (2 in) apart each way, and cover them with about 2 cm (¾ in) of soil. Germinate in a slightly heated greenhouse or even a frame, provided the latter is well covered with sacks or mats on frosty nights. This method of sowing early in boxes gives far more reliable results, at any rate on all but the lightest of soils, than the old-fashioned scheme of sowing out of doors in the autumn.

Sow Lettuces, Culinary Peas and Cauliflowers. If you want a really early outdoor supply of lettuces make a small sowing of a cabbage variety in seed boxes and place in a warm greenhouse to germinate. An average temperature of 13°C (55°F) will be sufficient to ensure this. Seedlings from this indoor sowing will be planted out later, after proper hardening.

It is also an excellent plan to make a sowing of an early culinary pea in boxes and germinate in the same way as the lettuces. These seedlings will also be planted outdoors later. If you happen to live in a very mild part of the country or have an unusually sheltered garden you may even make an outside sowing of peas on a border with a southerly aspect, but you must certainly choose a really hardy variety, such as Foremost or Meteor.

37

Cauliflowers require a long and steady season of growth if they are to be a real success and if you have a warm greenhouse you should certainly make a first sowing now. A temperature of 13 to 16°C (55 to 60°F) will be quite adequate for germination. It is even possible to germinate them satisfactorily in a frame with soil-warming cables. Sow the seeds as thinly as possible, either in deep seed trays or, if in a frame, directly in the soil in shallow drills.

Sow Cucumbers for an Early Crop. Sow a few cucumber seeds for an early crop if you have a well-heated greenhouse. Place the seeds singly in 8-cm (3-in) pots filled with John Innes or a peat seed compost and germinate in a temperature of 24°C (75°F) in a propagator, preferably with bottom heat. It is an excellent plan to half-fill the propagator with peat and plunge the pots to their rims in this. Cucumbers need more warmth than tomatoes in the early stages, as they must be kept in rapid growth.

Plant Jerusalem Artichokes. Plant Jerusalem artichokes at the

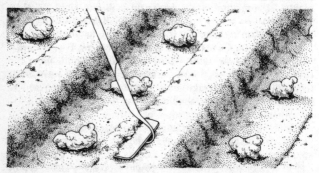

Planting Jerusalem Artichokes. Take out narrow trenches 10 cm (4 in) deep and 75 cm (2½ ft) apart and space the tubers 38 cm (15 in) apart in the rows. This vegetable will grow well even on poor soil

earliest opportunity. These are amongst the hardiest of all vegetables, and as they make a lot of tall, sunflower-like growth they may well be used as a windbreak in exposed gardens. They will grow almost anywhere, and good crops are to be had from soil that would be far too poor to produce potatoes. Simply plant the tubers 38 cm (15 in) apart in rows 75 cm (2½ ft) apart. Cover with 8 cm (3 in) of soil.

Prune Autumn-fruiting Raspberries. September-fruiting raspberries must now be cut right back to within 15 cm (6 in) of the ground. These varieties fruit on the young growth produced after pruning. The variety Lloyd George can also be pruned in this way for autumn fruiting, but is really more profitable as a summer fruiting variety, when it is pruned in August (see August, Second Week).

Continue to Force Seakale and Rhubarb. More roots can be treated as described (see November, Second Week).

Continue to Blanch Chicory. Further roots can be dug up and blanched as required (see November, General Work).

Start Second Early Vines into Growth. If you were afraid to start vines in January owing to lack of artificial heat it may well be possible to do so now. It is still necessary to maintain the same temperatures as before (see January, First Week), but with lengthening days and more sun heat this is not so difficult.

Strawberries Under Glass. If some strawberries have been grown in pots (see July, Fourth Week), bring a few into the greenhouse now and maintain a temperature of 10 to 16°C (50 to 60°F).

SECOND WEEK

Plant Anemones and Ranunculuses. This is an excellent time to make a planting of anemones of the St Brigid, de Caen and fulgens types, and also of turban ranunculuses for a summer display. The anemones should be 6·5 to 8 cm (2½ to 3 in) deep and the ranunculuses about 4 to 5 cm (1½ to 2 in) deep. The latter are queer-looking things, like dried-up claws, and the claws should be planted downwards. Space both subjects about 15 cm (6 in) apart each way.

Prune and Start Greenhouse Plants. Several well-known greenhouse plants require pruning now. Bougainvilleas should have last year's growth cut hard back unless you wish to retain some growths for extension. Bouvardias, gardenias, fuchsias, zonal and ivy-leaved pelargoniums should be cut sufficiently to give them a solid foundation for the coming season's growth and so prevent the least suspicion of untidiness. You can give all these plants water in gradually increasing quantity from now onwards as growth starts. A slightly higher temperature will also be all to the good, though it is not essential. All need as much light as they can get.

Sow Parsnips. If the weather is at all favourable do not hesitate to sow parsnips out of doors, for the longer and more steadily they can grow the better. However, there is no sense in sowing if the ground is sodden or frozen; it is better to wait two or three weeks than have all the seeds rot away. Sow in drills 2·5 cm (1 in) deep and about 38 cm (15 in) apart, scattering the seeds as thinly as possible, for later on the seedlings must be thinned to at least 23 cm (9 in) apart in the rows. Those who grow for exhibition very often make a hole for each parsnip with a large iron crowbar. This is driven in to a depth of about 60 cm (2 ft), the hole is then almost filled with fine potting soil, two seeds are sown, and a little more fine soil placed on top. The object of this is to encourage the tap root to grow straight down into the soft potting soil, and so obtain specimens of perfect shape. If both seeds germinate the weaker seedling is pulled out.

Lift and Store Parsnips. Parsnips that have been left in the ground all the winter will soon be starting to grow again, and it is best to lift them without delay and store in some cold place. A position beneath a north wall will do very well. It is only necessary to place the roots in a heap and cover them with a little soil; they are quite hardy and will not be injured by frost.

Plant Shallots. There used to be an old-time idea that shallots should be planted on the shortest day of the year. There are, no doubt, some gardeners who follow this out still, but my own opinion is that, at any rate around London and on heavy soils generally, it is much better to wait until the second week in February. Indeed, even then, I would not plant unless the surface of the bed can be broken down reasonably fine. The method of planting is simply to push good bulbs firmly into the soil until only the top third can be seen. Plant 23 cm (9 in) apart in rows 30 cm (1 ft) apart. Choose an open position and, for preference, ground that is well drained and has been adequately manured earlier in the winter.

Plant Out Spring Cabbages. Cabbages for a spring supply are sown in July or August and are usually planted out in early autumn in the beds in which they are to mature. But sometimes one cannot find sufficient room for all the seedlings, and if there are some still left in the seed beds, now is the time to get them planted, always provided the weather is reasonably good. These late plants are not likely to make such big hearts as the earlier ones, so it will be sufficient to plant them 25 to 30 cm (10 in to 1 ft) apart in rows 45 cm (18 in) apart.

THIRD WEEK

Sow Half-hardy Annuals and Greenhouse Plants. I usually make this week a busy one in the greenhouse, reserving it for sowing a great number of half-hardy annuals, greenhouse plants, etc. The half-hardy annuals are principally required for summer bedding, but some of them may also come in useful for potting later on and growing as greenhouse plants during the summer (see my notes on hardy annuals in the greenhouse, March, First Week).

The principal half-hardy annuals to be sown now are ageratum, amaranthus, anagallis, antirrhinum, *Begonia semperflorens*, brachycome, cobaea, cosmea, *Dianthus heddewigii*, eccremocarpus, kochia, limonium (statice), lobelia, marigolds of both French and African types, annual carnation, nicotiana, nemesia, *Phlox drummondii*, petunia, scarlet salvia, salpiglossis, schizanthus, ten-week stock and verbena. The greenhouse plants include balsam, begonia, celosia (including cockscomb), celsia, *Clerodendrum speciosissimum*, gloxinia, *Impatiens sultani* and *I. holstii*, mimulus, streptocarpus and trachelium. You may have sown some of these already (see January, Third Week), but even so plants from this later sowing will prove very useful for succession. Dahlias also do very well from a sowing made at this time, and make good strong plants for putting out early in June. They will all germinate in a temperature of 13 to 16°C (55 to 60°F).

For all these use either John Innes or a peat-based seed compost. Seed boxes or trays will do for all seeds, though perhaps it is a little better to have the really choice greenhouse seeds, such as celosias, begonias and streptocarpus, in seed pans. Whichever you use be sure to make them thoroughly clean by scrubbing them out with a stiff brush. Prepare the trays a day before you actually intend to sow the seeds and give the soil a thorough watering; then stand the trays on the staging to drain. Never fill a seed receptacle right to the rim; leave at least 0·5 cm ($\frac{1}{4}$ in) for watering. The day after watering sow the seeds very thinly and evenly, cover lightly with soil (a good general rule is to cover a seed with twice its own depth of soil), and then place a sheet of glass over each pan or tray and a large piece of brown paper over the lot. Any more water that may be needed must be given either from a can fitted with a very fine rose or else by holding the pan or tray almost to its rim in a tub of water.

Start Dahlia Tubers for Cuttings. If you wish to increase your stock of dahlias take the old dahlia tubers out of store and place them in boxes in the greenhouse to start into growth. Old apple

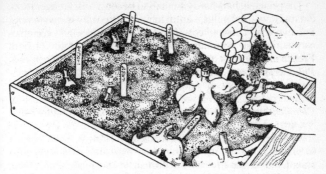

Starting Dahlia Tubers. Dahlia tubers can now be boxed up in old compost or peat and kept warm to encourage shoots for use as cuttings.

boxes serve very well for this purpose, or orange cases can be used – indeed, anything that is deep enough to take a dahlia tuber. Place a little old potting compost or moist peat in the bottom of the box, then stand the tubers on it, as many in a box as can be accommodated comfortably, and place more soil around them until the fleshy tubers themselves are just covered, but the stumps of last year's stems are exposed. Water the tubers in and place the boxes in any light or semi-light place. They can go under the greenhouse staging for the time being, but as soon as growth starts they must be brought out into full light or the shoots will be leggy and useless. Give more water as necessary, sparingly at first but much more freely when growth appears. Any temperature over 13°C (55°F) will be sufficient to start growth.

Pot Early Begonias and Gloxinia Tubers. If you were able to start begonia and gloxinia tubers into growth during January they will almost certainly need potting up by this time. It is not wise to leave them until their roots become matted together in the trays. Get them out when they have two or three leaves each and place them separately in the smallest sized pots that will accommodate them comfortably using John Innes potting compost No. 1 or a peat-based equivalent. The tubers should only just be covered with soil. Make them moderately firm, give them a thorough watering, and keep them in a temperature of 16 to 18°C (60 to 65°F) for a few days. Syringe every morning with slightly warm water to prevent flagging, and shade for a few days from strong direct sunshine.

Start Begonias, Gloxinias and Hippeastrums. A further batch of begonias, gloxinias and hippeastrums may be started into growth to provide a succession after those started in January (see January, Second and Fourth Weeks). Even if you were unable to start any then you may be safe in doing so now, for it will be easier to maintain the requisite temperatures.

Start Clivias and Vallotas. These plants may also be brought into growth now, but as they are never dried off to the extent of hippeastrums this simply means increasing the water supply a little and standing in a warmer part of the house. A temperature of 13 to 16°C (55 to 60°F) will be ample unless very early flowers are required.

Sow Early Celery. This is the time to make the earliest sowing of celery to give fully blanched stems by the end of August. I do not advise you to attempt this first sowing unless you have plenty of frame space available and are fairly accustomed to handling plants under glass. It is much easier to grow celery from a March sowing, and from this you should have good sticks by the end of September. However, if you intend to exhibit in some August shows a few sticks of celery may make all the difference. A temperature of 16 to 18°C (60 to 65°F) will be necessary for germination. The seeds should be sown as thinly as possible in John Innes seed compost. It is an advantage to cover each box with a sheet of glass and to place a sheet of newspaper or brown paper on top of this. Of course, an early variety should be chosen for this sowing.

Sow Maincrop Tomatoes. A second sowing of tomatoes (see January, Second Week) will provide you with good sturdy plants for planting in the greenhouse in May as soon as you have cleared it of bedding and early-flowering plants. Details of sowing are as before.

Pot Tomato Seedlings. Tomato seedlings from the January sowing should be potted separately in 8-cm (3-in) pots as soon as they have made two or three rough leaves each beyond the first pair of plain seed leaves. Transfer them carefully to these pots, using John Innes seed compost. Water freely and keep shaded from direct sunshine for a day or so until they get over the move. Later sowings may be pricked off into deeper boxes before potting, but I find that for the earliest crop it is better to pot separately as soon as possible.

Sow Turnips. Make a first sowing of turnips outdoors in a warm, sheltered place. Sow the seeds thinly in drills 1 cm ($\frac{1}{2}$ in) deep and 25 cm (10 in) apart. You should only sow a few seeds now and subsequently make small successional sowings every fortnight or so until the end of July, as by this method you will have a constant supply of young roots instead of a lot of old, tough and strongly flavoured ones.

Start Fruit in the Unheated Greenhouse. Give considerably less ventilation to the unheated glasshouses containing peaches, nectarines and apricots. By day the top ventilators may be opened a little if the weather is fine, but early in the afternoon the house should be closed completely. This will encourage the trees to start into growth.

FOURTH WEEK

Prick off Early Seedlings. It should now be possible to prick off some of the early seedlings such as begonias, gloxinias and streptocarpus which were sown in January (see January, Third Week). They will be very small and it may be necessary to use a small forked stick to lift them, but early pricking out before roots become matted together is amply repaid. Fill rather deep seed trays or big earthenware pans with the same kind of compost as that used for seed raising, and dibble the seedlings in about 5 cm (2 in) apart each way. Water freely and keep rather warm and shaded for a few days until they recover from the shift, after which they may be placed on the ordinary greenhouse staging in a temperature of about 16°C (60°F).

Plant Chives. Chives are not a very important vegetable crop, but a couple of clumps come in very useful for flavourings. This is the time of year to plant and to divide old clumps that have got overcrowded. Simply lift the plants and pull them apart, replanting small tufts about 25 cm (10 in) apart. Any ordinary soil and reasonably open position will do.

Plant Potatoes in a Sheltered Border. If you have a very sheltered border, preferably one with a south aspect, and you are not afraid to take a small risk, you can now make a first planting of early potatoes. They will need watching later on and you will probably have to protect the young shoots with dry straw or bracken, but if you are successful there is no reason why you should not be digging new potatoes early in June. Of course, for this first planting it is essential to choose a quick-growing variety such as Arran Pilot or Sharpe's Express. Also you should use only well-sprouted sets. Reduce the number of sprouts to two or three sturdy ones on each tuber. Plant in trenches about 13 cm (5 in) deep and 60 cm (2 ft) apart, setting the tubers 23 cm (9 in) apart with the eyes pointing upwards. Surround each tuber with a couple of handfuls of leaf-mould or moss peat and sprinkle a little potato fertilizer in the bottom of each trench; about 55 g per metre run (2 oz per yard). Then refill the trenches but do not firm the soil much. Plenty of good potato fertilizers can be bought ready to use, but if you prefer you can make your own with eight parts of superphosphate of lime, five parts of sulphate of ammonia and three parts of sulphate of potash. This mixture will keep for quite a long time in a dry place. If it sets hard after a few days, break it up thoroughly with the back of a spade.

Plant Out Autumn-sown Onions. Directly the soil is in good condition – that is to say, as soon as you can walk on it without it sticking to your boots – plant out seedling onions from the August sowing (see August, Fourth Week). The method is to

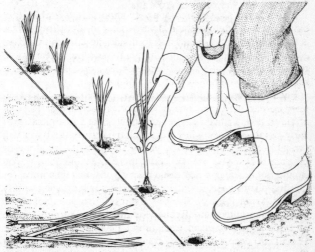

Planting Out Onions. The autumn-sown onions are planted out now by dropping them into 5-cm (2-in) deep holes and watering them in

plant with a small dibber, just dropping the seedlings into holes about 5 cm (2 in) deep. Plant 15 cm (6 in) apart in rows 30 cm (1 ft) apart. The position chosen should be fully open and the soil must have been well cultivated earlier in the winter – plenty of manure in the bottom spit and any quantity of wood ashes mixed with the surface soil. Onions growing in rough, hard soil are almost certain to be misshapen.

Prick off Lettuce and Cauliflower Seedlings. These seedlings from the sowings made three weeks ago should now be ready for pricking off into deeper seed boxes filled with the same kind of compost as that used in the seed trays. Lift the seedlings very carefully with a sharpened wooden label and dibble them in 5 cm (2 in) apart each way. Water freely and keep shaded for a day or so until they start to grow again.

Sow Parsley in a Sheltered Place. Make a small sowing of parsley in a warm, sheltered place. It is much too early yet for the main sowing, but plants raised now will be useful in early summer before the main crop is ready. Parsley seed is quite cheap, so there is no great loss even if the sowing does not prove a success.

Sow French Beans for Succession. Sow some more french beans in 20-cm (8-in) pots if you wish to keep up a successional supply under glass during the spring (see January, Fourth Week).

Sow Melons in a Heated Greenhouse. This is a good time to sow melon seeds. Sow them singly, 1 cm ($\frac{1}{2}$ in) deep, in small pots (those 6·5 cm, $2\frac{1}{2}$ in, in diameter will be admirable), and start them into growth in a temperature of 16 to 21°C (60 to 70°F). It is a good plan to plunge the pots to their rims in moist peat in a warm propagating case.

Prune Cobnuts and Filberts. Cobnuts and filberts must be pruned as soon as the small red female flowers can be seen. These are rather insignificant and you must look closely to find them. It is the male catkins that make the show. The leading shoots of established bushes which fill their space are shortened to a couple of buds each. If there is still room for the bushes to extend there is no need to prune these leaders at all, or at the most only to remove their tips. Side shoots are cut back to the first catkin, reckoning from the tip, or, if there are no catkins, to the first female flower. Some shoots may have catkins only. These should be left unpruned until the catkins fade and then be cut right back to two buds. There is no point in keeping them, as they will not produce any nuts. Badly placed branches which crowd up the centre of the bush should be removed altogether, even if this means using a saw. The ideal nut bush is roughly in the form of a goblet, with a short main trunk and branches radiating from it at regular intervals.

Spray Peaches and Nectarines Outdoors. If your outdoor peaches or nectarines were attacked by red spider the previous summer, spray them now with lime-sulphur wash at the usual winter strength advised by the manufacturers. This treatment will also check the leaf-curl disease.

FLOWERS, VEGETABLES AND FRUITS IN SEASON DURING FEBRUARY

Herbaceous Plants: *Adonis amurensis, Arisarum proboscideum, Bergenia ciliata, B. cordifolia, B. crassifolia, B. purpurascens, B. stracheyi, Euphorbia biglandulosa, Helleborus abchasicus, H. antiquorum, H. caucasicus, H. colchicus, H. corsicus, H. foetidus, H. guttatus, H. maximus, H. odorus, H. olympicus, H. orientalis* vars., *H. purpurascens, H. viridis, Iris unguicularis, Petasites fragrans, Pulmonaria angustifolia, P. rubra, P. saccharata, Ranunculus ficaria* vars., *Viola odorata* vars.

Hardy Bulbs, Corms and Tubers: *Chionodoxa luciliae, Crocus ancyrensis, C. aureus* and vars., *C. balansae, C. biflorus* and vars., *C. chrysanthus* and vars., *C. dalmaticus, C. etruscus, C. fleischeri, C. imperati, C. korolkowii, C. sieberi, C. tomasinianus, Cyclamen coum, Eranthis cilicica, E. hyemalis, E. sibirica, E. tubergenii,*

Erythronium dens-canis, Galanthus byzantinus, G. caucasicus, G. elwesii, G. ikariae, G. latifolius, G. nivalis in var., *G. plicatus, Hyacinthus azureus, Iris aucheri, I. bakeriana, I. danfordiae, I. histrioides, I. persica, I. reticulata, I. sindpers, Leucojum vernum, Merendera robusta, Narcissus bulbocodium* and vars., *N. cyclamineus* and vars., *N. minor* and vars., *N. pallidiflorus, N. pseudo-narcissus, N. tazetta* and vars., *Romulea bulbocodium, Scilla bifolia* and vars., *S. sibirica, S. tubergeniana, Tulipa biflora.*

Rock Plants: *Anemone blanda, Lithospermum rosmarinifolium* (shelter), *Omphalodes verna, Primula allionii, P. edgeworthii, P. juliae, P. juliana* vars., *Ranunculus calandrinioides, Saxifraga apiculata, S. borisii, S. burseriana* and vars., *S. elizabethae, S. haagii, S. irvingii, S. jenkinsae, S. juniperifolia, S. kellereri, S. marginata, S. oppositifolia* and vars., *Sisyrinchium grandiflorum, Synthyris reniformis, Viola labradorica.*

Evergreen Shrubs: *Azara integrifolia, A. microphylla, A. petiolaris, Camellia japonica* vars., *C. reticulata* and vars., *C. sasanqua* vars., *Daphne bholua, D. laureola, D. odora, Erica arborea* and vars., *E. carnea* and vars., *E. darleyensis, E. lusitanica, E. mediterranea, Garrya elliptica, Mahonia acanthifolia, M. aquifolium, M. bealei, M. japonica* and vars., *M. media* vars., *M. pinnata, Pieris japonica, Rhododendron arboreum, R.* Christmas Cheer, *R. leucaspis, R. moupinense, R. nobleanum, R. praecox, Ribes laurifolium, Sarcococca confusa, S. hookeriana, S. humilis, S. ruscifolia, Ulex europaeus* vars., *Viburnum burkwoodii, V. tinus* and vars.

Deciduous Shrubs: *Chaenomeles japonica* vars., *C. speciosa* vars., *Chimonanthus fragans, Cornus mas, Corylopsis griffithii* (shelter), *Corylus avellana* and vars., *C. maxima* and vars., *Daphne mezereum, Edgworthia papyrifera, Hamamelis intermedia* vars., *H. japonica* and vars., *H. mollis, H. vernalis, Lonicera fragrantissima, L. purpusii, L. standishii, Osmaronia cerasiformis, Prunus incisa praecox, Stachyurus praecox, Viburnum bodnan-*

tense, V. foetens, V. fragrans (farreri), V. grandiflorum.

Evergreen Trees: *Acacia dealbata, Rhododendron arboreum.*

Deciduous Trees: *Alnus incana* vars., *A. rubra, Corylus colurna, Magnolia campbellii, Populus tremula, Prunus cerasifera* and vars., *P. conradinae, P. davidiana, P. mume* vars., *P. pseudocerasus, P. subhirtella autumnalis, Salix aegyptiaca.*

Hardy Climbing Plants: *Clematis calycina, C. cirrhosa, Jasminum nudiflorum.*

Greenhouse Plants: *Acacia armata, A. baileyana, A. dealbata,* arum lilies, azaleas (Indian and Mollis), begonias (as January except Optima type), *Boronia heterophylla, B. megastigma,* bouvardias, *Browallia speciosa major, Brunfelsia calycina,* camellias, carnations (perpetual flowering), cinerarias (hybrids), clivias, *Coleus thyrsoideus, Columnea gloriosa, Coronilla glauca,* correas, cyclamen (Persian), epacris, freesias, gardenias, hyacynths, bulbous irises such as Wedgwood, *Jacobinia pauciflora, Jasminum mesnyi, Kalanchoe blossfeldiana,* lachenalias, narcissi, primulas (as January), *Reinwardtia trigyna, Schlumbergera buckleyi, Sparmannia africana,* tulips (early-flowering vars.), veltheimias, also forced shrubs such as almonds, cherries, deutzias, peaches and viburnums.

Vegetables in Store: Jerusalem artichoke, beetroot, carrots, onions, parsnips, potatoes, shallots, turnips.

Vegetables in the Garden: Jerusalem artichoke, broccoli (sprouting), Brussels sprouts, cauliflower (late), celery, coleworts, endive, kale, leeks, spring onions, parsnips, savoys, turnip tops.

Vegetables under Glass: Chicory, endive, lettuce, mushrooms, mustard and cress.

Fruits in Store: *Apples:* Adams' Pearmain (D), Annie Elizabeth (C), Barnack Beauty (CD), Beauty of Kent (C), Belle de Boskoop (CD), Brownlees' Russet (D), Claygate Pearmain (D), Cornish Gillyflower (D), Court Pendu Plat (D), Cox's Orange Pippin (D), Crawley Beauty (C), Delicious (D), Edward VII

(C), John Standish (D), King's Acre Pippin (D), Lane's Prince Albert (C), Laxton's Pearmain (D), Monarch (C), Newton Wonder (C), Norfolk Royal (D), Reinette du Canada (D), Rosemary Russet (D), Roundway Magnum Bonum (D), Saltcote Pippin (D), St Cecilia (D), Superb (D), Wagener (D), Wellington (C), Winston (D), Wyken Pippin (D). *Grapes:* Alicante, Gros Guillaume, Lady Downe's Seedling, Mrs Pince, Muscat of Alexandria, Prince of Wales. *Pears:* Bellissime d'Hiver (C), Bergamotte d'Esperen (D), Beurré Easter (D), Catillac (C), Joséphine de Malines (D), Olivier de Serres (D), Uvedale's St Germain (C).

Nuts in Store: Cobnuts, filberts, walnuts.

March

GENERAL WORK

Transplant and Divide Herbaceous Perennials. March is usually the best month during which to transplant the majority of herbaceous plants. There are a few exceptions, but they are not very important. Flag or German irises are usually planted by experts at the end of June because they will then give a full display of flowers the following year, but they can be transplanted with equal safety in March, the only drawback being that there will be few flowers the following summer. Similar remarks apply to pyrethrums, which are also moved by experts immediately after flowering. Peonies and eremuruses are often quoted as examples of plants that benefit greatly by autumn transplanting. My own opinion is that this is well enough on properly drained soil, but that even with these plants it is better to wait until March if one has to contend with heavy clay. The

53

actual moment during the month chosen for planting may be decided to some extent by opportunity and pressure of other work, but do not fail to seize any really good days early in the month or you may find that later on persistent rain holds you up.

When transplanting old clumps always break them up into smaller pieces, and if you have plenty of stock throw away the hard central portions of the clumps and keep only the young outside pieces. This is particularly important with vigorous spreading things such as Michaelmas daisies, heleniums, rudbeckias, and solidagos. Split up by hand where possible, and for very tough clumps use a couple of small border forks thrust back to back through the middle of the mass and then levered

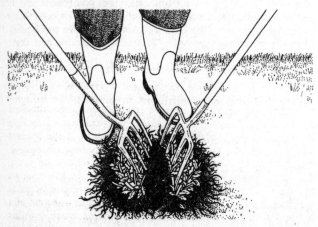

Dividing Herbaceous Plants. Particularly tough clumps of herbaceous perennials can be divided by thrusting two forks back to back through the centre of the clump and forcing them apart

apart. Only use a knife with plants that make a solid crown – for example, peonies, delphiniums, and Caucasian scabious – and even then be careful only to cut the crowns and not the roots; pull these apart.

Always replant with a spade or trowel and not a dibber. Prepare good wide holes, spread the roots out well, work some fine dry soil around them (it is an excellent plan to prepare a barrow-load of this in advance), and thoroughly firm the plants in.

Prune Roses. Continue to prune bush and standard roses (see November, General Work).

Lay Turves. This is a good month for turf laying, and also for repairing bare places in lawns. So, if you have any of this work to do, choose any day during March when the surface is dry enough to be walked on without sticking to your boots and it can be broken down reasonably well with the fork or rake. Beat the turves down on to the soil with a special wooden turf beater or roll them with a light roller, first in one direction and then transversely.

General Greenhouse Management. The greenhouse will now be filling with many more seedlings and young rooted cuttings than before. These must have plenty of light and air if they are to be kept short-jointed and sturdy and are not to be attacked by the deadly damping-off fungus. In consequence it may not be possible to do with much less artificial heat in the general utility greenhouse than in January or February because, though the days may be a little warmer, more ventilation must be given, and yet the temperature inside the greenhouse must still be at an average of 13 to 16°C (55 to 60°F) for the majority of popular greenhouse plants. If you have a separate house or a section of a house that can be devoted to seed germination, starting bulbs and tubers and rooting soft cuttings, this can be ventilated less and the necessary temperature of 16 to 21°C (60 to 70°F) maintained with considerably less artificial heat than formerly.

In the main greenhouse, in which you have flowering and foliage plants, seedlings, and cuttings that have been removed from the propagating box and are being hardened off, avoid sudden large rises of temperature caused by direct sun heat. On a bright, still day the thermometer may rise rapidly in an hour or so if you are not on the watch. Give increased top ventilation to counteract this, so avoiding rises of more than 3 or 4°C (10°F) and preventing serious scorching of both foliage and flowers.

Roses started in the greenhouse during January or February will benefit from an occasional spraying with a greenfly killer such as malathion or resmethrin. On warm, bright days many plants not in bloom will benefit from spraying with tepid water. It should be done in the morning, but not too early. Plants must not be sprayed while they are in bloom.

Harden Autumn Seedlings and Cuttings. Various seedlings and cuttings that have been in frames during the autumn and winter must now be hardened off. This simply means that more ventilation should be given, the lights being removed altogether during the day when the weather is mild and being tilted a little at night unless it is actually freezing or blowing very cold. The hardiest of these plants, and therefore the most able to stand exposure, will be pansies, violas, and violets. Antirrhinums (either from autumn seed or cuttings), penstemons, and calceolarias need a little more protection as yet.

Take Cuttings of Bedding and Greenhouse Plants. In a moderately heated greenhouse such popular bedding plants as heliotrope, marguerite, fuchsia and pelargonium (geranium) will be making suitable growth to provide cuttings. Secure these as soon as they are long enough. The actual length of the cutting will depend on the type of plant – for example, with geraniums, which have comparatively thick stems, cuttings 8 cm (3 in) in length are ideal, but 5-cm (2-in) cuttings will do for the thinner fuchsias and heliotropes. Prepare all by severing them cleanly immediately below a joint and then insert them in well-drained boxes or 10-cm (4-in) pots filled with a sandy compost, dropping them in just sufficiently deep to keep them erect. They can be rooted on the greenhouse staging if they are shaded during the day, but better results with all except geraniums are obtained by placing them in a propagating case, especially if this is over the heating apparatus.

You can propagate quite a number of popular greenhouse plants in precisely the same way. It is worth trying a few shoots of any perennial that is just making new growth. A few examples are abutilon, bouvardia, coleus, datura, eupatorium, gardenia, jacobinia, lantana, berried solanums, the double-flowered tropaeolums and petunia. All these should be kept as close as possible in a heated propagator until they are rooted. Winter-flowering begonias of the Gloire de Lorraine type make basal growths at this time of the year, and these can be secured as cuttings when 5 cm (2 in) in length.

If desired the base of each cutting can be treated with a root-forming hormone before insertion. This can be done either by

Taking Pelargonium Cuttings. Sturdy growths should be selected and prepared by removing the lower leaves and making a clean cut below a leaf joint to give an 8-cm (3-in) cutting. Insert in sandy compost

57

dipping it in powder containing the hormone or by leaving the cuttings to stand for a few hours in a very weak solution of the hormone. Suitable preparations can be purchased from a dealer in horticultural sundries.

Stop Early Carnations. Complete the propagation of perpetual-flowering carnations from cuttings as soon as possible. Cuttings that were rooted in December and January will be ready for stopping some time during the month. This simply means that the top of each cutting is broken off with a sideways movement. The effect of this is to make the plants produce side shoots. The right stage of growth for stopping is when the plant has made about seven joints; one complete joint is broken out.

Pot Chrysanthemum and Carnation Cuttings. You must continue to pot chrysanthemum and perpetual-flowering carnation cuttings as soon as they are well rooted (see January, General Work).

Perpetual-flowering carnations that were potted into 5-cm (2-in) pots in January and early February will also need a move on into 8- or 9-cm (3- or 3½-in) pots some time during the month. Use the same compost as before, but rather coarser in texture. Do not place the plants in a frame in the same way as the chrysanthemums, but stand them on the staging or a shelf in the greenhouse with an average temperature of 13°C (55°F), and as much ventilation as possible without cold draughts.

Chrysanthemum cuttings that were rooted during December and January should be ready for the second potting into 13-cm (5-in) pots quite early in the month. Use John Innes potting compost No. 2 or an equivalent mixture and pot a little more firmly. After potting place the plants in a frame but keep the lights on at first and have plenty of thick sacks or mats at hand to cover them on cold nights.

This is also a good time to purchase rooted cuttings of all kinds of chrysanthemums. Pot the cuttings up singly directly they arrive, and place them in the greenhouse, keeping them shaded from direct sunshine for a few days and spraying with slightly warm water every morning.

Take Chrysanthemum Cuttings and Split Border Kinds. The best way to grow outdoor chrysanthemums is from cuttings, and you can continue to take these throughout March. Instructions are as for indoor kinds (see December, Third Week). However, if you have no facilities for handling cuttings you can still get quite good results by treating the border chrysanthemums like ordinary herbaceous perennials, lifting the roots now and splitting them up into small pieces. Throw away the hard, woody stumps of last year's growth and keep only the young outer shoots. Plant these 45 cm (18 in) apart in the border or, if in rows, 30 cm (1 ft) apart in lines 60 cm to 1 m (2 to 3 ft) apart. Propagation of the main stock of late-flowering chrysanthemums should now be almost completed, but towards the end of the month you may take a few more cuttings to be flowered in 15-cm (6-in) pots.

Make Successional Sowings. Several vegetables that you have already sown will need to be resown during the month to provide a succession. You will need two or three more sowings of radishes as described in the notes for February, General Work. For the first three weeks of the month these should be made in a frame unless you are in an exceptionally favourable district, for radishes must grow rapidly to be of any use. At the end of the month you can make a sowing outdoors in a warm sheltered border. One or two small sowings of turnips (see February, Third Week) will ensure a constant supply in early summer. Mustard and cress may be sown quite frequently in a warm frame or greenhouse (see January, General Work). Make another sowing of lettuces in the greenhouse early in the month (see February, First Week). At the end of the month it will be safe to sow outdoors (see Fourth Week).

Prick off Seedlings. During the month many seedlings raised in the warm greenhouse or frame last month will be ready for pricking out. Usually the ideal time is when the seedlings have made two true leaves each in addition to the first seed leaves (these are quite different in character from the true leaves and can be distinguished quite easily). Monocotyledons, such as onions and leeks, make only one seed leaf and are pricked off as soon as they can be handled conveniently. However, if you followed my advice (see January, First and Fourth Weeks) and spaced the seeds singly, no pricking off will be necessary as the tiny plants will have plenty of room.

For general pricking off use John Innes or a peat-based seed sowing compost. Lift the seedlings with as little root injury as possible and dibble them in 5 cm (2 in) apart each way, making the soil firm around their roots. Water freely and shade for a few days while the tiny plants are recovering from the check of the move. You can either prick off into other boxes like those used for the seeds but preferably a little deeper, or else, if in frames, directly into a bed of fine soil. Among the seedlings needing this attention will be cauliflowers and lettuces sown under glass for planting out, tomatoes (unless you can pot them singly straight away to save time as I described in my notes for February, Third Week), and many half-hardy annuals and greenhouse plants.

Complete the Blanching of Chicory. Any remaining roots should be lifted and blanched before they restart into growth outdoors (see November, General Work).

Treat Peaches, Nectarines and Apricots according to Growth. Peaches, nectarines and apricots in an unheated glasshouse will come into bloom early in the month and will require hand-fertilization exactly as described in the notes for February, General Work. Later they must be disbudded little by little, as described in the same place.

Peaches and nectarines which were started in January should now have fruit well set, and you can begin to thin these; but do not complete the work as yet, because there is often a heavy natural fall during the stoning period (see April, General Work). Simply content yourself so far with reducing the number of fruits per cluster so that they have room to swell.

Start to Thin the Earliest Grapes. Some time during the month bunches of grapes in a fairly warm glasshouse will be ready for their first thinning. The ideal time to start is about a fortnight after the grapes first set. Use a special pair of grape scissors with pointed blades and start thinning at the bottom of the bunch. Leave the extreme point of the bunch, but remove all the berries that are within 2 cm ($\frac{3}{4}$ in) above it. Berries at the top of the bunch can be left almost twice as thick as this, those between being given an intermediate amount of room. Do not touch the berries by hand, but use a small forked stick to turn them if necessary.

Vines started into growth in February will be in need of pollination, training and stopping exactly as I described for the earliest vines (see February, General Work).

FIRST WEEK

Sow Sweet Peas Outdoors. If you were unable to sow sweet peas in the autumn or in January under glass you should certainly make an outdoor sowing at the earliest possible moment now. Some growers are successful with sowings made in the open as early as the second week in February, but my opinion is that little is gained in this way, and that the soil is much more likely to be in the right condition during March. Sow the seeds 2·5 cm (1 in) deep and 5 to 8 cm (2 to 3 in) apart in rows 25 cm (10 in) apart, with an alleyway at least 1·25 m (4 ft) wide between each pair of rows.

This is also the time to pinch out the tips of sweet peas sown in January, a task which must be done even if the peas are to be grown on the single stem (cordon) system. Side growths produce better flowers than the main stems.

61

Bed out Wallflowers, Forget-me-nots and other Spring Bedding Plants. If it was not possible to complete the planting of wallflowers, forget-me-nots, Canterbury bells, polyanthuses and double daisies in October, now is the time to get the plants into their flowering quarters. Do not delay this operation if weather and soil conditions are right (see October, General Work, for particulars).

Sow Annuals for the Greenhouse. A great many of the familiar hardy annuals that are grown for flowering in summer beds also make good greenhouse pot plants. Included under this heading are annual anchusa, browallia, calendula, annual chrysanthemum, clarkia, impatiens, larkspur, limonium, *Mesembryanthemum criniflorum*, mignonette, nasturtium, nemesia, nemophila, phacelia, salpiglossis, sweet scabious, ten week stocks, annual statice, ursinia and viscaria. Sow seed now in well-drained seed trays and germinate in the greenhouse in a temperature of 13 to 16°C (55 to 60°F). You will then have good strong plants starting to flower at the end of May, just when your greenhouse has been cleared of most of the winter and spring plants. Prick off the seedlings 5 cm (2 in) apart each way into similar soil and trays as soon as they have made two true leaves each.

Repot Foliage Plants and Ferns. Early March is a great time for potting, at any rate so far as summer and autumn-flowering plants are concerned, and also all plants that are grown principally for their foliage. Winter-flowering plants are a different matter, and are generally best repotted as soon as they have finished blooming. Now is the time to deal with palms, aspidistras, ferns of all kinds, including the so-called asparagus fern and *Asparagus sprengeri*, smilax, coleus, crotons, cacti and succulents generally, dracaenas, marguerites, fuchsias, pelargoniums (this genus includes the familiar bedding geranium) and heliotropes. It is usually advisable to give plants that are to be repotted a shift into a pot one size larger than that which they occupied before. If for any reason it is essential that the plants

Repot Foliage Plants. As soon as these have filled their pots with roots they can be transferred to pots one size larger. Tease some soil from the roots and work the new compost in with a small rammer

should be kept in the same size pot you must first reduce the size of the ball of soil around the roots. The way to do this is to tap the plant out of its old pot by rapping the rim of this upside down on the edge of the potting bench and holding one hand close up to the ball of soil to support it as it comes away. Then get a pointed stick and carefully loosen the soil around the edge of the ball without injuring the roots. If the compost is neither too wet nor too dry this can be done fairly readily. Do not remove all soil, but just sufficient to get a reasonable quantity of new compost into the new pot. Even when potting for a size larger receptacle it is advisable to loosen roots a little in this way. After potting always give the plants a thorough soaking with water at the same temperature as that of the house and then transfer them to a slightly warmer temperature than that in which they were growing previously. Syringe every morning with tepid water, and shade from direct sunshine. These special precautions need only be maintained for a week or ten days, after which normal conditions should be resumed. The idea is to prevent the leaves from flagging during such time as new roots are being formed, and to encourage rooting as much as possible.

A good general compost for most of this potting is John Innes potting compost No. 1. For some strong growing plants John Innes potting compost No. 2 will give better results and ferns will grow better in a peat-based mix or a mixture of 2 parts, by bulk, peat or leafmould, 1 part loam and 1 part coarse sand or charcoal.

Pot Rooted Cuttings. Another kind of potting which you should do at the earliest opportunity is that of late summer and early autumn rooted cuttings of tender bedding plants, including marguerites, geraniums, heliotropes, and fuchsias. These will be just starting into growth, and if you transfer them singly to 8- or 9-cm (3- to 3½-in) pots in the compost just mentioned they will soon grow into sturdy specimens. After potting, shade the plants for a few days, but stand them on the greenhouse staging in a light place as soon as growth recommences.

Sow Cauliflower, Broccoli and other Brassicas in a Frame. If you were not able to sow cauliflowers in the greenhouse (see February, First Week) you should now sow seeds in a frame. It is even worth making this sowing as an addition to the greenhouse one if you choose a rather later variety than that sown before, because you will then prevent any chance of a break in the supply of curds in late summer and autumn. Sow thinly, as advised for cabbages. Summer broccoli (calabrese) can be sown in the same way.

Brussels sprouts must have a long and steady season of growth if they are to be really successful. Sow now in boxes and germinate in a heated frame or in a slightly heated greenhouse. If you also want a supply of cabbages in midsummer, sow an early variety now under exactly the same conditions as the sprouts.

Sow Onions. A most important sowing for this first week in

March, if the weather is reasonably kind, is that of maincrop onions. Sow in drills 1 cm ($\frac{1}{2}$ in) deep. The drills themselves should be 23 to 30 cm (9 in to 1 ft) apart, the latter if you are growing big bulbs for exhibition. As I have already remarked, it is almost impossible to make the surface of the onion bed too fine and light, but there should be plenty of richness in the way of animal manure below. With the top 10 cm (4 in), mix only wood ashes and similar lightening things so that the bulbs can swell without restriction.

Sow Spinach in a Sheltered Place. A first sowing of summer spinach can be made in a sheltered border – preferably one with a southern aspect. Sow thinly in drills nearly 2·5 cm (1 in) deep and 30 cm (1 ft) apart. Other successional sowings will be made later, so this first sowing need only be a small one.

Sow Broad Beans and Celery. Make another sowing of broad beans in boxes for planting out (see February, First Week). If you were unable to make the first sowing through lack of heat you may yet manage this one, for it is possible to germinate the seeds now in a practically unheated house or in a frame with soil-warming cables.

This is the time to make the main sowing of celery for a supply from October on through the winter. Treat the seeds exactly as described for the earlier sowing (see February, Third Week).

Plant Rhubarb, Horseradish and Seakale. You can make a new rhubarb bed if you wish now, or transplant old roots from one part of the garden to another. Be certain to dig out a hole big enough to take all the roots and allow the crowns to be just level with the surface of the ground. It is a spade job and not one that can be done with a trowel. The ground should have been well manured first and the position may be open or slightly shaded, but preferably the former.

A few roots of horseradish are always useful, but you should be certain to plant them in an out-of-the-way part of the garden because once established it is extremely difficult to get rid of. The roots are planted with a dibber 30 cm (1 ft) apart each way, and are dropped right into the soil so that the crowns are 10 cm (4 in) beneath the surface. The only further cultivation that is necessary is an occasional hoeing to keep down weeds.

The seakale thongs that were removed earlier from the planting crowns and tied up in bundles (see November, Second Week) can also be planted outdoors to form new beds. Cut the roots into pieces about 15 cm (6 in) long and make a nick or sloping cut at the bottom end of each so that you may be certain to plant them the right way up. Plant with a dibber, making holes 15 cm (6 in) deep so that the cuttings are just level with the soil. Plant them 30 cm (1 ft) apart in rows 45 cm (18 in) apart.

New stocks can be obtained by sowing seeds outdoors now. Sow in drills 30 cm (1 ft) apart and 1 cm (½ in) deep.

Plant Early Cucumbers. Cucumbers raised last month (see February, First Week) will now be ready for planting. Prepare the bed in a greenhouse in which you can maintain a minimum temperature of 16°C (60°F). The bed can be on the ground or on staging, provided there is adequate light. Slates or sheets of corrugated iron make a good base. On this spread some straw for drainage and then spread a 15-cm (6-in) layer of rough turfy loam mixed with about one-third its own bulk of well-rotted stable manure and a good sprinkling of bonemeal and wood ashes. At intervals of 1 m (3 ft) make low mounds, each consisting of about 2 bucketfuls of the same compost, and plant a cucumber on the summit of each. Place a stake to each plant and make it secure to this. Train the main stem, as it grows, towards the apex of the house and tie laterals to horizontal wires stretched 38 cm (15 in) apart 23 cm (9 in) below the glass. Water the plants freely and spray them twice daily with tepid water to keep the atmosphere moist. Little air will be needed at first, but open the top ventilators when the temperature reaches 24°C (75°F).

Sow Cucumbers. Cucumbers may be sown at almost any time

of the year for successional cropping, but the average amateur gardener will find that a sowing made now will prove most useful for his general needs.

Plant Strawberries. The best time for planting strawberries is at the end of August or early September, but if for some reason it was not possible to complete planting then, the work may be finished in March. Do not allow these plants to bear any fruit in the first year. If plants are available in pots some more may now be brought into the greenhouse for succession (see February, First Week).

Spray Apple Trees. If apple blossom weevil has been troublesome (this is the pest which produces small white maggots which feed inside the opening flower buds, causing them to turn brown and become capped) spray with a suitable insecticide such as HCH, carbaryl or fenitrothion. If for any reason it was not possible to carry out tar oil spraying in winter, DNOC winter wash can be used now. This will kill aphids, capsid bugs, and many other pests, but not the apple blossom weevil. It is not as effective as tar oil in cleaning green scum, lichen and moss from the bark of old trees.

SECOND WEEK

Sow Herbaceous Perennials and Alpines. A great many herbaceous perennials and rock plants can be raised easily from seeds sown at this time of the year in either a frame or an unheated greenhouse. These include delphiniums, lupins, perennial gypsophilas, perennial statices, thalictrums, coloured primroses and polyanthuses, violas and pansies, campanulas, hypericums, meconopses, aquilegias, dianthuses, etc. I make no attempt to give a full list because it is really worth while trying anything of which you can obtain seed. The method is to sow thinly in well-drained trays or pans (the latter are better in some ways, especially if the seeds happen to be slow in germinating) filled with John

Innes seed compost. Cover the seeds to twice their own depth with very fine soil and then place them in the frame or greenhouse and shade from direct sunlight. Remove the shading as soon as the seedlings can be seen.

Auriculas may also be sown now, but are best in well-drained seed pans, as the seeds are slow and irregular in germination. Place the pans in a frame or greenhouse and water as necessary by partial immersion rather than from a watering can. Sow very thinly so that seedlings can be pricked off as they appear.

Sow Roses, Trees and Shrubs. This is also a good time to sow seed of roses and any other shrubs and trees that may be available. It is not worth sowing rose seed saved haphazard, but if you or any of your friends have made some special crosses, it is quite possible that they may yield good results. Do not expect too much, however. One really worthwhile rose out of a hundred seedlings is quite good going. All these seeds should be sown outdoors in a sheltered border of finely prepared soil without any manure, or at most a sprinkling of bonemeal. If the seed has been stratified (see November, General Work) rub the mass of sand, pulp and seed through the hands to separate the seeds roughly. Then everything can be scattered in the seed drills as evenly as possible. Sow in drills about 1 cm ($\frac{1}{2}$ in) deep and press the soil down fairly firmly on top of the seeds, but not so hard as to make it puddle. Many of the seeds may not germinate the first year, so be certain to sow in a place where you can leave them undisturbed if necessary.

Sow Cacti, Fuchsias and Geraniums. This is a good time to sow seeds of cacti and succulents, and also fuchsias and geraniums. Sow the seeds very thinly in well-drained pots, using a light, sandy compost. Germinate in a greenhouse in a temperature of about 16°C (60°F). The pots containing the fuchsia and geranium seeds can be covered with glass and brown paper, but the cactus and succulent seeds should only be covered with glass; they germinate better in the light.

Stop Chrysanthemums. Many exhibition chrysanthemums should be stopped now (chrysanthemum specialists' catalogues will list suitable varieties). Stopping simply means pinching the growing tip out of each plant with the object of making it produce side shoots. If your desire is to have very large blooms for exhibition each plant must be kept to one stem and this must not be allowed to carry more than one flower. In this case you must only keep the uppermost of the side shoots that form after stopping. Rub the others out at the earliest opportunity. If your object is to have several smaller flowers per plant, you may retain about three of the best side shoots after this first stopping.

Sow Herbs. Sundry herbs, including thyme, sage and marjoram, can be raised from seed sown in a frame or practically unheated greenhouse and treated in exactly the same way as the seed of rock plants or herbaceous perennials.

Sow Culinary Peas Outdoors. Make a first sowing of an early culinary pea outdoors where the plants are to grow. I find the best method is to scoop out a trench with a spade. It should be just the width of the spade (about 23 cm, 9 in) and not more than 8 cm (3 in) deep. Place the peas singly in this trench in two lines, one at each side, the peas themselves being about 8 cm (3 in) apart in the lines, and staggered on opposite sides of the trench. Then cover with 2·5 cm (1 in) of soil. The depression left will provide the tiny seedlings with some protection and will make watering a simple matter. Space the rows either 45 cm (18 in) apart, for dwarf varieties, or 1 m (3 ft) apart for the taller varieties. Do not sow all your early peas at once, or they will all mature at once. Practise successional sowing every fortnight or so.

Plant out Cauliflowers sown in September. Cauliflowers raised from a September sowing in a frame may now be planted outdoors if properly hardened off (see February, General Work). Lift the plants with as much soil and root as possible, and plant with a trowel on really good, well-dug soil. Allow 60 cm (2 ft) between the plants each way.

Plant Mint. If you want to make a new bed of mint now is the time to set about it. Lift some old plants or purchase the necessary roots; divide them up and spread them out thinly over the selected site, which should be in a reasonably open place, and cover with about 4 cm (1½ in) finely broken soil.

Sow Aubergines and Capsicums. For cultivation under glass sow aubergines and capsicums (sweet peppers) in John Innes or a peat seed compost and germinate in a temperature of 16 to 18°C (60 to 65°F).

Pot Early Tomatoes and make Further Sowings. Tomatoes from the January sowing (see January, Second Week) should now be ready for their second potting into 11- to 13-cm (4½- to 5-in) pots of John Innes potting compost No. 1 or an equivalent soilless mixture. Pot the plants rather firmly this time and shade for a day or so as before (see February, Third Week).

A sowing of tomatoes made now will provide good sturdy plants for planting outdoors in June. Sow the seeds exactly as before (see January, Second Week) and germinate them in the greenhouse in a temperature of about 16°C (60°F).

THIRD WEEK

Plant Autumn-sown Sweet Peas. Seize the first favourable opportunity to plant out sweet pea seedlings raised in pots in the autumn. Contrary to general practice when planting from pots, no attempt should be made to keep intact the ball of soil around the roots. Instead, very carefully shake the roots clear of soil and then plant equally carefully in deep holes prepared with a trowel. Spread the roots out and work fine soil around them, firming it thoroughly with the knuckles. For exhibition purposes the plants should be at least 23 cm (9 in) apart in the rows. Common practice is to grow double rows 30 cm (1 ft) apart with 1·5-m (5-ft) alleyways between.

Sow Hardy Annuals. This is a good time to make first sowings of all really hardy annuals, provided the soil is in reasonably good condition. Sow thinly broadcast and cover the seeds with fine soil to about twice their own depth. The seeds should be sown where the plants are to flower. If the seedlings are too thick some of them may be transplanted later on, but the best flowers will be obtained from the unmoved plants.

Among the best annuals for sowing now are sweet alyssum, bartonia, calendula, annual candytuft, annual chrysanthemum, clarkia, collinsia, *Convolvulus minor*, annual coreopsis, cornflower, eschscholzia, godetia, annual gypsophila, larkspur, *Lavatera rosea*, limnanthes, linum (scarlet flax), annual lupins, malope, mignonette, nemophila, nigella, phacelia, cardinal and Shirley poppies, annual rudbeckia, annual saponaria, annual sunflower, Virginian stock, and annual viscaria.

Sow Half-hardy Annuals in a Frame. If you have not a heated greenhouse and were therefore unable to sow half-hardy annuals as advised in my notes for February, Third Week, you can do so now in a frame. This should be in a sheltered place and it is all the better if soil-warming cables are installed. The seeds may either be sown directly in the frame or in boxes or pans as with greenhouse-germinated seeds. The latter method does make for easier handling later on. Dahlias usually germinate very well in a frame at this period and make good flowering plants by August.

This, I find, is a good time to make a first sowing of asters. Seed will germinate easily enough earlier in the year, but the plants tend to get too big by planting time, and are much more liable to damp off.

Plant Gladioli and Montbretias. Make a first planting of gladioli, but do not plant all the corms at once. It is much better to make successional plantings over a period of about a month or six weeks, because this will lengthen the flowering period. Cover the corms with about 8 cm (3 in) of soil. The small 'primulinus' and miniature varieties may be 8 cm (3 in) apart in rows 20 cm (8 in) apart, but the large-flowered gladioli should be at least 15 cm (6 in) apart in rows 30 cm (1 ft) apart – that is to say, if you want the flowers for cutting. If they are merely to be used for bedding or in groups in the herbaceous border, let them be at least 15 cm (6 in) apart each way.

Montbretias are also planted now, and all can go out at once. If you are purchasing dried corms, I advise you to start them into growth first in trays filled with a very light compost mainly consisting of peat and sand. Just bury them in this, water moderately, and place in a frame. Then, as soon as growth starts, transfer them to the beds in which they are to flower, planting carefully with a trowel and covering the corms with about 5 cm (2 in) of soil. A better method of culture is to obtain growing tufts (plants that have never been quite dried off) and plant these as advised for the started corms. Montbretias should be at least 10 cm (4 in) apart each way.

Start Cannas and Dahlias. Cannas and dahlias can now be started into growth in slightly heated greenhouses, in frames with soil-warming cables, or even in well-constructed frames standing in a really sheltered place. But beware of unheated frames as yet if the sides are thin or have gaps between the wood through which draughts can penetrate. The method of starting dahlias is exactly as in greenhouses (see February, Third Week), except that there is really no need to use boxes. The roots can simply be placed in the frames side by side and nearly covered with dry soil. Old canna roots may be in pots already. There is not any need to repot them for the moment, as this is better done after growth has restarted. If, however, you are purchasing new roots or are dealing with old bedding roots that have been overwintered in boxes, pot them singly in 15-cm (6-in) pots, in John Innes potting compost No. 1 or an equivalent peat-based mix.

Take Dahlia Cuttings. Dahlias introduced to the greenhouse last month will now be making growth, and you can obtain a first batch of cuttings. Sever the firm young shoots when they

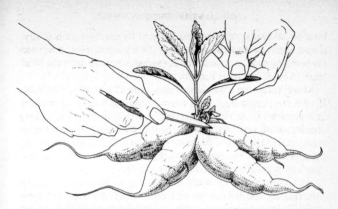

Taking Dahlia Cuttings. Sever the cuttings just above the tuber when they are about 5 cm (2 in) long. Do not remove them with a piece of tuber – this is wasteful and they will root just as well without

are about 5 cm (2 in) in length. Some recommend taking each cutting with a small piece of tuber, but I regard this as wasteful. If the cuttings are severed just above the tuber, leaving a tiny stump still attached to it, this stump will soon send out two or three more shoots which can in turn be taken as cuttings. If the shoot is severed with some of the tuber, no more cuttings will be obtained from there. The cuttings are prepared by trimming the base cleanly just below a joint, removing the lower leaves (if any), and inserting 2 cm (¾ in) deep in sandy soil. I find the simplest and quickest method in the long run is to put the soil into 6·5-cm (2½-in) pots and place one cutting in each. Then there need be no further root disturbance. The cuttings should be rooted in a propagating case with a temperature of 16 to 21°C (60 to 70°F). Any sufficiently deep box with a piece of glass on the top will serve. Water rather freely. If desired dahlia cuttings can be treated with a root-forming hormone prior to insertion as described on page 57.

Start Begonia and Gloxinia Tubers. If you have only a small greenhouse or one that is not too well heated, now is the time to start gloxinias and tuberous-rooted begonias into growth. I have already given full particulars regarding this (see January, Second Week) and there is nothing further to be said, except that you will find it a good deal easier to maintain the required temperature of 13 to 16°C (55 to 60°F) in March than in January. Make use of sun heat during the day by closing the ventilators early in the afternoon. An excellent plan with houses that are not too well heated is to have heavy blinds which can be rolled down right over the glass as soon as the sun sets.

Pot Begonia and Gloxinia Tubers. Tubers that were started in January and potted for the first time in February (see February, Third Week) will almost certainly need a move into their flowering pots, 10 to 15 cm (4 to 6 in) in diameter, according to the size of the plants. Use the same compost and treat as before. Tubers set in fibre in February to start growth will probably be ready for first potting.

Pot Greenhouse Annuals. If you were able to pot some annuals for the greenhouse in February (see February, First Week), the finest should now be ready for a further shift into 18- to 20-cm (7- to 8-in) pots, still using John Innes potting compost No. 1 or a peat-based equivalent.

Remove Vegetable Seedlings to Frame. Onions and leeks sown in the greenhouse in January (see January, First and Fourth Weeks), also cauliflowers, peas, lettuces and broad beans sown in February (see February, First Week) will now be better in a frame, where they can be hardened off for planting outdoors in April. Ventilate cautiously at first and be ready with sacks for cold nights, but gradually accustom the plants to full exposure.

Sow Carrots and Leeks Outdoors. If the soil is in good working condition, make a small sowing of stump-rooted carrot outdoors, but choose a sheltered place. Sow very thinly, either broadcast or in rows 23 cm (9 in) apart, and cover with 0·5 cm

($\frac{1}{4}$ in) of soil. The main sowings will be made in April (see April, Second Week).

As already explained, the best leeks are raised under glass (see January, Fourth Week), but if you do not possess a greenhouse, or even a frame in which you can install soil-warming cables, you can still have quite good leeks of your own raising by sowing outdoors now. Sow thinly in rows 30 cm (1 ft) apart and cover with 0·5 cm ($\frac{1}{4}$ in) of fine soil.

Plant Early Potatoes. Even if you are not favoured with a particularly sheltered border you may now make a first planting of early potatoes. I have already given full particulars of the method to be followed in the notes for February, Fourth Week.

Prick off Early Celery. Celery from the February sowing will be in need of pricking off into deeper seed boxes filled with John Innes potting compost No. 1 or a peat-based equivalent. Dibble the seedlings 5 cm (2 in) apart each way. Water freely and return to the greenhouse in an average temperature of about 13°C (55°F) for the time being, but gradually harden them off so that you can remove the boxes to a frame later (see April, Second Week).

Protect Early Fruit Blossom. Outdoor peaches and nectarines should now be coming into flower, and it is an excellent plan to protect these by hanging fine mesh netting in front of the trees. It might seem that this would afford no protection at all, but actually it makes quite a difference, causing eddies and preventing the slow, unbroken flow of air which always accompanies the worst frosts.

FOURTH WEEK

Clip Ivy on Walls. It is an excellent plan to clip ivy growing on walls at this time of the year. The work can be done very quickly with a pair of shears. Simply clip off the leaves, leaving the stems practically bare, and then brush them down with a stiff broom, getting out all dead leaves and dirt. The plants will look very bare at first, but will soon get new leaves and will be much better for a clean up.

Plant Tigridias. Tigridias are not everybody's flower, but they are very lovely and even though the individual blooms only last a day, they are followed by a succession of others. The bulbs are barely hardy and must be given a sheltered and sunny position. Plant now, placing the bulbs 8 cm (4 in) deep and about 15 cm (6 in) apart each way. Alternatively, tigridias can be grown in a sunny, unheated greenhouse, five bulbs in a 15-cm (6-in) pot in John Innes potting compost No. 1 or a peat-based potting compost.

Plant Carnation Layers. Early autumn is usually considered the best time for planting rooted border carnation layers, but in very exposed places I prefer to pot the layers in the autumn and keep them in a cold frame during the winter. Then they are planted outdoors at this time of the year, when conditions are getting steadily more favourable.

Sow Spinach Beet. This is a very useful form of beetroot grown for its leaves, which are used like those of spinach. Sow now in drills 2·5 cm (1 in) deep and 45 cm (18 in) apart and thin out the seedlings to 23 cm (9 in) apart. This plant is sometimes known as perpetual spinach, because it keeps on cropping all the summer and autumn and most of the winter as well.

Sow Lettuces Outdoors. Unless the weather is exceptionally bad or your garden is very cold, it should now be safe to make a first sowing of lettuces outdoors. You can choose a cabbage or a cos variety according to taste. Sow the seeds very thinly in drills 1 cm ($\frac{1}{2}$ in) deep and about 30 cm (1 ft) apart for the large varieties, or 23 cm (9 in) apart for the Tom Thumb type.

Sow Broad Beans and Peas Outdoors. This is usually a good time to make the first sowing of broad beans outdoors. The place chosen must be open, and really well cultivated. Sow the seeds 15 cm (6 in) apart in drills rather over 2·5 cm (1 in) deep and about 60 cm (2 ft) apart. The dwarf varieties can be grown as close as 38 cm (15 in) between the rows, but it is a mistake to crowd the bigger kinds.

Make a second sowing of an early culinary pea exactly as advised in my notes for the Second Week in this month.

Sow Celery and Celeriac in a Frame. Celery may be sown in a frame in a very sheltered position and, for preference, with soil-warming cables installed. Sow thinly either directly in soil in a frame or in seed trays. Plants from this sowing will provide a succession for planting out after those raised earlier in the greenhouse (see February, Third Week).

Celeriac, which is a moderately good substitute for celery and has the advantage that it will grow on soil that would be much too poor for that crop, is also sown now. The seeds are treated in exactly the same way as those of the celery.

Sow French Beans for Succession. You may now make a third sowing of beans in 20-cm (8-in) pots for cropping under glass (see January, Fourth Week, and February, Fourth Week). At this season it will be possible to maintain the necessary temperature in a well-made frame placed in a sheltered but sunny position and covered with sacks at night.

Sow Cucumbers in a Heated Frame. Good cucumbers can be grown in frames with soil-warming cables as well as in heated greenhouses. If sown now they will start to bear in June, just when the earliest hothouse cucumbers are getting past their first vigour. Spread compost prepared as for glasshouse cucumbers (see First Week), with a low mound in the centre of the space covered by each light. Sow two seeds on the centre of each mound. If both germinate, pull out the weaker seedling.

Plant Melons. Melons raised in a warm greenhouse in February (see February, Fourth Week) will be ready for planting. The method followed is exactly the same as for cucumbers (see First Week), and similar watering and spraying must be carried out.

Graft Apples and Pears. Apple and pear stocks that are well

77

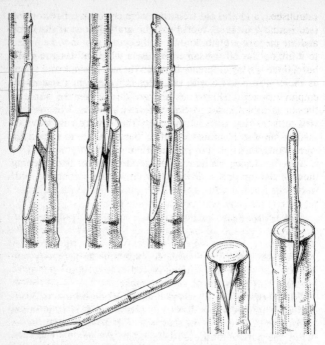

Grafting. a) Whip and Tongue Graft: This graft can be used where the stock and scion are of the same size or where the stock is only slightly thicker. Corresponding cuts are made as shown in both scion and stock and the two are joined together, bound with raffia and covered with grafting wax. **b) Rind Graft:** This is used where the stock is much thicker than the scion (as is the case when trees are reworked). The prepared scion is inserted into the slit made in the bark of the stock. The union is then bound with raffia and covered with wax. With both grafts the unions should be inspected regularly and the raffia cut and replaced should it constrict the scion established, and also old trees that were cut back for reworking (see January, General Work) may be grafted now. If the stock and the piece of growth, known as the scion, that is to be joined to it are not far off the same size, use a whip and tongue graft, but if there is a big difference between the size of stock and scion, as there is sure to be with old trees that are being reworked, employ the method known as rind grafting. Cover the whole of the cut surface and the part immediately above and below it as well with grafting wax, making everything quite airtight.

Start Vines in Unheated Vineries. It is now safe to encourage vines to start into growth even in quite unheated vineries. This is done by closing ventilators altogether at night and opening those at the top only a little by day. Spray every morning with water that is just slightly warm.

FLOWERS, VEGETABLES AND FRUITS IN SEASON DURING MARCH

Herbaceous Plants: *Adonis amurensis, Bergenia ciliata, B. cordifolia, B. crassifolia, B. ligulata, B. purpurascens, B. stracheyi, Doronicum austriacum, D. caucasicum* and vars., *D. cordatum, Helleborus abchasicus, H. antiquorum, H. atrorubens, H. corsicus, H. guttatus, H. niger, H. odorus, H. olympicus, H. orientalis* and vars., *H. viridis, Iris unguicularis, Pulmonaria angustifolia, P. officinalis, P. rubra, P. saccharata, Primula vulgaris* and vars. (primrose and polyanthus), *Ranunculus ficaria* (celandine) garden vars., *Viola odorata* vars.

Hardy Bulbs, Corms and Tubers: *Anemone coronaria* and vars., *A. fulgens, Chionodoxa luciliae, C. sardensis,* crocuses (large flowered), *Crocus balansae, C. biflorus, C. candidus, C. chrysanthus* and vars., *C. corsicus, C. etruscus, C. minimus, C. sieberi, C. susianus, C. vernus* vars., *C. versicolor, Cyclamen coum, C. libanoticum, Eranthis cilicica, E. hyemalis, E. tubergenii, Erythronium dens-canis, Galanthus latifolius, G. plicatus,* hyacinths (large flowered), *Hyacinthus azureus, Ipheion uniflora, Iris aucheri, I. sindpers, Leucojum vernum, Narcissus bulbocodium, N. minor,* narcissus hybrids in variety, *Romulea bulbocodium, R. clusiana, R. requienii, Scilla bifolia, S. sibirica, S. tubergeniana, Tulipa kaufmanniana, T. kolpakowskiana, T. saxatilis.*

Rock Plants: *Anemone apennina, A. blanda, A. nemorosa* vars., *A. ranunculoides, Daphne blagayana, Gentiana acaulis* and vars., *G. verna, Hepatica acutiloba, H. transsilvanica* and vars., *H. triloba* and vars., *Lithospermum rosmarinifolium* (shelter), *Morisia monantha, Primula allionii, P. cortusoides, P. denticulata* and vars., *P. juliae, P. juliana* vars., *P. marginata, P. sonchifolia, Pulsatilla vernalis, P. vulgaris, Ranunculus calandrinioides, Sanguinaria canadensis, Saxifraga apiculata, S. arco-valleyi, S. aretioides, S. borisii, S. boydii, S. burseriana* and vars., *S. elizabethae, S.* Faldonside, *S. griesbachii, S. haagii, S. irv.ngii, S. jenkinsae, S. juniperifolia, S. lilacina, S. marginata, S. oppositifolia* and vars., *S. paulinae, S. petraschii, S. porophylla, S. sancta, S. scardica, Sisyrinchium grandiflorum, Soldanella alpina, S. minima, S. montana, Synthyris reniformis, Viola labradorica.*

Hardy Aquatic and Bog Plants: *Caltha palustris, C. polypetala, Primula rosea.*

Evergreen Shrubs: *Arctostaphylos manzanita, Azara integrifolia, A. microphylla, A. petiolaris, Berberis buxifolia, B. linearifolia, Camellia japonica* vars., *C. reticulata* vars., *C. saluenensis, C. williamsii* vars., *Daphne bholua, D. hybrida, D. laureola, D. odora, D. tangutica, Erica arborea* and vars., *E. carnea* vars., *E. darleyensis, E. lusitanica, E. mediterranea, Mahonia aquifolium, M. bealei, M. japonica* and vars., *M. napaulensis, M. repens, Pieris floribunda, P. japonica, P. taiwanensis, Rhododendron arboreum, R. barbatum, R. calophytum, R. ciliatum, R. cilipinense, R. grande, R. hippophaeoides, R. leucaspis, R. lutescens, R. praecox, R. racemosum, R. strigillosum, R. sutchuenense, Ulex europaeus* vars., *Viburnum burkwoodii, V. tinus.*

Deciduous Shrubs: *Chaenomeles japonica, Colletia infausta,*

Cornus mas, Corylopsis griffithii, C. pauciflora, C. platypetala, C. spicata, Daphne mezereum, Forsythia intermedia vars., *F. ovata, F. suspensa, Lonicera fragrantissima, L. standishii, L. syringantha, Magnolia stellata, Osmaronia cerasiformis, Prinsepia sinensis, Prunus spinosa* (sloe, blackthorn), *P. tenella, P. tomentosa, Salix gracilistyla, Spiraea thunbergii, Stachyurus praecox, Viburnum bodnantense, V. foetens, V. grandiflorum.*

Evergreen Trees: *Arbutus andrachne.*

Deciduous Trees: *Acer opalus, A. rubrum, Alnus cordata, Magnolia campbellii, M. mollicomata, Parrotia persica, Prunus blireana, P. cerasifera* vars., *P. communis* (almond), *P. conradinae, P. dasycarpa, P. davidiana, P. incisa, P. mume, P. persica* and vars. (peach), *P. subhirtella* and vars., *P. triloba, P. yedoensis, Salix caprea.*

Hardy Climbing Plants: *Clematis calycina, Ercilla spicata.*

Greenhouse Plants: Abutilons, acacias, arum lilies, astilbes, azaleas (Indian and mollis), *Begonia manicata, Boronia megastigma,* camellias, carnation, (perpetual flowering), cinerarias (hybrids), clivias, *Coleus thyrsoideus,* correas, epacris, freesias, gardenias, hippeastrums, hyacinths (large flowered), *Jacobinia pauciflora,* lachenalias, *Leucocoryne ixioides,* lilies of the valley, *Lilium harrisii,* narcissi (including trumpet daffodils), polyanthuses, primroses, *Primula malacoides, P. obconica, P. sinensis, P. stellata, Reinwardtia trigyna, Rhipsalidopsis gaertneri,* rhododendrons, roses, tulips (earlies and May flowering), veltheimias, wallflowers, also such shrubs as cherries, deutzias, genistas, lilacs and peaches, all grown in pots.

Vegetables in Store: As January but also parsnips.

Vegetables in the Garden: Broccoli (sprouting), cabbage (sown July, August), cauliflower (late), kale, leeks, spring onions, rhubarb, seakale, spinach beet, turnip tops.

Vegetables under Glass: Carrots, lettuce, mushrooms, mustard and cress, radish.

Fruits in Store: *Apples:* Adams' Pearmain (D), Annie Elizabeth (C), Barnack Beauty (CD), Beauty of Kent (C), Belle de Boskoop (CD), Bramley's Seedling (C), Brownlees' Russet (D), Cornish Gillyflower (D), Court Pendu Plat (D), Crawley Beauty (C), D'Arcy Spice (D), Edward VII (C), John Standish (D), King of Tompkin's County (D), Lane's Prince Albert (C), Laxton's Pearmain (D), Monarch (C), Newton Wonder (C), Norfolk Royal (D), Ontario (CD), Roundway Magnum Bonum (D), St Cecilia (D), Sturmer Pippin (D), Superb (D), Wellington (C), Winston (D), Wyken Pippin (D). *Grapes:* Gros Guillaume, Lady Downe's Seedling, Muscat of Alexandria, Prince of Wales. *Pears:* Bellissime d'Hiver (C), Bergamotte d'Esperen (D), Beurré Easter (D), Catillac (C), Joséphine de Malines (D), Olivier de Serres (D), Uvedale's St Germain (C), Winter Nelis (D).

April

GENERAL WORK

Mow Lawns More Frequently. From April onwards lawns will require mowing more frequently. There is a widespread belief that the mowing machine should be put away during the winter, but this is entirely erroneous. It is folly to mow when the surface is frozen, and side-wheel mowers should not be used when it is soft after heavy rain, but well-oiled, easy-running roller machines can be used without damage even when the ground is fairly wet. Occasional winter mowing keeps the lawn neat and prevents the deterioration of the sward. In unmown lawns coarse grasses tend to take the place of fine ones. During the winter one mowing per month will probably be ample, but from now onwards grass will be growing rapidly and the mower must be used to keep it reasonably close. Give a dressing of a good proprietary lawn fertilizer or of a mixture of two parts of sulphate of potash, one part of sulphate of ammonia, two parts of dried blood, and twenty parts of silver sand, well blended and applied at the rate of 170 g per square metre (6 oz per square yard).

This is the time of year at which the various patent worm killers may be used most effectively. Choose a day when the soil is likely to be moist to a considerable depth and be sure to soak the worm killer well into it.

Complete Planting of Herbaceous Perennials. There is still time to plant hardy herbaceous perennials moved from the open ground, but the sooner the work is completed the better, for the plants will now be making quite a lot of growth. (For details see March, General Work.) Container-grown plants can be moved at any time provided they are sufficiently well established in their containers to be moved with roots and soil intact.

Plant Gladioli for Succession. Throughout the month you should continue to plant gladioli in small batches for succession, as already explained in my notes for March, Third Week.

Plant Alpines. Alpine plants are almost invariably grown by nurserymen in small pots and can be transplanted to the rock garden from these at any time of the year, provided sufficient care is taken. But April is the ideal month, and the one in which there is least risk. Even plants grown in the open ground can be shifted now, unless they happen to be in flower – for example, aubrietas, arabis and early saxifrages – when they should be transplanted as soon as they have finished flowering. When planting from pots, simply tap the plants out, remove the crocks from the bottom of the root ball, and loosen the mass a little with the fingers, but not so much as to damage any of the roots. Plant with a trowel and make firm. Only when planting in a scree is it advisable to shake all the soil from the roots and then spread these out carefully in the new compost.

Plant Evergreen Shrubs. This is the best time for planting evergreen shrubs lifted from the open ground, but if continued spells of cold east wind should follow planting it may be necessary to erect some kind of protection around the shrubs, either by making screens of sacking or placing wattle hurdles or evergreen boughs in position, paying particular attention to the east and north sides. Later on, as the weather becomes warm, a nightly spray with tepid water will do good, and mulching will help to keep the soil moist.

Propagate Shrubs by Layering. Layering is a very simple method of propagating quite a number of shrubs, fruit trees, etc. It is worth trying practically any variety, with the exception of the big fruits such as apples, pears, cherries and plums, and also very hard-wooded shrubs such as hawthorn and beech.

Layering Shrubs. Many shrubs can be propagated by layering, but in particular rhododendrons. The shoot to be layered is pulled down to the ground and a slit made in the underside. It is then firmly pegged down and covered with a few inches of soil.

Many evergreens grow freely from layers; rhododendrons, for example, and also laurels and aucubas. Rambler roses form roots without difficulty, and so do many of the more vigorous climbing varieties.

The method is similar with all these. Choose a good, supple

branch or stem, preferably one formed last year, make an upward incision through one of its joints, not too near the tip but at a point that can easily be bent down to soil level, press the cut portion of stem into the soil and hold it in position with a wire or wooden peg or a heavy stone. If the soil is very heavy or poor, make up a good mixture of loam, peat and sand in about equal parts, and peg the layer into this. Keep well watered during the summer and by the autumn the branch will have formed roots round the cut surface and can be detached from the parent plant and established on its own.

General Greenhouse Management. There will now be much less difficulty in maintaining sufficient temperature in the greenhouse. It may even be necessary to have some temporary shading for a good many plants during the hottest part of the day, especially in small houses which heat up very quickly, but permanent shading will not be needed as yet. It is not wise to have the temperature running much above 21°C (70°F) in the general utility greenhouse in April, which means ample top ventilation on all sunny and fairly still days. Do not use the side ventilators yet, nor leave the door open, for fear of admitting damaging draughts.

Bedding plants and half-hardy annuals generally must be gradually hardened off. Later in the month (see Third Week) you should remove them to frames, if possible, but you must prepare them gradually for this in the early part of the month by giving increased ventilation whenever the weather is favourable, and keeping them as close to the glass as possible. In a mixed greenhouse it is sometimes difficult to reconcile the needs of all the plants at this stage, but much can be done by erecting shelves, a little below the top ventilators, where the plants that need cool conditions can be placed. Those varieties that require warmth can be kept on the staging and as near to the heating apparatus as possible.

From now onwards you will have to keep a sharp look-out for

pests such as greenfly, thrips, and red spider mites. Should any of these appear, fumigate at once with an appropriate fumigant – HCH for greenfly and thrips and azobenzine for red spider mites. To obtain good results with fumigation, make sure that the greenhouse is as air-tight as possible. Close down all ventilators and doors, and leave the house closed for several hours. Plants which are to be fumigated should never be dry at the roots and treatment should not be carried out in bright sunlight. Alternatively, some insecticides, including malathion, are available as aerosols which are very effective in greenhouses.

The main batch of calceolarias, hippeastrums and autumn-sown schizanthuses will be approaching their flowering period and will benefit by fairly constant feeding, provided you use only weak manure water or light applications of fertilizer. The former should only just colour the water, but where proprietary fertilizers are concerned you should consult manufacturers' instructions and certainly not exceed them. I find that it is better to halve the strengths they recommend but to apply a little more frequently.

Harden off Plants in Frames. Onion, leek, cauliflower, pea, broad bean and lettuce seedlings in frames (see March, Third Week) will require full ventilation whenever the thermometer is above freezing point and the wind is not very cold. They must be hardened off fully for planting out later in the month (see Third Week). Similar remarks apply to violets, violas, pansies, penstemons, autumn-sown antirrhinums and other nearly hardy plants, but more tender kinds must still be ventilated with some caution.

Prick off Seedlings. Throughout the month you will be kept busy pricking off many seedlings from sowings made earlier (see March, General Work, for details).

General Potting. In addition to pricking off there will be a considerable amount of potting to do. Seedlings pricked off earlier may be getting overcrowded. Pot them singly into 6·5- to

8-cm (2½- to 3-in) pots directly their leaves touch. The later chrysanthemum and carnation cuttings will be needing a move (see January, General Work, and March, General Work), while dahlia cuttings can be potted into 8-cm (3-in) pots directly they are rooted, unless you inserted them singly in pots, in which case no further move will be needed as yet. This also applies to miscellaneous greenhouse plant cuttings such as abutilons, petunias and daturas (see March, General Work). Begonias and gloxinias started as tubers in January and February, and already potted once, will be in various stages of growth, and the same applies to many other young greenhouse plants and tomatoes. The safe plan is to tap a typical plant out of its pot occasionally and examine the roots. If the soil is just nicely moist right through you can do this quite easily without disturbing the plant at all. Simply turn the pot upside down, place one hand over the soil, and give the rim of the pot a sharp rap on the edge of the potting bench or greenhouse staging. As soon as you see white rootlets forming freely all round the side of the pot ball, transfer the plants to larger receptacles. The usual practice is to shift from 8-cm (3-in) pots into 10- to 13-cm (4- to 5-in) pots, and from these into 15- to 18-cm (6- to 7-in) pots, or, in the case of tomatoes, directly into the 25-cm (10-in) pots or large boxes in which they will fruit. But too big a shift at one time is not generally desirable. By this stage most plants will appreciate a richer soil mixture such as John Innes potting compost No. 2 or even No. 3 for the really strong growing plants such as chrysanthemums. Most plants should be returned to the greenhouse immediately after potting, but chrysanthemums are better in an unheated frame, where they may be hardened off gradually.

Repot Indian Azaleas and Camellias. Both Indian azaleas and camellias may be repotted if necessary as soon as they have finished flowering. Use a compost of lime-free loam and peat in equal parts with half a part of sand and a good sprinkling of bonemeal. At the most only use a pot one size larger than that

occupied formerly – it is all the better if they can go back into
the same size pots after teasing out some of the old soil with the
point of a stick. After potting the plants must be returned to the
greenhouse for a few weeks and should be sprayed every morning with tepid water.

Prune Azaleas, Genistas and Deutzias. As soon as they have
finished flowering remove the faded flower heads from Indian
azaleas and cut back the flowering branches of deutzias and
genistas quite close to the base.

Take Cuttings of Winter-flowering Begonias. It should be possible to take further cuttings of winter-flowering begonias during
the month (see March, General Work). Semi-tuberous rooted
begonias of the Optima type will now be starting into growth
again, and you may encourage them to do so by giving them
rather more water. As soon as the basal growths are a couple of
inches in length you can remove some of them as cuttings,
treating them exactly as you would the other winter-flowering
types.

Rest Freesias, Lachenalias, Arum Lilies and Cyclamen. Freesias
and lachenalias that have been flowering during the winter must
now be allowed to go to rest gradually. To effect this, place them
on a shelf quite near the glass and gradually reduce the water
supply. Rather similar remarks apply to arum lilies that have
been used for winter flowering. These cannot be stood near the
glass, but they must be kept in a cooler atmosphere. Old cyclamen that have finished flowering may be treated just like freesias,
but the young seedlings must be kept growing.

Take Cuttings of Bedding and Greenhouse Plants. It is still
possible to take cuttings of bedding and greenhouse plants in
exactly the same manner as I described in the notes for General
Work during March. It is true that the bedding plants will be
comparatively late in flower, but they may be none the less
useful for that. Some late-struck fuchsias, geraniums, and salvias
make admirable pot plants for the greenhouse in autumn. Con-

tinue to take cuttings of dahlias as they become available (see March, Third Week).

Stop Early-Flowering Chrysanthemums. From time to time during the month you should pinch out the growing tips of the rooted cuttings of early-flowering chrysanthemums required for spray flowering. The ideal moment to do this is when the cuttings are well rooted, growing freely, and are about 15 cm (6 in) in height. Most February- and March-rooted cuttings will reach this stage before the end of April. Note particularly that this stopping applies only to plants that are to be grown for garden decoration or to produce a lot of flowers. The object is to produce a number of branches on each plant, and with this end in view the plants will be stopped again in June. With plants that are grown for large individual flowers, either for exhibition or for cutting, a different method is followed (see May, Third Week), and they must not be stopped now.

Much the same applies to the later varieties that are to flower under glass in the autumn but if some of these are required for exhibition on a particular date in October or November the time of stopping may need to be varied according to variety and locality. Commercial suppliers of chrysanthemums usually give detailed stopping instructions in their catalogues and these are useful as a guide but may need to be modified to suit local conditions. If plants are required solely for decoration or as cut flowers and the precise date at which they attain their peak of perfection is not important the late-flowering varieties can be treated in the same way as the earlies, that is, stopped when they are well rooted and growing freely.

Prepare Celery Trenches. Some time during the month you should prepare the trenches for celery. They will not actually be wanted until June, but it is an advantage to prepare them well in advance so that manure and soil may become blended together. The trenches should be 38 cm (15 in) wide for single rows and 45 cm (18 in) wide for double rows, and they must be at least 1 m (3 ft) apart. You can use the ground between the trenches for various salad crops. Remove the soil to a depth of 45 cm (18 in) and then break up the bottom as deeply as possible with a long fork, mixing well-rotted manure or decayed vegetable refuse with it. Place a layer of manure and good top-spit soil in about equal parts 23 cm (9 in) deep on top of the forked subsoil and a further layer of 15 cm (6 in) of good top-spit soil on top of this. This, you will see, leaves you with a depression about 8 cm (3 in) deep in which the celery will be planted later on. This shallow trench gives some protection to the young plants and makes it very easy to flood them with water.

Make Successional Sowings. You will need to make sundry successional sowings during the month if you wish to maintain an unbroken supply of vegetables later on. In the main these are the same as for last month (see March, General Work). Radishes and mustard and cress may now be sown outdoors, but choose a warm, sheltered place for preference. You should make two further sowings of lettuce at fortnightly intervals (see March, Fourth Week). Similar instructions apply to spinach (see March, First Week). A further sowing of broad beans outdoors (see March, Fourth Week) made towards the end of the month will ensure a crop in the early autumn. Further sowings of carrots will be necessary, but these I have dealt with separately (see Second Week). Most important of all are at least two sowings of peas (see March, Second Week). These are treated as before, but after mid-April it is best to use a second early or maincrop variety rather than an early kind bred to grow and flower in the relatively cool days of spring.

Train and Topdress Early Cucumbers. Side shoots formed on the main stems of cucumbers planted in March (see March, First Week) must be stopped from extending too far or there will soon be such a mass of foliage in the house that the plants will get unhealthy. Pinch out the soft tip of each side shoot as soon as it carries two tiny fruits, or when it is 60 cm (2 ft) in length if it reaches that before it has two fruits. If secondary side shoots appear, pinch them when they have made a couple of leaves. The tip of the main stem must be pinched out as soon as it reaches the apex of the house.

Keep a sharp watch and as soon as white rootlets appear on the surface of the bed give a topdressing, a couple of inches thick, of a mixture of equal parts of good fibrous loam and well-rotted manure. Repeat this later if necessary. The plants will want a lot of water now that they are growing freely. You should also spray them twice daily with tepid water and damp down the paths as well to maintain plenty of moisture in the atmosphere. Open the top ventilators a little when the thermometer reaches 24°C (75°F). A light permanent shading on the glass will be advisable from now onwards. You can use ordinary lime-wash with a little white of egg mixed in to make it stick or one of the proprietary shading compounds. Spray the glass quite lightly with this. Heavy shading is not desirable as yet.

Cucumbers growing in frames (see March, Fourth Week) are trained in a slightly different manner from those growing in greenhouses. The tip of each plant is pinched out when it has made four leaves. Then the laterals which form are trained evenly over the bed, being held in position with wooden or wire pegs, and are stopped again as soon as they reach the edge of the frame or interfere with neighbouring plants. Sublaterals, bearing flowers and subsequently fruits, are pinched from time to time one or two leaves beyond the flowers to prevent gross overcrowding with foliage. Later on some old growths that have finished bearing may be cut out to make room for new growths (see June, General Work).

Water the frame plants freely and ventilate very sparingly on mild days only. Spray overhead when closing for the day in sunny, warm weather.

Train and Pollinate Melons. The training of melons (see March, Fourth Week) is not unlike that of cucumbers. It is, however, necessary to restrict each plant to about four fruits. These should be spaced as evenly as possible over the plant. There are two kinds of flowers, male and female, and only the latter will produce fruits. You can recognize the females because each will have a tiny fruit on its stalk just beneath the petals. These flowers

Pollinating Melon Flowers. The female flower (recognized by the presence of an immature fruit behind the petals) should be dusted with pollen from the male flower to ensure that fruit is set

must be pollinated by hand, and all on any one plant at the same time. You can arrange to get four suitable blooms open at once by judicious pinching. Backward blooms can be hastened by stopping the shoots on which they are growing one leaf beyond the flower, while forward blooms can be retarded by allowing the shoot to grow unstopped. Scatter pollen from the male blooms on the females when the sun is shining.

Management of the Vinery. The vinery, whether heated or unheated, will require fairly constant attention throughout the month. In unheated houses growth can be encouraged now by giving less ventilation and rolling down blinds (see notes on starting begonias and gloxinias, March, Third Week) an hour before sunset, so as to trap sun heat for the night. In a heated vinery growth will be in full swing, and will be in various stages according to the time at which the house was closed. Some vines will be in flower, and will need a slightly higher temperature and a drier atmosphere; more ventilation should be given and spraying with water discontinued for the time being (see February, General Work). These will also require training and stopping, as I explained in the same place. Other vines a little more advanced will be in need of fruit thinning, as described in the notes for March, General Work. The earliest vines, started in January, will be forming their pips (this is technically known as stoning), and you must make every effort to avoid severe fluctuations of temperature. A minimum night temperature of 16°C (60°F), rising to 27°C (80°F) by day with direct sun heat is ideal.

Thin Peaches and Nectarines. In the warm greenhouse or conservatory peaches and nectarines will have completed stoning by this period, and it will be all the better if you can increase the temperature by 5°C (10°F) by day and night. Thinning can be completed as soon as the stones are formed. You can easily ascertain how far things have gone by removing a typical fruit and cutting into it. If the stone is hard and almost full size, with a well-developed kernel, the stoning period is over. Leave an average of one fruit per 30 cm sq (1 sq ft) of tree area. Peaches in unheated houses should be nicely set and you can start thinning as advised in the General Notes for March.

FIRST WEEK

Sow Grass Seed. This is usually the most favourable time for sowing grass seed, but wait a little if the ground is sticky. Rake the surface of the ground quite level and scatter the seed as evenly as possible at the rate of 25 to 55 g per square metre (1 to 2 oz per square yard). Cover with a light sprinkling of fairly dry soil or by raking lightly to mix the seed with the soil. If grass seed is obtained pre-treated with a good bird repellant no further protection against birds will be necessary, but otherwise bird scarers or black thread stranded between small sticks should be used.

Apply Tonk's Fertilizer to Roses. Give all your roses a dressing of Tonk's fertilizer. It will provide them with most of the food they require throughout the summer. You can purchase this fertilizer ready for use, or, if you prefer, you can make it yourself. The ingredients are twelve parts of superphosphate of lime, ten parts of nitrate of potash, two parts of sulphate of magnesium, one part of sulphate of iron, eight parts of gypsum. Mix thoroughly, crush up fine, and use at the rate of 110 g per square metre (4 oz per square yard).

Prune Flowering Shrubs. Shrubs to prune now include the hardy fuchsias such as *F. magellanica*, *F. gracilis* and *F. riccartonii*; *Buddleia variabilis*, and its varieties, *Leycesteria formosa*, *Perowskia atriplicifolia*, *Romneya coulteri* and *R. trichocalyx*, also all varieties of cornus and salix (willow) grown for bark effects. With all these pruning should be hard, last year's growth being cut back quite close to the older wood, but with the buddleias you can allow a few branches to remain at three-quarter length to build up a main framework of growth if a large bush is required (for method see February, First Week).

Pot Cyclamen Seedlings. If you were able to raise cyclamen from seeds last summer (see August, Second Week), the seedlings will now be ready for transferring singly to 8-cm (3-in) pots filled with John Innes potting compost No. 1 or an equivalent mixture. The tubers should be kept on the surface of the soil, not buried. Pot moderately firm, water freely, and then stand the plants on a shelf or staging in a light, airy part of the greenhouse. The temperature should not fall below 10°C (50°F). An average of just over 16°C (60°F) is ideal at this stage.

Sow Zinnias in a Frame. If you make a sowing of zinnias in a warm, sheltered frame and keep the seedlings growing strongly without check, the plants will flower by July. The secret of success with zinnias is to maintain steady growth. Any kind of check is fatal, and sometimes it is almost impossible to avoid a check with seedlings from an earlier sowing. Sow thinly in boxes or directly in the frame and cover with 0·5 cm ($\frac{1}{4}$ in) of fine soil.

Lift Celery and Leeks. If there are still celery and leeks left in the ground from last year, lift these and lay them in behind a north wall or in any other cool place. This simply means digging a shallow trench, laying the leeks and celery in this with their tops exposed, and covering them with a little soil.

Feed Spring Cabbages. Give spring cabbages – that is, cabbages which are now nearing maturity – a topdressing of nitrate of soda, at the rate of 14 g per square metre ($\frac{1}{2}$ oz per square yard), and hoe it in. A further dressing can be given in about three weeks' time.

Plant Second Early and Maincrop Potatoes. If the weather is good and the soil works well, there is no point in delaying the planting of second early and maincrop potatoes. These crop more heavily than the earlies and therefore require more room. Allow at least 1 m (3 ft) between the rows and 30 cm (12 in) between the tubers in the rows. I find that it is simplest and most satisfactory to plant with a spade, making the holes just deep enough to allow the tops of the tubers to be covered with 8 cm (3 in) of soil. If the soil is inclined to be harsh and stony, surround each planting set with a few handfuls of peat or leafmould. Maincrop potatoes take longer to mature than second earlies, and will give a good succession in spite of the fact that they are planted at the same time.

Protect Early Potatoes. Keep a close watch on the earliest potato bed now, for shoots may soon appear and, if they do, they will certainly need protection. The simplest method is to pull some soil over them with a draw hoe; or, if you prefer, you can scatter some dry straw or bracken over them.

Plant Onion Sets. These are small onion bulbs especially prepared for spring planting. Space them 10 to 15 cm (4 to 6 in) apart in rows 30 cm (1 ft) apart, barely covering the little bulbs with soil. The bed should be prepared as for seed-raised onions.

Sow and Plant Globe Artichokes. The globe artichoke can be raised from seed, though a better method is to propagate selected varieties by suckers as the best forms do not come true from seed. However, if you would like to try seed, now is the time to sow it, either in a frame or a sheltered border. Sow in drills 20 cm (8 in) apart and cover very lightly.

The best globe artichokes are propagated by suckers or offsets, and this is the time to plant them. Choose a really good piece of ground, well worked and thoroughly manured, and plant the suckers firmly 1 m (3 ft) apart each way. This will seem a lot of space, but it is really necessary because the globe artichoke grows into a very large plant and will not give good results if crowded.

Sow Kohl Rabi. Kohl rabi is useful as a substitute for turnips in seasons or places where the soil is too dry for the latter crop. This is the time to sow the seeds, in shallow drills 38 cm (15 in) apart.

Sow and Plant Asparagus. Asparagus can be raised from seed sown now in a sheltered border outdoors, but it is a slow process, for three or four years must elapse before the roots are large enough for cutting to start.

The best method of making new asparagus plantations is by planting sturdy roots. There are many different ways of growing asparagus but one of the best is that in which the crowns are planted in single rows about 1 m (3 ft) apart, with 30 cm (1 ft) between each plant. The crowns are put into a shallow trench, spreading the roots out as widely as possible, and then covering them with fine soil until they are 10 cm (4 in) below the surface. Two-year-old crowns can be used, although commercial growers often prefer to use one-year-old plants.

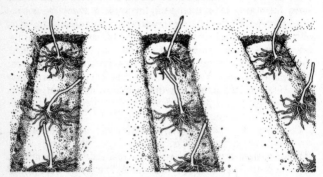

Planting Asparagus. New asparagus beds can be made at this time by planting sturdy roots 10 cm (4 in) deep and 30 cm (1 ft) apart in rows which are 1 m (3 ft) apart

This method of growing in flat beds is suitable where drainage is good, but on heavy or poorly drained soils a raised bed is better, making it about 15 cm (6 in) above the level of the surrounding ground.

Plant Cucumbers. Cucumbers from a March sowing (see March, First Week) will now be ready for planting in a heated greenhouse.

Spray Gooseberries and Black Currants. If your gooseberries have suffered in the past from attacks of mildew, spray them, a few days before the flowers expand, with lime sulphur wash or dinocap at the usual strength recommended by the manufacturers.

Black currants sometimes get very badly attacked by a minute pest which breeds within the buds and causes them to swell up to a great size. This condition is appropriately known as big bud, and if any of your black currants are suffering from it you should spray them at once with lime sulphur wash at twice the normal winter strength recommended by the manufacturers. The effect of this will be to scorch the tiny leaves that are just appearing, but the bushes will recover later on and the mites will be killed.

Finish Grafting Fruit Trees. Early April is a good time for grafting fruit trees in the open – but the earlier the better. I have already given instructions for this operation in March, Fourth Week.

SECOND WEEK

Plant Violets. It is time to make a new violet bed out of doors to provide clumps for forcing next winter. If cuttings were rooted the previous autumn, as described in the notes for September, General Work (and there is no better way of growing good, clean violets), the old clumps that have been flowering during the past winter can be discarded altogether. However, if you have no cuttings you will have to be satisfied with young rooted pieces pulled from the outside of the old clumps to make the new plantation. The central portion of each clump should be thrown away, however, for it is unlikely to give good results another season. Whether you use rooted pieces pulled off the clumps or rooted cuttings the method of making a plantation is the same. Choose a partially shaded border and rather heavy, rich soil if there is any choice in the matter. Plant the big single varieties 23 cm (9 in) apart in rows 30 cm (1 ft) apart and the doubles 15 cm (6 in) apart in rows 23 cm (9 in) apart.

Sow Hardy Annuals. Seed of the various hardy annuals will usually germinate more readily and certainly in mid-April than in March, particularly if the soil tends to be heavy and cold. I gave particulars for an early sowing in the notes for March, Third Week, and these apply with equal force now, except that a number of other kinds can be sown, notably nasturtiums of all types, calandrinia, sweet sultan, layia, leptosiphon, canary creeper, *Tagetes signata pumila*, *Mesembryanthemum criniflorum*, ursinia, venidium, dimorphotheca, salpiglossis and jacobaea. In sheltered gardens it is even possible to sow a number of half-hardy annuals outdoors with success, but if your garden is at all exposed I advise you to leave this until the first week in May. Given cloche protection, however, immediate sowing is possible.

Start Achimenes and Hippeastrums for Succession. A second batch of achimenes (see February, First Week) started now will ensure a succession of flowers in late summer and early autumn.

Start any remaining hippeastrum bulbs into growth now to provide late flowers (see January, Fourth Week).

Pot Seedlings of Glasshouse Plants. Begonias, gloxinias and streptocarpuses raised from seed in January and pricked off in February or early March (see February, Fourth Week) will probably be in need of first potting into 8-cm (3-in) pots. Use John Innes potting compost No. 1 or an equivalent soilless mixture and stand in a light, well-ventilated place in a temperature between 13 and 16°C (55 and 60°F).

Sow French Beans under Glass. If you want a supply of French beans in July make a sowing now in seed boxes or pots; the latter method has the advantage that it avoids any root disturbance later on. Place one seed in each 6·5-cm (2½-in) pot, or in boxes plant the seeds 5 cm (2 in) apart each way. Cover with 2 cm (¾ in) of soil and germinate in the greenhouse or in a frame with soil-warming cables. A temperature of about 13°C (55°F) is necessary for germination, but no harm will be done if it happens to fall a little below this occasionally. Frost, however, will kill the bean. The seedlings will be hardened off later on for planting out in late May (see May, Fourth Week).

Sow Maincrop Carrots. Now is the time to make the maincrop sowing of carrots. For this you will need an intermediate or long variety instead of the stump-rooted type. Sow thinly in drills about 1 cm ($\frac{1}{2}$ in) deep and 30 cm (1 ft) apart. It is quite a good plan to make a small successional sowing of a stump-rooted variety as well and repeat a fortnight or three weeks later, as from these sowings you will have tender young roots after midsummer, but before the main crop is ready. These small varieties need only be sown in drills 23 cm (9 in) apart.

Sow Salsify. Salsify is by no means everybody's vegetable, but food experts think a lot of it. Sow the seed now in shallow drills 30 cm (1 ft) apart. You must choose an open part of the garden and ground that has been well dug and manured, though preferably a year previously. The roots may be forked and useless if grown on freshly manured ground, and for this reason many gardeners plant salsify on the ground occupied by celery trenches the previous year, with no further manuring except a dusting of bonemeal in the autumn and an occasional sprinkling of a compound fertilizer while the plants are in growth.

Sow Winter Greens. All kinds of winter greens should now be sown. Brussels sprouts, cauliflower, broccoli and cabbages, either to follow the early sowing made under glass (see March, First Week) or as a first sowing, and borecole (kale), savoy and late sprouting broccoli for the first time. The simplest and most economical method is to sow broadcast as thinly as possible on a finely prepared seed bed and cover with fine soil, which can be sifted over the seeds, to a depth of about 0·5 cm ($\frac{1}{4}$ in). Of course, you must take care to keep each patch quite separate and to label it clearly, because seedlings of winter greens are very much alike and you may find difficulty in identifying them later on if you get the seeds mixed. Note particularly that there are early, mid-season and late varieties of most of these brassica crops and that, by including some of each, the season of use can be greatly extended. Winter hearting cauliflowers succeed best in the milder parts of the British Isles and elsewhere it is probably best to settle for summer and autumn varieties, perhaps deep freezing any surplus for winter and spring use. Broccoli varieties divide into relatively quick maturing calabrese types for use in summer or early autumn, to slow-growing sprouting broccoli which takes the best part of a year to mature and is, therefore, valuable for spring use. Cabbages for spring cutting are also available but should not be sown now (see July, Third Week).

Sow Celery in Frame. To supplement earlier sowings of celery made in a warm greenhouse, or as an alternative to these if they could not be made, celery may now be grown in an unheated frame. The method is just the same as before (see February, Third Week), the seed being sown thinly in well-drained seed trays filled with John Innes seed compost.

Prick off Cabbages, Cauliflowers, etc. Cabbage, cauliflowers, broccolis and Brussels sprouts raised in frame or greenhouse in March (see March, First Week) will be in need of pricking off, 8 cm (3 in) apart each way, in a frame or, provided the weather is mild and they have been properly hardened off, in a sheltered border outdoors.

Plant out Vegetable Seedlings. Culinary peas, onions, leeks, cauliflowers, broad beans and lettuces raised in the greenhouse and transferred to a frame last month for hardening off (see March, Third Week) may now be planted out in the beds in which they are to mature, provided the weather is fairly mild. If it is frosty or winds are cold, wait a further week. All the ground should have been well dug and manured. The position chosen for the cauliflowers should be sheltered from north and east if possible. Exhibition leeks are usually grown in trenches prepared exactly as for celery (see April, General Work), but quite good leeks can also be grown in ordinary beds if the plants are dropped into holes about 23 cm (9 in) deep made with a dibber. With this exception, all other planting of seedlings mentioned above is with a trowel. Planting distances are as follows:

Vegetable	Space between plants	Space between rows
Broad Beans	15 cm (6 in)	60 cm (2 ft)
Cauliflowers	60 cm (2 ft)	60 cm (2 ft)
Celery	30 cm (1 ft)	1 m (3 ft)
Leeks	23 cm (9 in)	45 cm (18 in)
Leeks for exhibition	30 cm (1 ft)	45 cm (18 in)
Lettuces	15 to 23 cm (6 to 9 in)	30 cm (1 ft)
Onions	23 cm (9 in)	30 cm (1 ft)
Peas	10 cm (4 in)	45 cm to 1 m (18 in to 3 ft)

Sow and Pot Aubergines and Capsicums. Make a further sowing of aubergines and capsicums (see March, Second Week) to give plants to be grown outdoors. Pot singly, in 8-cm (3-in) pots in John Innes potting compost No. 1, the seedlings from the March sowings.

Place Early Tomatoes in Final Pots. Tomatoes from a January sowing should now be ready for their final pots. You can, if you prefer, grow them in boxes or plant them out directly into a border of compost prepared on the staging, or on the floor if the house is a light one with low walls or glass right to ground level. Nevertheless, I think 23- or 25-cm (9- or 10-in) pots are best for the first crop, as plants seem to come to maturity more rapidly. John Innes potting compost No. 2 is suitable.

Spray Apples and Pears. If apples were attacked last year by scab disease, spray now with lime sulphur wash, dispersible sulphur or captan as recommended by the manufacturers. Pears similarly attacked should be treated with Bordeaux mixture rather than lime sulphur, as the latter is inclined to cause scorching. Bordeaux mixture should be used as recommended by the manufacturers; it is not safe to use it later than this, and captan should replace it where necessary.

THIRD WEEK

Thin Hardy Annuals. Hardy annuals sown in March outdoors where they are to bloom (see March, Third Week) will be in need of a first thinning out. Simply pull out the feeblest seedlings until the remainder are left a clear 5 to 8 cm (2 to 3 in) apart each way and have room to develop. A further thinning will be necessary in May. You can transplant some of the seedlings elsewhere if you wish, but as a rule those with long, unbranched tap roots do not recover well from the shift. These include annual lupins,

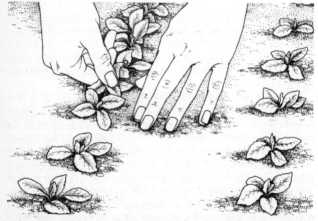

Thinning Annuals. The seedlings of hardy annuals should be thinned to a suitable spacing as soon as they are large enough to be handled

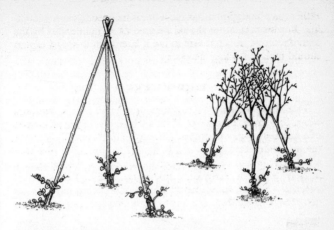

Growing Sweet Peas on Tripods. Three canes tied together in the form of a tripod are a pleasing and effective way of supporting the plants

eschscholzias, poppies, clarkias, godetias, gypsophilas, Virginian stocks, and mignonette. Be sure to firm the soil around the seedlings you leave.

Plant out and Stake Sweet Peas. Sweet peas raised in the greenhouse during January will be ready for planting out, provided they have been hardened off properly. The method to follow is exactly the same as that for planting out September-sown sweet peas (see March, Third Week).

Sweet peas planted in March should be well established, and it will be time to provide each plant with a bamboo cane at least 2·25 m (7 ft) long. This must be pushed really firmly into the soil, and it is a good plan to link all the canes together at the top with string or wire, securing this at each end to a stronger post. You should reduce the number of shoots to one per plant, choosing the sturdiest, and lead this towards its cane with raffia or string.

If the March-sown peas (see March, First Week) have made 5 to 8 cm (2 to 3 in) of growth, as they should by this time, pinch out the tip of each plant. These late-sown peas are usually grown naturally on bushy pea sticks and are not trained to a single stem on bamboos, so there will not be any need to reduce the number of shoots that form as a result of the stopping. They look well in small groups or climbing up tripods among herbaceous plants, or may be trained on screens, pergolas and arches with other climbers including roses.

Plant Violas and Pansies. Plant out violas and pansies, both seedlings and rooted cuttings, if they have been properly hardened off. A rather cool, semi-shaded position is best, though both plants will grow in full sun. The drawback is that they tend to finish flowering sooner. Well-worked, rather liberally manured ground will ensure fine blooms. Plant with a trowel and water in freely.

Start Dahlias in Frames. If you were unable to start dahlias early, as recommended in the February and March notes (see February, Third Week and March, Third Week), you can do so now in an unheated frame. Simply arrange the roots close together in a frame and cover the tubers with light soil. Water moderately, but give increasing supplies as growth commences. Cover the frame with plenty of sacks every night, and remove these in the morning, unless it is very frosty.

Prune Forsythias. This is the time to prune forsythias if you want to keep them as moderately small specimens, or to train them against a wall. The method is to cut back as many as possible of the flowering branches to younger stems that have not yet flowered or to new shoots just starting. Where wall specimens are concerned any small laterals that have not flowered and cannot conveniently be tied in can be cut back severely.

Prune Evergreens grown for Foliage. Hardy evergreen shrubs that are grown principally for their foliage, either in hedges or as topiary specimens, can also be pruned with safety. If there is any really hard cutting back to be done, this is certainly the time to do it. Light trimming can be practised during the summer, but severe pruning is out of place then. Old, worn-out laurel hedges can often be renovated by cutting them back to within a foot of the ground at this time of the year. Of course, the stumps look terrible for a while, but given a little luck and some warm, showery weather, they will soon be a forest of healthy new shoots, with fine, vigorous leaves.

Transfer Bedding Plants to Frames. You may now transfer most of the bedding plants and half-hardy annuals, which till now have been in the greenhouse, to frames for the next stage in hardening off. For the first few days after this move you should keep the frames closed, and cover them well with sacks at night. Then admit a little air by day if it is fine, steadily increasing the amount until by the end of the month the lights are removed altogether for several hours on all mild days. Be particularly wary of days when the sky clears and the wind drops towards evening. At this time of year these signs often precede frost, and lights should be temporarily closed. Your object should be thoroughly to accustom the plants to full exposure, day and night, by the end of May.

If no frame is available, place the young plants in the coolest part of the greenhouse, possibly near the door, and a little later stand them in a sheltered, preferably sunny, place outdoors and cover them at night, whenever the weather is cold, with polythene supported on some kind of temporary framework to keep it off the plants.

Sow Vegetable Marrows, Ridge Cucumbers and Melons. Later on you are sure to want vegetable marrows, and you may be glad of a few ridge cucumbers as well. Sow some seeds now, singly, in 6·5- to 8-cm (2½- to 3-in) pots, and germinate them in the greenhouse or in a frame with soil-warming cables in a temperature of 16°C (60°F) or thereabouts. They will germinate more quickly if you cover the pots with a piece of brown paper, but this must be removed as soon as the seed leaves appear. Melons that are to be grown in a frame should also be sown now and germinated in exactly the same way.

Sow Parsley Outdoors. Make a small sowing of parsley outdoors to provide a successional crop after that sown in February (see February, Fourth Week). Details of sowing are exactly as before, except that there is no need now to choose a specially sheltered or warm position for the sowing.

FOURTH WEEK

Plant Antirrhinums and Penstemons. Antirrhinums raised in the autumn from seeds or cuttings and also penstemons from autumn cuttings may be planted in their flowering quarters if they have been thoroughly accustomed to full exposure.

Take Chrysanthemum Cuttings for Dwarf Plants. This is the time to start taking cuttings of chrysanthemums that are to make dwarf specimens in pots. You can root them in boxes or beds of soil exactly as the earlier chrysanthemum cuttings, though I think a better method is to insert them singly in 6·5-cm (2½-in) pots, or three round the edge of an 8-cm (3-in) pot. Allow them to root either in a cool greenhouse or a frame. By no means all varieties are suitable for this method of culture but lists are given in the catalogues of most chrysanthemum nurseries.

Sow Greenhouse Primulas. Make a first sowing of the various primulas that flower in the greenhouse during winter, for example, *Primula sinensis* and its variety *stellata*, *P. obconica*, and *P. kewensis*. Do not sow all your seeds of the first three now, however, but keep some for a second batch in June (see June, Third Week). Sow the seeds thinly in John Innes or a soilless seed compost. I think they are better sown in well-drained pots or pans rather than boxes. Cover the seeds very lightly with fine soil and germinate in the greenhouse in a temperature of about 16°C (60°F). Cover each seed vessel with a pane of glass until germination takes place. If water is needed, give this by holding the pots nearly to their rims in a tub and not by watering overhead.

Sow Annuals for the Greenhouse. You can now make a second sowing of hardy and half-hardy annuals, for flowering in pots in the greenhouse (see February, Third Week, and March, First Week). Plants from this late sowing will provide a succession of flowers after the first batch is over.

Sow Runner Beans. Make a small sowing of runner beans in exactly the same way as the early sowing of French beans (see Second Week). If you germinate them in the greenhouse you will have some nice forward plants for putting out the first week in June, and these will give you a crop of beans several weeks earlier than would be possible from the earliest outdoor sowing.

Sow Globe Beetroot. You can now make a sowing of globe beetroot in a fairly sheltered border out of doors. This earliest sowing need not be a very large one, as it will be followed by another in May, and also by a much bigger sowing of long beet in the same month. Sow the seeds 5 cm (2 in) deep in rows 30 cm (1 ft) apart. I find the most economical method is to place three seeds every 15 cm (6 in) along the rows and then reduce the seedlings to one at each point later on.

Sow Endive. Make a small sowing of endive; it makes a welcome change from lettuce in summer salads. Sow the seeds thinly in drills 1 cm ($\frac{1}{2}$ in) deep and 30 cm (1 ft) apart.

Spray Gooseberries. If you considered it necessary to spray your gooseberries with lime sulphur before flowering (see April, First Week), you should certainly repeat the treatment as soon as the petals have fallen and you can just see the tiny, fertilized fruits. But for this second spraying you must use the lime sulphur at summer strength, or, alternatively, use dinocap. Consult manufacturer's instructions regarding these.

Remove Greasebands from Trees. You should now remove and burn greasebands that have been round the main trunks or branches of apples, pears, and other fruit trees since September.

Thin Outdoor Peaches and Nectarines. The young fruits on outdoor peaches and nectarines should now be about the size of marbles and you must start to thin them out. The work is done in exactly the same way as with indoor peaches (see March, General Work), and so I need not go into it again in detail here. Do not forget that there may be a natural fall during the stoning period with outdoor peaches and nectarines just as with glasshouse-grown varieties, and that it is not wise to complete thinning until this is over. Disbudding, that is, removal of unwanted young shoots, is carried out with the outdoor trees as with those in the orchard house.

Apricot trees may be allowed to carry more fruits, about 30 per square metre (3 or 4 per square foot) and disbudding is nothing like so drastic, well-placed laterals being merely stopped and not rubbed right out.

FLOWERS, VEGETABLES AND FRUITS IN SEASON DURING APRIL

Herbaceous Plants: *Adonis vernalis, Anchusa officinalis, Bellis perennis monstrosa* (double daisy), *Bergenia ciliata, B. cordifolia* and vars., *B. crassifolia, B. purpurascens, B. stracheyi, Brunnera macrophylla, Cheiranthus allionii* (Siberian wallflower), *C. cheiri* (wallflower), *Doronicum austriacum, D. caucasicum, D. cordatum, D. pardalianches, D. plantagineum, Dracunculus vulgaris, Helleborus atrorubens, H. corsicus, H. orientalis* and vars. (Lenten rose), *Heuchera tiarelloides, Iris chamaeiris, I. ensata, I. innominata, I. japonica,* myosotis hybrids (forget-me-nots), *Polygonatum hybridum, P. multiflorum* (Solomon's seal), *P. odoratum, P. verticillatum, Primula vulgaris* and vars. (primrose and polyanthus), *Pulmonaria angustifolia, P. officinalis, P. rubra, P. saccharata.*

Hardy Bulbs, Corms and Tubers: *Allium neapolitanum,
Anemone coronaria* and vars., *A. fulgens* and vars., *Chionodoxa
luciliae, C. sardensis, Convallaria majalis* (lily of the valley),
crocuses (large flowered), *Cyclamen libanoticum, C. orbiculatum,
C. repandum, Endymion hispanicus, E. non-scriptus* (bluebell),
*Erythronium californicum, E. dens-canis, E. grandiflorum, E.
hartwegii, E. hendersonii, E. revolutum, E. tuolumnense, Fritillaria acmopetala, F. assyriaca, F. citrina, F. imperialis, F.
meleagris, F. persica, F. pudica, F. pyrenaica, F. recurva, F.
ruthenica,* hyacinths (large flowered), *Ipheion uniflorum, Iris
bucharica, I. melanostricta, I. orchioides, Leucojum vernum,
Muscari armeniacum, M. botryoides, M. comosum, M. latifolium,
M. moschatum, M. racemosum, Narcissus bulbocodium, N.
minor,* narcissus hybrids in var. (including trumpet daffodils),
*Puschkinia scilloides, Romulea clusiana, R. requienii, R. rosea,
Scilla bifolia, S. sibirica, Tecophilaea cyanocrocus* (shelter),
*Trillium erectum, T. grandiflorum, T. ovatum, T. recurvatum, T.
sessile, T. undulatum, Tulipa biflora, T. clusiana, T. dasystemon,
T. didieri, T. eichleri, T. fosteriana, T. greigii, T. hageri, T.
kaufmanniana, T. linifolia, T. orphanidea, T. praestans, T.
primulina, T. pulchella, T. saxatilis, T. sylvestris, T. tarda, T.
viridiflora,* tulips in var. (early singles and doubles, Mendels and
Triumphs).

Rock Plants: *Aethionema pulchellum, Alyssum saxatile* and
vars., *A. serpyllifolium, A. spinosum, Androsace carnea, Anemone
apennina, A. ranunculoides, Arabis albida* and vars., *Arctostaphylos uva-ursi, Armeria caespitosa, Aubrieta deltoidea* and
vars., *Bellis perennis* vars., *Bellium bellidioides, Chiastophyllum
simplicifolium, Corydalis cheilanthifolia, C. wilsonii, Daphne
blagayana, D. cneorum, D. tangutica, Draba aizoides, D. aizoon,
D. bruniifolia, D. bryoides, D. dedeana, D. imbricata, D. poly-
tricha, Epigaea repens, Epimedium grandiflorum, E. pinnatum,
E. rubrum, E. versicolor* and vars., *Gentiana acaulis, G. verna,
Geum borisii, G. montanum, Iberis saxatilis, I. sempervirens, Iris*

pumila and vars., *Lathyrus vernus*, *Lithospermum rosmarinifolium* (shelter), *Mazus pumilio*, *M. reptans*, *Morisia monantha*, *Omphalodes cappadocica*, *O. verna*, *Papaver alpinum*, *Primula allionii*, *P. auricula* and vars., *P. cortusoides*, *P. denticulata* and vars., *P. frondosa*, *P. juliae*, *P. juliana* hybrids, *P. marginata*, *P. minima*, *P. prolifera*, *Pulsatilla vernalis*, *P. vulgaris*, *Ranunculus alpestris*, *R. amplexicaule*, *R. glacialis*, *R. gramineus*, *R. pyrenaeus*, *Sanguinaria canadensis*, *Saxifraga arco-valleyi*, *S. aretioides*, *S. boydii*, *S. decipiens* in var. (mossy saxifrages), *S. hypnoides* (mossy saxifrages), *S. lilacina*, *S. marginata*, *S. oppositifolia* and vars., *S. petraschii*, *S. sancta*, *Shortia galacifolia*, *S. uniflora*, *Soldanella alpina*, *S. montana*, *Synthyris reniformis*, *Tiarella cordifolia*, *Viola biflora*, *V. gracilis* and vars.

Hardy Aquatic and Bog Plants: *Caltha palustris* and vars., *C. polypetala*, *Cardamine pratensis plena*, *Chrysosplenium oppositifolium*, *Dodecatheon meadia* and vars., *Peltiphyllum peltatum*.

Evergreen Shrubs: *Arctostaphylos manzanita*, *Berberis buxifolia*, *B. darwinii*, *B. hookeri*, *B. linearifolia*, *B. lologensis*, *B. pruinosa*, *B. sargentiana*, *B. stenophylla*, *B. verruculosa*, *Camellia japonica* vars., *C. reticulata* vars., *C. saluenensis*, *C. williamsii* vars., *Ceanothus arboreus*, *C. rigidus*, *Choisya ternata*, *Coronilla glauca*, *Daphne burkwoodii*, *D. cneorum*, *D. tangutica*, *Erica arborea*, *E. australis*, *E. cárnea* and vars., *E. darleyensis*, *E. mediterranea*, *Euphorbia wulfenii*, *Mahonia aquifolium*, *M. repens*, *M. undulata*, *Osmanthus delavayi*, *Osmarea burkwoodii*, *Photinia serrulata*, *Pieris floribunda*, *P. formosa*, *P. japonica*, *P. taiwanensis*, *Prunus laurocerasus* and vars., *Rhododendron agrophyllum* (shelter), *R. arboreum*, *R. augustinii*, *R. calophytum*, *R. campanulatum*, *R. campylocarpum* and hybrids, *R. ciliatum*, *R. concatenans*, *R. decorum*, *R. falconeri*, *R. fictolacteum*, *R. hippophaeoides*, *R. hodgsonii*, *R. impeditum*, *R. intricatum*, *R. neriiflorum*, *R. racemosum*, *R. rubiginosum*, *R. scintillans*, *R. sinograande*, *R. spinuliferum*, *R. thomsonii*, *R. valentinianum*, *R. williamsonianum*, *Rosmarinus officinalis*, *Skimmia japonica*, *Vi-*

burnum burkwoodii, *V. tinus*, *Vinca major*, *V. minor*.

Deciduous Shrubs: *Chaenomeles japonica*, *C. speciosa*, *Colletia infausta*, *Cytisus ardoinii*, *C. monspessulanus*, *C. praecox*, *Elaeagnus multiflora*, *Enkianthus campanulatus*, *Forsythia intermedia* and vars., *F. suspensa*, *F. viridissima*, *Fothergilla gardenii*, *Magnolia stellata*, *Prunus glandulosa*, *P. tenella*, *P. triloba*, *Rhododendron albrechtii*, *R. quinquefolium*, *R. schlippenbachii*, *R. vaseyi*, *Ribes sanguineum* and vars., *R. speciosum*, *Rubus spectabilis*, *Spirea arguta*, *S. prunifolia*, *S. thunbergii*, *Ulex europaeus plenus*, *Viburnum carlesii*, *V. judii*, *Xanthorrhiza apiifolia*.

Evergreen Trees: *Arbutus andrachne*, *Drimys winteri*, *Michelia doltsopa*.

Deciduous Trees: *Acer circinatum*, *A. opalus*, *A. platanoides*, *A. rubrum*, *Amelanchier canadensis*, *A. laevis*, *A. lamarckii*, *A. ovalis*, *Magnolia denudata*, *M. kobus*, *M. liliiflora*, *M. salicifolia*, *M. sargentiana*, *M. soulangiana*, *M. veitchii*, *Malus aldenhamensis*, *M. atrosanguinea*, *M. baccata*, *M. floribunda*, *M. lemoinei*, *M. niedzwetzkyana*, *M. prunifolia*, *M. purpurea*, *M. robusta*, *M. sargentii*, *M. scheideckeri*, *M. spectabilis*, *M. tschonoskii*, *M. yunnanensis*, *Prunus avium*, *P. cerasus* vars., *P. communis*, *P. incisa*, *P. lannesiana* (Japanese cherry), *P. mahaleb* and vars., *P. mume*, *P. persica* and vars., *P. sargentii*, *P. serrulata* and vars. (Japanese cherries), *P. subhirtella*, *P. yedoensis*, *Pyrus communis* (pear).

Hardy Climbing Plants: *Akebia quinata*, *A. trifoliata*, *Clematis alpina*, *C. armandii*, *Ercilla spicata*, *Stauntonia hexaphylla*.

Greenhouse Plants: Abutilons, acacias, arum lilies, astilbes, azaleas (Indian and mollis types), *Begonia manicata*, *Boronia megastigma*, *Brunfelsia calycina*, calceolaria (herbaceous), *Cantua buxifolia*, carnations (perpetual flowering), celsias, cinerarias (hybrids), clivias, *Columnea banksii*, *C. gloriosa*, *Coronilla glauca*, *Crossandra infundibuliformis*, *C. subacaulis*, *Cuphea ignea*, *Cytisus canariensis*, *Deutzia gracilis*, *Dicentra spectabilis*, freesias, gardenias, hippeastrums, hyacinths (large flowered), *Hydrangea macrophylla hortensia* in var., ixias, *Jacobinia pauciflora*, lachenalias, *Lampranthus* species, *Leucocoryne ixioides*, *Lilium longiflorum*, pelargoniums (show and regal), *Prostanthera violacea*, *Reinwardtia trigyna*, *Rhipsalidopsis gaertneri*, rhododendrons, roses, schizanthus and other annuals (see list, September, First Week), stephanotis, tulips (Cottage and Darwin).

Vegetables in Store: Same as March.

Vegetables in the Garden: Broccoli (sprouting), cabbage (sown in July and August), cauliflower (late), kale, leeks, lettuce, spring onions, rhubarb, seakale, spinach beet, turnip tops.

Vegetables under Glass: French beans, carrots, cucumbers, lettuce, mustard and cress, radish.

Fruits in Store: *Apples:* Allen's Everlasting (D), Annie Elizabeth (C), Barnack Beauty (CD), Belle de Boskoop (CD), Bramley's Seedling (C), Brownlees' Russet (D), Cornish Gillyflower (D), Crawley Beauty (C), D'Arcy Spice (D), Edward VII (C), King of Tompkin's County (D), Laxton's Pearmain (D), Monarch (C), Newton Wonder (C), Ontario (CD), Sturmer Pippin (D), Wagener (C), Winston (D). *Grapes:* Mrs Pince, Prince of Wales. *Pears:* Bergamotte d'Esperen (D), Catillac (C), Joséphine de Malines (D), Uvedale's St Germain (C).

Fruits under Glass. Strawberries.

May

GENERAL WORK

Thin and Stake Herbaceous Perennials. It is usually a mistake to allow herbaceous perennials to retain all the growth they produce. Much better results can be obtained by thinning out the shoots a little at this time of the year. Delphiniums and Michaelmas daisies in particular repay rather drastic thinning. Retain some of the sturdiest shoots and nip off the rest. Before the stems get too long and begin to flop about, place bamboo canes in position and loop the stems to these. Usually it is best to have several canes per plant, thrust in close to the clump but leaning outwards towards the top so that, as growth extends and is tied to the canes, it will be spread out and get its full ration of light and air. As an alternative to this method of staking, twiggy branches may be pushed into the soil around the plants; as the plants grow they will obscure the branches and be supported by them.

Thin out Rose Growth. It is an excellent plan to examine rose bushes and standards occasionally during the month and to pinch out any badly placed or overcrowded shoots. Those growing inwards and so tending to crowd the centre of the plant are the ones most likely to cause trouble later on.

Keep a Watch for Greenfly. Greenfly is likely to make its first appearance during the month. Keep a sharp look out for this pest especially on the young growths of roses and fruit trees. At the outset it is easy enough to kill all the insects by spraying once or twice with a reliable aphicide such as dimethoate, formothion, menazon, pirimicarb or resmethrin. The first three are systemic, which means that they enter the sap of the plant where they gradually decompose but cannot be washed off by rain. If used on fruit crops, care must be taken not to eat the fruits until the prescribed safety period, printed on the label, has elapsed.

Kill Slugs. Slugs are also likely to be much in evidence now and may do a lot of damage to tender seedlings, lettuces, delphiniums, etc., unless you take measures against them. There are numerous propriatary pellets which may be sprinkled round plants to protect them. An effective home-made slug killer can be prepared by mixing 25 g of metaldehyde with 1·6 kg of bran (1 oz of metaldehyde to 3 lb of bran). Place this in small heaps, protected by small pieces of slate, where slugs have been feeding.

Use Lawn Sand on Weedy Lawns. May is a good month for using lawn sand or finely powdered sulphate of ammonia to kill small, broad-leaved weeds on the lawn. What actually happens is that the chemical lodges on broad leaves and scorches them but slips harmlessly off the upright narrow blades of grass. It is most effective in dry weather. If you use sulphate of ammonia, be certain to distribute it as evenly as possible and not to use more than 14 g per square metre ($\frac{1}{2}$ oz per square yard). You can give a second application a few weeks after the first provided there has been some rain meanwhile to wash the former dose away. Commercial lawn sand should always be used strictly according to the manufacturer's instructions.

An alternative and even more effective method is to use one of the selective hormone weed killers such as MCPA or 2, 4-D. These are sold under various trade names and for lawn use are generally offered in liquid form (see p. 8).

Feed Plants that are in Full Growth. It is a very good plan to feed plants that are growing fast. At this time of the year most herbaceous plants are making a big effort and many of them are forming their flower stems. Spring-sown vegetables are also growing freely and need plenty of nourishment. Early in the month give all such plants a small topdressing of a compound, quick-acting fertilizer and hoe this in. There are plenty of good fertilizers on the market for this purpose or, if you prefer, you can make your own mixture with seven parts of superphosphate of lime, three parts of sulphate of ammonia, two parts of sulphate of potash and one part of steamed boneflour well mixed and applied at the rate of 85 g per square metre (3 oz per square yard). Repeat the application after about three weeks. The mixture mentioned above is suitable for a great variety of plants, but for vegetables grown principally for their leaves, and also peas, you can increase the proportion of sulphate of ammonia to five parts with advantage. An alternative to dry feeding of this kind is to use a liquid fertilizer every 7 to 14 days, diluted according to the maker's instructions.

Plant Aquatics. May is the best month of the year for planting water lilies and other aquatic plants. These may either be planted direct in soil, spread on the bottom of the pool to a depth of at least 15 cm (6 in), or they may be planted in baskets or pots which are then sunk into position. If you adopt the former method, empty the pool first, place the soil in position and plant the roots with a trowel exactly as if you were dealing with herbaceous perennials. Then run a little water into the pool, but

117

only a few inches at first. Add more as the plants grow, the idea being to keep the leaves of water lilies just floating on the surface. If the plants are placed in baskets or pots these may stand on bricks temporarily to keep the crowns near the surface. When growth is well started the bricks are removed.

Planting Aquatics. Aquatic plants such as water lilies are most conveniently planted in special baskets. The basket is first lined with hessian to retain the soil in which the plants are set. The soil, in turn, is covered with gravel to avoid disturbance.

Harden off Bedding Plants in Frames. During the early part of May bedding plants in frames must receive as much ventilation as possible, though it is still unwise to expose any of them to frost. Take the lights right off by day if the weather is fine, but replace them in the afternoon should there be a threat of frost. A clearing sky in the afternoon is to be regarded with suspicion at this time of the year, as, more often than not, it is an indication that there will be a sharp frost at night. Geraniums, fuchsias and marguerites, also almost all half-hardy annuals sown in February (see February, Third Week), should be fully hardened off and ready for the open ground by the last week in May; but it is advisable to give dahlias, heliotropes, scarlet salvias and cannas a further week as they are more susceptible to cold.

General Greenhouse Management. As sun heat gains still more in power you will have to be increasingly careful in shading plants. Foliage plants in general, and particularly many ferns, suffer a lot if exposed too long to intense light and heat. Tuberous-rooted begonias also take it badly, and gloxinias appreciate a measure of shade.

Another consequence of the increased sun heat is that plants will require considerably larger supplies of water. This is particularly so with cucumbers and tomatoes. The earlier raised plants should be growing very freely and will transpire a lot of water on a warm day. You must certainly examine all the plants in your greenhouse daily. It does not follow that all the plants will require water every day, though it is quite possible some will, but you should examine the soil carefully to make quite certain how things are. Where plants in clay pots are concerned, rap these with a hard piece of wood such as a cotton reel pushed on to the end of a thin bamboo cane, or the leg bone of a chicken. If the pot gives a ringing note the soil within it is dry, but if it has a dull heavy sound the soil is probably moist enough. I say 'probably' because the test is valueless if the pot happens to be cracked. Broken pots always give a dull note, so see that you are not misled. Plastic pots cannot be tested in this way.

More ventilation can be given by day and usually it is safe to give a little ventilation at night, but I still prefer to rely exclusively on the top ventilators, except with plants that have been grown under cool conditions from the outset. Side ventilators are well enough in the summer, but in the spring they are liable to cause damaging draughts. One thing that you must particularly guard against from now onwards is a sudden rise of temperature early in the morning. As soon as direct sunlight first strikes the greenhouse, this quick rise in temperature is likely to take place. A vast amount of damage in amateurs' greenhouses must be done every year during the spring and summer on bright mornings between about 5 and 8 a.m.

Pot on Spring-rooted Pelargoniums and other Greenhouse Plants. If you struck cuttings of fuchsias and pelargoniums in March (see March, General Work) and you wish to grow on some of the plants in pots for autumn and winter flowering, they will need potting now into 13-cm (5-in) pots. Use John Innes potting compost No. 1 or a soilless equivalent. Pinch the points out of fuchsias to encourage bushy growth. Return the plants to the greenhouse for a week or so after potting. At the end of the month they may go to a sunny frame for the summer. Similar remarks apply to rooted cuttings of coleuses and other greenhouse plants. Some of the later cuttings of all these plants will be in need of a first potting into 8-cm (3-in) pots.

Cuttings of winter-flowering begonias rooted last month (see April, General Work) must be potted as soon as they are well rooted. Pot them singly in 8-cm (3-in) pots, using the same compost as that used for the pelargoniums and fuchsias. Place them on the staging in the greenhouse with an average day temperature of 18°C (65°F), not falling below 13°C (55°F) at night, and shade from direct sunshine.

Allow Nerines, Arums, Freesias and Lachenalias to go to Rest. Gradually reduce the amount of water given to nerines, and place the plants in the sunniest part of the greenhouse. The object of this is to ripen the bulbs and allow them to go to rest. The foliage will gradually turn yellow and die down. Freesias and lachenalias (see April, General Work) will benefit from a similar thorough baking on a shelf near the glass or in some such sunny place. Once their foliage dies down no water need be given until July or August. Arum lilies must also be allowed to go to rest (see April, General Work). This now applies to the later batches that have flowered in a cool house as well as to the earlier forced roots. Do not attempt to bake them in the sun after the fashion of nerine bulbs, but simply reduce the water supply gradually and then, when the foliage dies down, lay the pots on their sides and give no more water until August.

Pot and Stop Perpetual-flowering Carnations. Carnations grown from cuttings taken during the winter and early spring are all likely to be ready for their final move into pots 15 to 18 cm (6 to 7 in) in diameter some time during the month. Do the work as soon as the 8-cm (3-in) pots are comfortably filled with roots but before they show the slightest tendency to become pot bound. Use John Innes potting compost No. 2. Pot firmly and then arrange the plants in a frame, keeping the lights on if it freezes or the wind is very cold, but removing them altogether when it is mild.

From time to time break out the ends of the first side shoots resulting from the earlier stopping (see March, General Work). The ideal time to do this is when the shoot has made about eight joints, and two complete joints should be broken out. Do not deal with more than one shoot per plant at a time but spread the work over a period so that the plant does not suffer any severe check to growth.

Thin out Chrysanthemum Growths. During the month chrysanthemums that were stopped during March and April will be making new growths – known as 'breaks'. You will have to decide just how many of these you require per plant and then rub the rest out as soon as possible. The actual number retained will depend upon the type of chrysanthemum and the purpose for which you are growing it. With exhibition Japanese chrysanthemums that are being grown for the biggest flowers possible, only one shoot must be retained per plant. If prize winning is not the main object you may be satisfied to leave three stems per plant, and this is usually the ideal number to leave on incurved varieties that are being grown for exhibition. The reason for leaving more with these is that great size is not desirable, quality and form are the imperative points and these are best obtained by having several blooms per plant. Decoratives that are being grown for cutting may also have three stems from the present stopping. They will be allowed to carry still more when they break again (see June, General Work).

Stop Exhibition Chrysanthemums. Some varieties may need to be stopped at some time in May so consult the stopping lists given in the catalogues of chrysanthemum specialists (see April, General Work).

Make Successional Sowings. Once again there will be a number of sowings to be made during the month to provide a succession of vegetables after those raised from earlier sowings. Lettuces, spinach, turnips, radishes and mustard and cress should be sown exactly as explained in the notes for April, General Work, with the exception that it is now more than ever advisable to sow the three first-named in a partially shaded position. They will not stand a great amount of summer heat, as this makes them run to seed. You should make a couple of sowings of maincrop peas to give you a chance of continuing the crop well on into the autumn. Make a further sowing of endive (see April, Fourth Week) towards the end of the month, and another sowing of kohl rabi about the middle of the month (see April, First Week).

Stake Culinary Peas. Successional batches of culinary peas will be growing freely during the month and these must be staked as soon as they are a couple of inches in height. Even the dwarf peas should have small brushy twigs to keep them erect. At the same time draw a little soil into a ridge on each side of the row. This will serve to protect the young plants and will also make a trough into which you can pour water and liquid manure later on.

Earth up Early Potatoes. As the earlier crops of potatoes push their shoots through the ground draw more soil around them for protection. A few degrees of frost will injure these shoots and there can be no certainty about the weather until May is well advanced. The very earliest outdoor crops, in sheltered borders (see February, Fourth Week) will be well advanced in growth and it will not be possible to protect them with soil alone. Keep some dry straw, bracken, or evergreen boughs at hand and strew these thickly over the bed when frost threatens.

Potatoes in frames must be ventilated as freely as possible on all mild days, but be sure to place the lights in position again early in the afternoon if frost threatens. Incidentally, it is wasteful

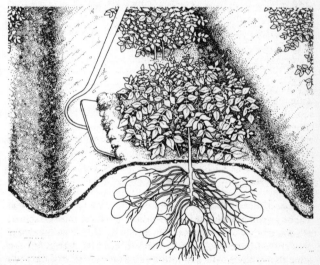

Earthing Up Potatoes. Protect early potatoes by drawing soil up around the stems as they grow

to lift whole roots of frame potatoes when the tubers form. Scrape away the soil from them as they grow, remove the biggest tubers and then return the soil once more. The smaller tubers will continue to swell and you can collect them later on. You should be able to pick the first tubers early this month.

Thin Onions and Root Crops. Various crops sown in drills out of doors will be in need of thinning during the month. The sooner this can be started the better, once the seedlings can be clearly seen, but I do not advise you to complete the thinning all at one operation as there may be some casualties yet.

Recommended thinning distances are as follows:

Vegetable	Distance between plants
Artichoke, Globe	15 cm (6 in)
Asparagus	30 cm (1 ft)
Carrots (Stump-rooted)	8 cm (3 in)
Carrots (Long or intermediate)	10 cm (4 in)
Kohl rabi	23 cm (9 in)
Leeks	10 cm (4 in) These will be transplanted in July
Lettuces	15 to 30 cm (6 in to 1 ft) depending on the variety
Onions	15 to 23 cm (6 to 9 in)
Turnips	10 cm (4 in)

It is always advisable to increase these distances if you wish to have large vegetables for exhibition. Seedlings of lettuce may be transplanted elsewhere if you water them in well. The seedlings of root crops are not of any value for transplanting. Pull out the weakest and least promising seedlings first, and be careful not to disturb those you leave more than you can help. Make the loosened soil firm again with the knuckles. This is particularly important with onions, as the dreaded onion fly frequently lays its eggs in the loose soil caused by careless thinning.

As a further precaution against this pest sprinkle 4% calomel dust along the rows of onions, keeping it in a narrow band on each side of the plants.

Protect Brassica Seedlings from Flea Beetles. Lightly dust all seedlings of cabbage, broccoli, cauliflower, Brussels sprouts, kale, turnip, swede and other brassicas with HCH, carbaryl or derris to kill flea beetles before they have a chance to do any harm. The treatment can be repeated occasionally if any flea beetles are seen or if small holes appear in the leaves.

Feed, Disbud and Pollinate Tomatoes. Tomatoes will be in various stages of growth. The earliest will have set some fruits by this time, later batches may be just coming into flower, while yet others from March sowings will be ready for potting on into 13-cm (5-in) pots early in the month. With all these you must remove side shoots regularly.

It is advisable to continue to pollinate flowers by hand either by tapping the plants or by scattering dry pollen from flower to flower with a soft paintbrush. This is most effective if done about midday when the sun is shining.

The earliest plants will benefit from a topdressing of old, well-rotted manure thoroughly broken up and spread evenly all over the existing compost to a depth of about 2·5 cm (1 in). You can give additional food in liquid form once a week. There is nothing better than a good proprietary fertilizer for this purpose – only be sure to use it weak. I prefer to dilute with twice as much water as the manufacturers recommend and then give the feed rather more frequently. If you prefer to make your own mixture use three parts of superphosphate of lime, two parts of sulphate of ammonia, and two parts of sulphate of potash well mixed and dissolved in water at the rate of 1 teaspoonful per gallon (4·5 litres).

Keep the main stems tied up regularly and pinch out the points of the most forward plants as soon as they reach the ridge.

Train and Feed Melons. You will now be able to see the result of your pollination last month (see April, General Work). If sufficient fruits have set on each plant, well and good; but if only one or two have set, remove them and start all over again, fertilizing the requisite number of female flowers all on the same day. As soon as white rootlets appear on the surface of the bed, topdress with 2·5 cm (1 in) of well-rotted manure thoroughly broken up. Water very freely. Continue to pinch out the points of side shoots so that the house does not get overcrowded with foliage. Maintain a rather moist atmosphere and a day temperature averaging 21°C (70°F).

Train and Feed Cucumbers. Cucumbers in heated greenhouses and frames will be in various stages of growth. All will require regular training and stopping as already described (see April, General Work), and all must be watered freely and ventilated very sparingly. A damp, warm atmosphere is what the cucumber likes, and only on really mild days should a little air be admitted. From this time onwards a permanent shading of lime wash will be needed on the glass to prevent sun scorch.

The earliest plants in full bearing will need regular feeding with liquid fertilizer used according to makers' instructions. Choose one with approximately equal proportions of nitrogen, phosphoric acid and potash. If you note white rootlets on the surface of any of the beds, topdress at once with an inch-thick layer of old manure, well broken up.

Mulch Fruit Trees. Spread a fairly thick layer of well-rotted farmyard or stable manure, or failing this spent hops (not hop manure, which contains chemicals), around fruit trees and bushes of all types, also raspberries. This is known technically as a mulch, and it is very valuable for three reasons: it provides the trees with much-needed nourishment while they are in growth; it helps to retain moisture in the soil by preventing surface evaporation, and it also keeps down weed growth.

Disbud and Thin Peaches, Nectarines and Apricots Outdoors.
During the month peaches, nectarines, and apricots on walls
will be growing freely, and you must continue to disbud them
in the same way as those grown under glass (see February,
General Work). The fruits must also be thinned a little, but do
not complete this process until the stones are formed (see April,
General Work).

Management of Fruit Under Glass. Peaches and nectarines
that were started into growth in January will be ripening their
fruits during May and you must no longer spray them with water.
Ventilate as freely as possible without letting the temperature
fall below 16°C (60°F) by day or 10°C (50°F) by night. Later
trees will be in various stages of growth and will require thinning,
disbudding, and so on, as described in my notes for General
Work during March and April. Apricots should be thinned
moderately if overcrowded, and laterals must be pinched from
time to time to prevent unnecessary formation of wood.

Treatment of Vines. Outdoor vines will be growing freely now
and you must regulate their growth in much the same manner as
that of indoor varieties. Reduce the number of laterals to one
per spur, retaining those that are showing flower trusses. Stop
them beyond the truss but before they have grown so far as to
interfere with neighbouring vines or the laterals from other rods.

Indoor vines will be in various stages of growth according to
the time at which you started them, and I refer you to my notes
in the General Work for February, March and April for information on such matters as pollination, stopping and thinning.
The earliest vines started in January will now be starting to ripen,
and you must give increased ventilation, using side ventilators
as well as those at the ridge. This, of course, applies in measure
to all vines under glass now that the weather is getting warmer,
but in particular to the earliest, because a heated, stagnant
atmosphere is a certain cause of cracking. There is no need to

keep the evaporating trays filled with water any longer for early vines as a rather dry atmosphere is an advantage. Keep the top ventilators a little open throughout the night, even though this necessitates the use of a little more artificial heat when the weather is cold.

FIRST WEEK

Plant Dahlia Tubers Outdoors. If you have not been able to start dahlia tubers into growth in either a greenhouse or frame you can plant them outdoors now. Cover the tubers with 8 cm (3 in) of soil and then they will be quite secure against frost. It will be some weeks before shoots appear above ground.

Sow Hardy and Half-hardy Annuals. If you want flowers of hardy and half-hardy annuals outdoors in early autumn, now is the time to sow them. The seeds should be scattered broadcast where the plants are to flower and should be covered lightly with soil exactly as described for earlier sowings (see March, Third Week, and April, Second Week).

Spray Roses. Give roses an early spraying with benomyl to prevent black spot disease establishing itself on the young leaves. A systemic insecticide such as dimethoate, formothion or menazon can be used at the same time to kill early aphids.

Sow Cinerarias. Sow a few seeds of cinerarias if you want to have plants in flower by December. The seeds will want a little warmth to encourage germination so early, but the ordinary greenhouse temperature of 13 to 16°C (55 to 60°F) will be ample. Sow very thinly in well-drained pans, using John Innes or a soilless seed compost. Cover lightly with fine soil and sand, and shade until germination begins.

Plant out Winter Greens. Winter green crops from early sowings, and particularly cauliflowers and Brussels sprouts sown in March (see March, First Week) should be planted outdoors in their permanent quarters at the first opportunity. Of course, they must be properly hardened off first, but it should be easy to accomplish this by early May.

It is better to plant with a trowel rather than with a dibber, even though the work is done more rapidly with the latter tool. Usually it is sufficient to plant 60 cm (2 ft) apart in rows 75 cm (2½ ft) apart, but these distances may need to be varied a little according to the size of the varieties you are growing. Seed packets usually give adequate information on these points.

Sow Dwarf French Beans. It should be safe to make a sowing of dwarf French beans in the open, if you were not able to raise any plants under glass last month. Sow the seeds singly about 15 cm (6 in) apart in drills 5 cm (2 in) deep. An economical method is to have two drills about 23 to 30 cm (9 in to 1 ft) apart, then an alleyway about 75 cm (2½ ft) wide, then another couple of rows, and so on.

Sow Maincrop Beetroot. Early May is the time to sow the main crop of beetroot. For this you should choose a long-rooted or intermediate beet rather than a globe variety, unless your ground happens to be very shallow. Sow the seeds in drills 2·5 cm (1 in) deep and 30 cm (1 ft) apart. If you space the seeds, which are quite large, at about 5 cm (2 in) apart it will be a very simple matter to thin the seedlings to about 15 cm (6 in) later on.

Start to Cut Asparagus. From now onwards, for something like six weeks, you should be able to cut good asparagus from established beds. It is, however, a great mistake to cut any shoots at all until the roots are well established. I certainly do not advise you to cut a single shoot until the second year after planting, and it may even be worth waiting until the third year.

Cover Strawberry Beds. Place clean straw around and between strawberry plants. The object of this is twofold: mainly to protect the fruits later on from mud splashings, but also to provide a mulch and so conserve soil moisture, a most important point in the cultivation of good strawberries. Alternatives to loose straw are special strawberry mats that can be purchased from

Cutting Asparagus. The shoots of asparagus are best cut 8 cm (3 in) below soil level when they are about 10 cm (4 in) high

some fruit specialists or the rolls of black polythene film sold for use as soil covering to prevent weeds growing and to conserve soil moisture.

Ring Unfruitful Apples and Pears. Apple and pear trees that persistently refuse to blossom and bear fruit can often be made fruitful by checking the flow of food from the leaves to the roots. This is done by removing a ring of bark around the main trunk or low down on each main branch. Now is the time to do it, and the method is to cut out a strip of bark, 0·5 cm ($\frac{1}{4}$ in) wide, down to the wood and right round the branch or trunk. You should understand, however, that ringing will only be of assistance if the trees are failing to flower as well as to fruit. If they bloom freely but yet bear no crop the cure must be sought elsewhere. It may be that the trees lack suitable 'mates' for cross pollination, that the position is too exposed, or that the trees are undernourished.

Spray Apple Trees against Scab. It is at just about this time that the expanding blossom buds on apple trees reach the point

130

of development described by growers as 'pink bud stage'; that is, the first trace of pink petal colouring can be seen. This is the ideal moment for applying a second application of lime sulphur, dispersible sulphur, or captan as a preventive of scab disease. You must not delay beyond this stage or the disease may spread rapidly, particularly in warm, humid weather. The actual details of application are exactly the same as for the earlier spraying (see April, Second Week).

SECOND WEEK

Plant Early-flowering Chrysanthemums. By this time early-flowering chrysanthemums raised from cuttings taken in February and March should be sufficiently hardened off to be planted outdoors in the beds in which they are to flower. Choose a good open place and well-manured, deeply cultivated ground if you want blooms of the highest quality. For cutting it is best to have the plants in beds by themselves, 38 cm (15 in) apart in rows 60 to 75 cm (2 to 2½ ft) apart; but they can also be used to fill up spaces in the herbaceous border, in which case they should be spaced 38 cm (15 in) apart each way. Plant with a trowel, taking care to make holes large enough to accommodate all roots without doubling or twisting. Make moderately firm and water freely if the soil is dry.

Plant out Seedlings of Hardy Perennials, etc. If you were able to sow hardy perennials and alpines in a greenhouse or frame in March (see March, Second Week) you may now plant the seedlings outdoors. Place them in a nursery bed where they can grow on undisturbed throughout the summer. The soil should be good but not heavily manured – indeed, it is better that it should have no manure at all for alpines. Set the plants in lines about 30 cm (1 ft) apart leaving from 8 to 30 cm (3 in to 1 ft) between the plants according to the nature of their growth. Violas, primroses and polyanthuses succeed best in a partially shaded place, but the other plants mentioned in my March notes prefer a reasonably sunny position. Similar remarks apply to herbs raised from seed and also to hardy perennials raised from root cuttings (see January, General Work).

Remove Greenhouse Plants to Frame. You can further clear the greenhouse by removing a good many of the winter and spring-flowering plants to frames; but keep plenty of sacks at hand for use at night during the first week or so, as we often have treacherous weather about the middle of May. In addition to forced bulbs, shrubs, and bedding plants, about which I have already given advice (see April, General Work and Third Week), you can now clear out arum lilies, freesias, vallotas and any perpetual-flowering carnations that have for the time being finished flowering. It is not worth keeping the various greenhouse primulas, cinerarias and calceolarias for another year after they have finished flowering. All these should be raised annually from seed.

If no frame is available it will be wise to leave plants where they are for a further fortnight, except in the mildest parts of the country where they can be stood outdoors now.

Greenhouse cyclamens, both seedlings raised last August (see August, Second Week) and old flowering plants, will also be better in a shady frame during the summer. The old corms must be kept practically dry from now onwards until the middle of August, but the seedling plants should be maintained in growth all the time, and that means an ample water supply.

Prick out Winter Greens. It is a mistake to let winter green crops get overcrowded in the seed beds. Prick out all the seedlings from the April sowing (see April, Second Week) into a nursery bed in the open. This should be well broken down on the surface and fairly rich. Plant the seedlings 8 cm (3 in) apart in lines 20 cm (8 in) apart. Do the same to any seedlings left over from the March sowings, but give these rather more room.

Sow Chinese Cabbage. This is more like a cos lettuce than a cabbage. Sow thinly in rows 30 cm (1 ft) apart where plants are to mature.

Prick off and Plant Celery. Celery sown last month (see April, Second Week) will require pricking off into a frame. Give the seedlings plenty of space for they will be growing fast now. Planting 10 cm (4 in) apart in rows 15 cm (6 in) apart will not be overdoing it. Ventilate carefully at first but very freely after a week or so.

It will not be possible to keep the earliest celery (see February, Third Week) in boxes or frame beds any longer without risk of checking them severely in transplanting, so get them out into the trenches now (see April, General Work). There is still danger of frost sufficient to kill the plants, so you must keep some protection at hand. The simplest and best method is to draw up some soil to form a ridge on each side of the shallow trench and then to rest some ordinary frame lights on this, so converting the whole trench into a temporary frame. Set the plants 30 cm (1 ft) apart in a single line down the middle of the trench if it is a narrow one, or in two lines, one at each side of the trench, if it is a wide one. Water in really freely. Celery loves moisture and will fail if allowed to get dry.

Sow Sweet Corn. Sweet corn may be sown out of doors where the plants are to grow. Drop the seeds in pairs 30 cm (1 ft) apart in the row and allow 2 ft between the rows. Thin out later to one plant at each station.

Sow Chicory. Chicory is often neglected by amateurs, but it is a most useful vegetable and a welcome change from seakale and endive in the winter and spring. It is blanched and eaten raw or cooked. Sow seeds now in a sheltered place and on rich, deeply dug ground. Sow sparingly in drills 1 cm ($\frac{1}{2}$ in) deep and 30 cm (1 ft) apart.

Plant Tomatoes in Unheated Greenhouses. When you have cleared the greenhouse sufficiently you can plant it with tomatoes for a late summer crop. Little or no artificial heat will be needed for these from now onwards if you are careful with ventilation and you have stout hessian blinds that can be lowered over the glass on frosty nights. The tomatoes can be grown in pots as advised for the early crops (see March, Second Week), or you can have them in boxes, on a bed of soil made up on the staging, or in a border on the floor. In any case the plants should be at least 30 cm (1 ft) apart in rows which should be 75 cm (2½ ft) apart. An alternative method, which certainly makes working easy, is to have two rows quite close together (say 38 cm, 15 in, apart) and then an alleyway 1 m (3 ft) wide. Make the soil very firm around the roots. The best compost is good fibrous loam, with a little well-rotted manure, or John Innes potting compost No. 3. Water the plants in freely after planting or potting, and provide each with a small bamboo cane for support.

Pot and Harden Off Aubergines and Capsicums. Plants from the first sowings (March, Second Week) should now be moved into 15- or 18-cm (6- to 7-in) pots and John Innes potting compost No. 2. Seedlings from the second sowing (see April, Second Week) should be potted singly in 8-cm (3-in) pots and John Innes potting compost No. 1, and should be gradually hardened off in readiness for planting outdoors in early June. Pinch out the tips of all aubergine plants when 15 to 20 cm (6 to 8 in) high.

Spray Pear Trees. By this time most of the blossom will probably have fallen from pear trees, and it will be necessary to spray again, this time with captan, if there is much danger of scab attacking the trees during the summer. The ideal period is between a week and ten days after blossom can first be shaken from the topmost branches. The details of application are exactly the same as before flowering (see April, Second Week). If caterpillars have been troublesome in previous years, it is also an excellent plan to spray with a good insecticide, such as derris, or to mix such an approved insecticide with the fungicide according to manufacturers' instructions.

Dust Strawberries to Protect them from Disease. If you have had any trouble with mildew on strawberries, now is the time to take preventive measures by dusting the leaves thoroughly with benomyl, flowers of sulphur or dinocap. Benomyl also gives good control of botrytis, a disease that causes the fruits to rot; or, alternatively, spray with captan or thiram.

THIRD WEEK

Clear Beds for Summer Bedding. Next week it will be time to make a start at planting the summer bedding subjects and so some time this week you must clear the beds of their spring occupants. Lift daffodils, hyacinths and tulips as carefully as possible with all the roots that you can get and heel them in temporarily in any out-of-the-way, but preferably sunny, place. Heeling in simply means making a trench about 15 cm (6 in) deep, laying the bulbs in this with their leaves exposed to sun and air and covering the roots and bulbs with soil which should be made moderately firm. It is useless to take the bulbs up and dry them straight away, for they have not yet finished their growth and would be too weak to do any good another year, but

Heeling In Bulbs. Bulbs which have been growing in land needed for summer bedding can be lifted, with as much root as possible, and replanted in an out-of-the-way corner to finish ripening

if heeled in as described, some, at least, will give flowers next season.

Remove Side Shoots from Sweet Peas. Early sweet peas that are being grown on the single stem (cordon) system will need regular attention from now on in the way of removal of all side shoots and tendrils. Be careful not to pinch out flowering stems by mistake; it is quite easy to tell these, as the flower buds are evident even at an early stage.

The later peas will be in need of staking and tying in (see April, Third Week).

Stop Chrysanthemums. If early-flowering chrysanthemums required for specimen blooms and planted out last week are not showing a break bud – that is to say, a flower bud – at the extremity of the central growth, stop them now by pinching out the tip and first pair of leaves. Note well that this instruction applies only to plants that are being grown for large specimen blooms. If your object is to have a big number of comparatively small flowers, two stoppings are necessary, one in April (see April, General Work) and the other in June (see June, General Work).

Pot Late-flowering Chrysanthemums. It should now be possible to get most of the late-flowering chrysanthemums, including Japanese exhibition varieties, incurves, decoratives, and singles, into their final flowering pots. Exception, of course, must be made for late cuttings, some of which may as yet be barely rooted. Flowering pots for the early-rooted cuttings should be 20 to 23 cm (8 to 9 in) in diameter according to the strength of the plants, while for late March cuttings, 15-cm (6-in) pots should prove adequate. John Innes potting compost No. 3 is the best for all these different kinds.

Pot Begonias, Gloxinias, etc. Begonias, gloxinias and streptocarpuses from an early sowing (see January, Third Week) should be ready for removal to their flowering pots. Do not be in a hurry, however, if roots are not showing freely around the sides of the present balls of soil. Over-potting does no good – but then neither does overcrowding. The flowering pots should be 13 to 15 cm (5 to 6 in) in diameter. Use John Innes potting compost No. 1 or an equivalent soilless mixture as before (see April, Second Week). Water freely, place in the greenhouse, and shade from direct sunshine.

Sow Runner Beans Outdoors. It is now time to make a good sowing of runner beans in the open. Sow the seeds individually or in pairs about 20 cm (8 in) apart in two lines 25 cm (10 in) apart. If you require more than one double row, leave an alleyway of at least 2 m (6 ft) wide between each set. Cover the seeds with 5 cm (2 in) of soil. If you sow the seeds in pairs and they all germinate you will need to single the seedlings out later on.

Plant out Celeriac. Celeriac raised from seed in March (see March, Fourth Week) may now be planted outdoors. Choose an open position and reasonably rich soil and plant 30 cm (1 ft) apart in rows 45 cm (18 in) apart.

Plant Melons and Cucumbers in Frames. Melons raised in the greenhouse last month (see April, Third Week) may be planted in frames. Prepare a compost as described for cucumbers (see March, First Week) and allow one plant for each full-sized garden light 2 m by 1·25 m (6 ft by 4 ft). Plant on a small mound of compost in the centre of the space covered by the light. Pinch out the point of each plant when it has made about five leaves.

Cucumbers raised from seed last month (see April, Third Week) for cultivation in unheated frames may also be planted in exactly the same way as melons. Subsequent training is the same as for cucumbers in frames (see April, General Work).

Spray Raspberries, Loganberries and Blackberries. Raspberries and loganberries and also to a smaller extent blackberries, sometimes suffer severely from a disease known as cane spot. Purplish patches of decayed tissue appear on the canes, gradually encircling them and cutting off the supply of sap. If you have had any of this trouble in former years, spray now with lime

137

sulphur wash at twice the ordinary summer strength or with thiram.

Start to Pick Green Gooseberries. It is usually possible to get a first picking of green gooseberries at about this time. The fruits will still be very small and immature and it would be foolish to strip the branches as yet, but if you remove a few here and there where they are overcrowded it will give the remainder a chance to develop more fully and will give you the opportunity of enjoying an early gooseberry pie. This thinning can be repeated from time to time as the fruits increase in size until eventually they are spaced out evenly 5 to 8 cm (2 to 3 in) apart for ripening.

FOURTH WEEK

Plant out Bedding Plants and Half-hardy Annuals. If the weather appears reasonably settled and you have followed out instructions regarding hardening off, now is the time to plant out the majority of bedding plants and half-hardy annuals. As I mentioned in the General Notes for this month, I make exception for dahlias, heliotropes, scarlet salvias and cannas, all of which are very susceptible to the cold and are better kept where they can be protected easily until the first week in June. Plant with a trowel, giving roots plenty of room and firming the soil thoroughly round them. Water in liberally if the soil is dry.

Plant Window Boxes and Hanging Baskets. This is also the time to fill window boxes, hanging baskets and ornamental vases with their summer occupants. To hang over the edge you can have ivy-leaved pelargoniums, trailing lobelia, *Campanula isophylla, Lysimachia nummularia aurea, and Asparagus sprengeri,* while good plants of erect habit for this purpose are zonal pelargoniums, marguerites, fuchsias, petunias and bedding calceolarias. Give the plants a thorough watering after planting. The hanging baskets must be well lined with sphagnum moss or punctured black polythene to prevent the soil from washing through.

Plant out Chrysanthemums for Lifting. It is possible to grow many of the late decorative chrysanthemums without keeping them in big pots all the summer. Plants from 10- to 13-cm (4- to 5-in) pots are planted outdoors now exactly like the early border varieties (see Second Week) and are allowed to grow on in the open ground until September or early October, when they are lifted, carried into the greenhouse, and either placed in big boxes or planted in beds of soil. One great advantage of this method is that plants do not need constant watering during the summer. An alternative method is to plant in wire or plastic baskets and sink these in the soil. Some roots will probably grow out into the surrounding soil but it is still easier to lift plants grown in this way than those planted out straight into the soil.

Start Last Batch of Achimenes. A final batch of achimenes (see February, First Week), started now, will carry the display of flowers well on into the autumn.

Prick off Primulas. Greenhouse primulas sown in April (see April, Fourth Week) will need to be pricked off into other boxes or seed pans by this time. Use the same compost as for seed sowing and space the seedlings about 4 cm (1½ in) apart each way. Water them in well and then place them in a sheltered frame. The plants will be better in frames for the rest of the summer. Ventilate rather sparingly at first, but freely once the seedlings take hold of their new soil.

Sow Vegetable Marrows and Ridge Cucumbers Outdoors. Vegetable marrows and ridge cucumbers can now be sown outdoors where the plants are to grow. Sow the seeds singly or in pairs about 1 m (3 ft) apart, cover them with 2·5 cm (1 in) of soil, and then invert flower pots over them as an additional protection. It is common practice to prepare vegetable marrow beds by building up a mound of turves, but in view of the fact that the plants can do with any amount of moisture, it is really much better to dig out a large hole and fill this with the chopped turves, or, better still, a mixture of turfy loam and manure. It is then a comparatively simple matter to flood the bed from time to time with water. Ridge cucumbers are better on low mounds of turf and dung, for they need all the sun they can get to make them grow rapidly. Still, do not build up the mounds too steeply or watering will be a problem.

Plant out French Beans. If you were able to raise some French beans in boxes last month (see April, Second Week), and have hardened the plants carefully in a frame, you may now plant them out with safety. Choose a reasonably sheltered place and be ready to cover the plants at night with some sheets of brown paper should the weather turn suddenly frosty. Plant the beans 15 cm (6 in) apart in rows 45 cm (18 in) apart.

Spray Apples against Scab, Sawfly and other Troubles. By this time the blossom will probably be falling freely from all but the latest-flowering apples. About ten days after it can first be shaken from the topmost branches is the ideal time to give yet one more spraying with lime sulphur wash, sulphur, or captan as a protection against scab disease (see April, Second Week, and May, First Week). Where lime sulphur is used, it should be applied at a weaker strength than before, otherwise there is danger of scorching the leaves, particularly on the sensitive varieties, such as Cox's Orange Pippin. You should consult the manufacturer's instructions on this point, for different brands may vary in strength. If in former years maggots have been found in the young apple fruits during June and many of these fruits have fallen off in consequence, the trees should be sprayed with HCH, dimethoate or fenitrothion now. The pest involved is the apple sawfly. The small caterpillars of the codling moth also eat their way into apples but the attack comes a little later. Codling moth caterpillars usually bore right into the core of the apple. Sawfly larvae often leave a ribbon-like scar on the skin of the apple and the sticky frass they produce has an unpleasant smell.

Thin out Raspberry Canes. Look over the raspberry plantation and reduce the number of new canes if these are very numerous. There is no point in having more than six canes per plant, and these should be quite close to the clump for preference. Raspberries have a habit of sending up suckers all over the bed, and unless you remove them from the alleyways it may be almost impossible to get between the canes to pick fruit later on.

Thinning Raspberry Canes. As new canes are produced on raspberry plants keep a look-out for any which are weak and spindly and remove these to avoid overcrowding. Leave six good canes on each plant

FLOWERS, VEGETABLES AND FRUITS IN SEASON DURING MAY

Herbaceous Plants: *Adonis autumnalis, Aquilegia chrysantha, A. longissima, A. skinneri, A. vulgaris* vars., aquilegias (long-spurred hybrids), *Aster subcaeruleus, Astrantia carniolica,*

Baptisia australis, Bellis perennis vars. (daisy), *Brunnera macro-phylla, Centaurea montana, Cheiranthus allionii* (Siberian wall-flower), *C. cheiri* (wallflower), *Dicentra eximia, D. formosa, D. spectabilis, Doronicum austriacum, D. caucasicum, D. cordatum, D. pardalianches, D. plantagineum, Eremurus elwesii, E. hima-laicus, E. robustus, Euphorbia amygdaloides, E. characias, E. cyparissias, E. griffithii, E. mellifera, E. pilosa major, E. poly-chroma, E. wulfenii, Galax aphylla, Geranium macrorrhizum, G. phaeum, G. psilostemon, Hemerocallis dumortieri, H. flava, H. middendorffii, Incarvillea delavayi, I. mairei, Iris douglasiana, I. gatesii, I. germanica* vars. (flag or German iris), *I. hoogiana, I. innominata, I. japonica, I. orientalis, I. pallida, I. pseudacorus, I. susiana, Lychnis viscaria* vars., *Meconopsis betonicifolia, M. cambrica* and vars., *M. grandis, M. quintuplinervia, M. sheldonii, M. superba, Mertensia sibirica, M. virginica, Myosotis* hybrids (forget-me-nots), *Orchis elata, O. maderensis, Paeonia anomala, P. emodi, P. mlokosewitschii, P. obovata, P. officinalis* and vars., *P. peregrina, P. tenuifolia* and vars., *P. wittmanniana, Papaver orientale* and vars. (oriental poppy), *Polygonatum multiflorum* (Solomon's seal), *P. odoratum,* pyrethrum hybrids, *Ranunculus aconitifolius flore pleno, Saxifraga umbrosa* (London pride), *Smilacina racemosa, Stachys macrantha, Trollius europaeus* and vars., *T. ledebouri, Verbascum phoeniceum, Veronica gentianoides,* violas (bedding), *Viola tricolor.*

Hardy Bulbs, Corms and Tubers: *Allium aflatunense, A. neapolitanum, A. oreophyllum* and vars., *A. siculum, Anemone coronaria* and vars., *A. fulgens, Calochortus amabilis, Convallaria majalis* (lily of the valley), *Cyclamen repandum, Endymion hispanicus, E. non-scriptus* and vars. (bluebell), *Erythronium americanum, E. californicum, E. dens-canis, E. grandiflorum* and vars., *E. hendersonii, E. revolutum, E. tuolumnense, Fritillaria acmopetala, F. citrina, F. imperialis* and vars., *F. meleagris* vars., *F. pontica, F. pudica, F. pyrenaica, Hermodactylus tuberosus,* hyacinths (large-flowered hybrids), *Iris cristata, Ixiolirion mon-*

tanum and vars., *Leucojum aestivum, Muscari armeniacum, M. botryoides, M. comosum monstrosum, Narcissus jonquilla* vars., *N. poeticus recurvus* and Double White, *Ornithogalum montanum, O. nutans, O. umbellatum, Romulea rosea, Trillium erectum, T. grandiflorum, T. recurvatum, Tulipa acuminata, T. batalinii, T. gesneriana, T. hageri, T. linifolia, T. sprengeri, T. tubergeniana, T. whittallii,* tulips (cottage, Darwin, Rambrandt and parrot).

Rock Plants: *Achillea tomentosa, Aethionema coridifolium, A. grandiflorum, A. oppositifolium, Alyssum saxatile* and vars., *A. spinosum, Androsace carnea, A. helvetica, A. lactea, A. sarmentosa* and vars., *A. sempervivoides, Aquilegia alpina, A. caerulea, A. glandulosa, Arabis albida* and vars., *A. alpina, A. aubretioides, Arctostaphylos uva-ursi, Arenaria balearica, A. laricifolia, A. montana, A. purpurascens, Armeria caespitosa, A. maritima* and vars., *Asperula hirta, Aster alpinus* and vars., *A. subcaeruleus, Astilbe simplicifolia, Aubrieta deltoidea* and vars., *Bellium bellidioides, Campanula garganica* and vars., *Cheiranthus alpinus, Chiastophyllum oppositifolium, Cornus canadensis, Corydalis cashmeriana, C. cheilanthifolia, Cypripedium acaule, C. calceolus, C. pubescens, Daphne cneorum, Dianthus gratianopolitanus, Edraianthus graminifolius, E. pumilio, E. serpyllifolia, Epigaea repens, Erinacea pungens, Erinus alpinus* and vars., *Gentiana acaulis, G. verna, Geum borisii, Haberlea ferdinandi-coburgii, H. rhodopensis, Hebe catarractae, Helianthemum apenninum, Houstonia caerulea, Hutchinsia alpina, Iberis correaefolia, I. gibraltarica, I. saxatilis, I. sempervirens, Iris chamaeiris, I. cristata, I. gracilipes, I. pumila, Isopyrum thalictroides, Lathyrus vernus, Lithospermum diffusum* and vars., *L. purpureo-coeruleum, Lychnis alpina, Mazus pumilio, M. reptans, Morisia monantha, Myosotis rupicola, Oenothera caespitosa, Omphalodes luciliae, O. verna, Oxalis adenophylla, Penstemon rupicola, P. scouleri, Phlox adsurgens, P. amoena, P. divaricata laphamii, P. douglasii, P. subulata* and vars., *Potentilla alba, P. aurea, P. cuneata, P.*

fragiformis, Primula auricula and vars., *P. farinosa, P. frondosa, P. involucrata, P. juliae, P. pubescens, P. sieboldii, Ramonda myconi, R. nathaliae, R. serbica, Ranunculus alpestris, R. gramineus, Saxifraga cochlearis, S. decipiens* vars., *S. granulata plena, S. hypnoides* vars., *S. moschata* vars., *S. primuloides, Schizocodon soldanelloides, Shortia galacifolia, S. uniflora, Silene acaulis, Sisyrinchium bermudiana, S. filifolium, Tanakaea radicans, Tiarella cordifolia, Trollius pumilus, Veronica pectinata, Viola cornuta* and vars., *V. cucullata, V. gracilis* and vars., *V. hederacea.*

Hardy Aquatic and Bog Plants: *Caltha palustris* and vars., *C. polypetala, Cardamine pratensis plena, Dodecatheon clevelandii, D. hendersonii, D. meadia, Geum rivale, Hottonia palustris, Iris laevigata, I. pseudacorus, Myosotis palustris, Primula chionantha, P. helodoxa, P. japonica, P. prolifera, P. pulverulenta* and vars., *P. rosea, P. secundiflora, P. sikkimensis, Ranunculus aquatilis.*

Annuals: Hardy varieties sown in September (see list, September, First Week).

Bedding Plants: *Cheiranthus allionii* (Siberian wallflower), double daisies, forget-me-nots, wallflowers.

Evergreen Shrubs: *Andromeda polifolia,* azaleas (evergreen hybrids), *Berberis candidula, B. darwinii, B. gagnepainii, B. hookeri, B. lologensis, B. stenophylla* and vars., *B. verruculosa, Buddleia globosa, Ceanothus dentatus, C. impressus, C. rigidus, C. thyrsiflorus, C. veitchianus, Choisya ternata, Crinodendron hookerianum, Daphne collina, D. tangutica, Erica mediterranea, E. veitchii, Ledum groenlandicum, Leiophyllum buxifolium, Leucothoe catesbaei, Mahonia undulata, Olearia gunniana, O. lyrata, O. scilloniensis, O. stellulata, Osmarea burkwoodii, Photinia serrulata, Pieris formosa* and vars., *Pyracantha angustifolia, P. atalantioides, P. coccinea* and vars., *P. rogersiana, P. watereri, Rhododendron argyrophyllum, R. augustinii, R. calostrotum, R. campylocarpum, R. caucasicum, R. cinnabarinum, R. decorum, R. dicroanthum, R. elliottii, R. falconeri, R. fictolacteum,*

R. fortunei hybrids, *R. griffithianum, R. haematodes, R. han-
ceanum, R. impeditum, R. intricatum, R. johnstoneanum, R.
lacteum, R. loderi, R. macabeanum, R. mucronulatum, R. niveum,
R. obtusum, R. orbiculare, R. pemakoense, R. ponticum* hybrids,
*R. racemosum, R. repens, R. rubiginosum, R. russatum, R.
sargentianum, R. scintillans, R. sinogrande, R. soulei, R. triflorum,
R. wardii*, also many hybrid rhododendrons, *Rosmarinus
officinalis, Skimmia reevesiana, Sophora microphylla, S. tetra-
ptera, Ulex europaeus plenus, Viburnum burkwoodii, V. rhytidophyllum, V. utile, Vinca major, V. minor, Yucca whipplei.*

Deciduous Shrubs: Azaleas (deciduous hybrids), *Caragana
arborescens, C. pygmaea, Collettia infausta, Cornus florida, C.
kousa, C. nuttallii, Cotoneaster multiflorus, Cytisus albus, C.
ardoinii, C. beanii, C. dallimorei, C. decumbens, C. kewensis,
C. praecox, C. purgans, C. purpureus, C. scoparius* and vars.,
*Deutzia gracilis, D. lemoinei, Dipelta floribunda, Enkianthus
campanulatus, Exochorda giraldii, E. korolkowii, E. macrantha,
E. racemosa, Fothergilla major, Fremontia californica* (shelter),
*Genista hispanica, G. lydia, G. pilosa, Kerria japonica, Kolkwitzia
amabilis, Leptospermum scoparium, Lonicera syringantha, L.
tatarica, Magnolia liliiflora, M. obovata, M. sieboldii, M. wilsonii,
Paeonia delavayi, P. lutea, P. suffruticosa* and vars., *Piptanthus
laburnifolius, Poncirus trifoliata, Rhododendron calendulaceum,
R. japonicum, R. kaempferi, R. luteum, R. molle, R. nudiflorum,
R. quinquefolium, R. schlippenbachii, Rhodotypos scandens, Ribes
speciosum, Robinia hispida, Rosa banksiae, R. cantabridgiensis,
R. cinnamomea, R. ecae, R. hugonis, R. laevigata, R. omeiensis,
R. pimpinellifolia, R. primula, R. sericea, R. xanthina, Rubus
deliciosus, R.* Tridel, *R. trilobus, Spiraea arguta, S. prunifolia
plena, S. vanhouttei, Staphylea colchica, Syringa chinensis, S.
josiflexa, S. persica, S. prestoniae, S. reflexa, S. vulgaris* in var.
(lilac), *Tamarix tetrandra, Vaccinium corymbosum, Viburnum
carlcephalum, V. carlesii, V. macrocephalum, V. plicatum* and
vars., *Xanthoceras sorbifolia.*

Evergreen Trees: *Arbutus andrachne, A. hybrida, A. menziesii, Drimys winteri, Embothrium coccineum* and vars., *Magnolia nitida, Michelia doltsopa.*

Deciduous Trees: *Aesculus hippocastanum* (horse chestnut), *A. octandra, Amelanchier alnifolia, A. canadensis, A. laevis, A. ovalis, Cercis siliquastrum, Crataegus lavallei, C. monogyna* and vars. (hawthorn), *C. oxyacantha* and vars. (hawthorn), *Cydonia oblonga, Davidia involucrata, Halesia carolina, H. monticola, Laburnum anagyroides, L. watereri* and vars., *Magnolia denudata, M. sargentiana, M. sieboldii, M. soulangiana, M. tripetala,* malus (as April but also *M. coronaria* and *M. ioensis*), *Meliosma beaniana, Mespilus germanica* (medlar), *Paulownia fargesii, P. tomentosa, Prunus avium* (gean), *P. lannesiana* vars. (Japanese cherries), *P. mahaleb pendula, P. padus* (bird cherry), *P. serrulata* vars. (Japanese cherries), *P. virginiana, Robinia pseudoacacia* (false acacia), *Sorbus alnifolia, S. americana, S. aria, S. aucuparia, S. cashmeriana, S. decora, S. esserteauana, S. intermedia, S.* Joseph Rock, *S. sargentiana, S. scopulina, S. torminalis, Viburnum lantana, V. lentago.*

Hardy Climbing Plants: *Clematis alpina, C. armandii, C. chrysocoma, C. macropetala, C. montana* and vars., *Schizandra chinensis, S. grandiflora, Wisteria floribunda* and vars., *W. sinensis* and vars., *W. venusta.*

Greenhouse Plants: Abutilons, *Allemanda cathartica, Aphelandra squarrosa,* astilbes, begonias (tuberous rooted), *Begonia coccinea,* boronias, bougainvilleas, *Brunfelsia calycina,* calceolarias (herbaceous), *Callistemon speciosus, Cantua bicolor, C. buxifolia,* carnations (perpetual flowering), celsias, chorizemas, cinerarias (hybrids), clianthus, *Coronilla glauca,* correas, *Crossandra infundibuliformis, C. subacaulis, Cuphea ignea, Epacris longiflora, Erica cavendishiana, E. pageana,* fuchsias, gerberas, gloxinias, *Haemanthus katharinae,* heliotrope, *Hibiscus rosa-sinensis,* hippeastrums, *Hydrangea macrophylla hortensia* in var., *Hymenocallis calathina, H. eucharidifolia, H. macrostephana,*

H. speciosa, ixias, *Lampranthus* species, lantanas, *Lilium longi-florum*, *L. regale*, marguerites, *Medinilla magnifica*, pelargoniums (show, regal, zonal and ivy leaved), *Prostanthera violacea*, roses, schizanthus and other annuals (as April), stephanotis, strelitzias, streptocarpus.

Vegetables in Store: Potatoes.

Vegetables in the Garden: Asparagus, broccoli (sprouting), cabbage (sown July and August), lettuce (sown under glass in February), spring onions, mustard and cress, radish, rhubarb, seakale, spinach (sown in March).

Vegetables under Glass: French beans, carrots, cucumbers, lettuce, mushrooms, mustard and cress, potatoes, radish.

Fruits in Store: *Apples:* Allen's Everlasting (D), Annie Elizabeth (C), Cornish Gillyflower (D), D'Arcy Spice (D), Newton Wonder (C), Ontario (CD), Sturmer Pippin (D).

Fruits Outdoors: *Gooseberries* (green).

Fruits under Glass: *Strawberries.*

June

GENERAL WORK

Spray against Pests. Aphids (greenfly, blackfly etc.) are likely to become more of a nuisance this month unless you take appropriate measures to destroy them at the first sign of attack (see May, General Work). Caterpillars may also put in an appearance now. Usually they can be poisoned before they have done much damage by spraying with one of the numerous insecticides available such as derris, HCH or malathion. Continue to use metaldehyde and bran or a proprietary slug bait against slugs (see May, General Work).

Red spider can become a nuisance on fruit trees at this time of year, infecting the under sides of the leaves and causing them to turn a mottled greyish-gold colour. If this occurs spray at once with derris, dimethoate or malathion and repeat after ten days or a fortnight.

Trim Hedges. You can trim evergreen hedges lightly at any time during the month. If you grow *Berberis darwinii* as a hedge, the best time to trim it is immediately the flowers fade. Cut the flowering shoots back sufficiently to give the hedge a neat appearance.

Continue to Feed Plants in Full Growth. Herbaceous plants and vegetables that are growing freely will be all the better for one or two more applications of a quick-acting fertilizer and some soakings with weak liquid manure (see May, General Work).

Remove Runners from Violets and Strawberries. If left to their own devices, violets will make innumerable runners during the summer and early autumn. You should remove these, cutting them off close to the main clump.

Similar remarks apply to the runners produced by strawberries, unless you require some for propagation (see July, First Week).

Disbud Roses for Exhibition. Roses will be forming their flower buds freely throughout the month, and if you want some big blooms for exhibition or cutting you must disbud large-flowered (hybrid tea) varieties from time to time. This simply means that out of each cluster of buds only the big terminal one must be retained, all the side buds being nipped out at as early a stage as possible.

Stake and Disbud Border Carnations. Border carnations will be forming their flower stems and these must be staked as necessary. Beginners often go wrong over this. The natural habit of the border carnation is to arch its flower slightly and not hold it stiffly erect. This you must allow it to do, and any ties you make must be sufficiently low down the stem not to interfere with its natural arching habit. If you make ties all the way up to the bud, rain will collect in the expanding flower and spoil the petals and hot sun will complete the damage.

Another important task if you want to have really fine blooms

Disbudding Roses. If large-flowered roses are being grown for exhibition, suitable stems should be disbudded; that is, side buds should be removed and only the terminal one left to develop

is to remove the side shoots that form on the flower stems and to remove all flower buds except the terminal one on each stem, exactly as advised for roses.

Pot on Perpetual-flowering Carnations and Chrysanthemums. If you did not pot on all the young stock of perpetual-flowering carnations last month (see May, General Work) you should certainly complete the work before the end of June. Deal with the most forward plants first and gradually work through the whole batch. Continue to stop first laterals a few at a time as they make their eighth joint.

Backward or late-struck chrysanthemums should also be dealt with at the earliest opportunity (see May, Third Week). Very late cuttings of special varieties grown for forming dwarf specimens in 13- to 15-cm (5- to 6-in) pots (see April, Fourth Week) must be placed in their flowering pots as soon as they have filled their first 8-cm (3-in) pots with roots.

Stop Early-flowering and Decorative Chrysanthemums. If you are growing some early-flowering chrysanthemums with the object of getting a large number of comparatively small flowers (see April, General Work, and also May, Third Week), the plants will require a second stopping some time during this month. The ideal time is when the most forward side shoots caused by the first stopping are 30 cm (1 ft) in length; but stopping must be completed by the end of the month. Precisely similar remarks apply to the late-flowering decoratives and singles, except that these are almost always better for two stoppings, whether the object in view is to get a lot of medium-size blooms or only a few big ones. If the latter is your aim, then you must reduce the number of side shoots that grow after the stopping, keeping only from six to a dozen per plant according to its strength.

General Greenhouse Management. As the weather gets warmer ventilation must become even more free. Keep a sharp watch on the thermometer at the beginning of the month, however, and be ready to close the ventilators quite early if it shows a tendency to drop rapidly, for early June nights can be very treacherous. The night average at this time of the year for the majority of popular greenhouse plants should be 16°C (60°F). Keep the top ventilators open a little at night when the weather is mild and ventilate really freely by day as soon as the thermometer registers 18°C (65°F). Side ventilators and doors can be opened wide on hot, sunny days.

Plants that are still making growth or are producing flowers must be watered with increasing freedom as the days become hotter, but some greenhouse plants will be going to rest (see p. 120). It is advisable to examine pot plants daily during the summer. Watering is best done in the morning.

Earth up Potatoes. The earthing up of all March and April planted potatoes must be completed during this month. This is not a task to be finished at one operation. Better results are obtained by drawing the soil up round the potato stems a little at a time. Go over them about three times in all, eventually leaving the bed in a series of broad, flat-topped ridges.

Blanch Leeks. If you planted leeks in trenches during April (see April, Second Week) you must start to blanch them as soon as they are well established and growing freely. The best method is to make tubes out of stiff brown paper, slip one of these over each plant, fastening it to a bamboo cane and drawing a little soil up around its base. The tubes should be about 15 cm (6 in) in length and about 8 cm (3 in) in diameter to ensure adequate blanching.

Make Successional Sowings. Successional sowings are almost precisely the same as those for last month (see May, General Work). Lettuces, endive, radishes, mustard and cress, turnips, should still be sown at intervals. It is too late to sow maincrop peas, but it is not a bad plan to make a sowing at the beginning of the month of a second early variety which will mature more rapidly. Choose a fully open place for this last crop, for late-sown peas in the shade are certain to be ruined by mildew. All the salad vegetables, and also turnips, will be better in a rather shady place.

Plant Winter Greens. Throughout June you should miss no opportunity of planting out all manner of winter greens, including Brussels sprouts, broccoli, kale and savoy. Usually these should be planted about 60 cm (2 ft) apart in rows 75 cm (2½ ft) apart, but, as different varieties grow to varying sizes, you should consult the seedsman's notes on the seed packet regarding this. Make the soil really firm around the roots; none of the cabbage family does well in loose soil, and for this reason the beds should be well trodden before planting. Then after planting, run a hoe through the surface to leave a dust mulch.

Lift Autumn-sown Onions as Required. During June the bulbs of autumn-sown onions (see August, Fourth Week) will have attained sufficient size to be used. Do not lift the whole crop yet, however, for the bulbs will not be properly ripened. Simply dig up a few onions at a time as you require them.

Stake Culinary Peas. Peas sown last month must be staked in the same way as the earlier batches (see May, General Work).

Feed and Fumigate Tomatoes under Glass. The earliest tomatoes (see January, Second Week) will be ripening freely, while even the latest batches planted last month (see May, Second Week) will be setting fruits during the month. All must be watered freely – they will need supplies every day when the weather is warm – and should be fed regularly as I described in my notes for last month (see May, General Work). Plants in flower should be pollinated, as explained in the same place; while training, stopping at the apex of the house, and the removal of all side shoots must proceed as before. A topdressing of well-rotted manure will help the later plants.

Whitefly may become a nuisance now. If it does, fumigate at once with lindane smokes, putting the pellets or canister on the path in the evening, setting light to them, and then keeping the house closely shut up until the morning. Repeat twice, at intervals of four or five days, to catch the adult flies as they emerge from the scales which are unaffected by the fumigant. Alternatively spray with malathion or resmethrin.

Ventilate very freely, keeping the top ventilators partly open during mild nights, and opening doors as well as side ventilators on very warm days. Cut back some of the lower leaves on early plants to expose the fruits to the light and so hasten ripening.

Train and Feed Melons. Melons in the heated greenhouse should be swelling well by now and you must sling the fruits up in special melon nets to take their weight off the stems. Gradually reduce the amount of atmospheric moisture and give increased ventilation, but without reducing the average day temperature of 21°C (70°F). This will assist ripening.

Melons in frames (see May, Third Week) will be making side shoots as a result of having their points pinched out. Retain four per plant and train them to the four corners of the bed, pegging them down to its surface. Pinch out their points when they reach the limits of the bed. Sublaterals will be formed.

Fertilize about half a dozen female flowers at the same time (see April, General Work). Keep the plants well watered and top dress the bed with 2·5 cm (1 in) of well-rotted manure as soon as white rootlets appear on the surface.

Train, Feed and Renovate Cucumbers. Cucumbers in greenhouses and frames will be in various stages of growth, and I refer you to my previous notes for details of treatment (April, General Work, and May, General Work). Some of the earliest plants in the warm greenhouse will be getting past their prime, but they can be renovated a lot and induced to go on bearing for another month or so by cutting out old laterals that have borne fruit and training young laterals in their place. See that shading material does not get washed off the glass. Strong sunshine may do a lot of damage. Keep the atmosphere really moist by frequent spraying with water and by wetting the paths.

Finish Thinning Outdoor Peaches, Nectarines and Apricots. You will be able to complete the thinning of peaches, nectarines and apricots on walls as soon as the stones are formed (see May, General Work). Continue to disbud the two first named and to pinch the laterals of apricots to encourage fruit spurs to form.

Spray Raspberries Against Fruit Maggots. If you have had trouble in previous years with maggots in the ripe fruits of raspberries spray twice during June with derris, fenitrothion or malathion; the first time when the raspberry flowers are beginning to fall and the second when the earliest fruits turn pink. Do not eat fruits for one week after using fenitrothion.

Management of Fruit Trees Under Glass. There is little to add to my remarks on this subject in May (see May, General Work). Ventilation can be very free whenever the weather is mild, and you may open side ventilators by day as well as those at the ridge. Ripening can be assisted by removing a leaf here and there to expose fruits to the sun, or propping them forward with the aid of ordinary wooden plant labels.

As soon as you have cleared the earliest trees of their fruits, recommence spraying at least twice a day with clean water. There is no better preventive of red spider and thrips, two pests that always prove troublesome in a dry atmosphere.

Treatment of Vines. Continue to train outdoor vines and pinch out the tips of secondary laterals when they have made one leaf. This will prevent the vines from getting overcrowded with foliage. The earliest varieties will need thinning (see March, General Work).

Indoor vines will be in various stages of growth and once again I refer you to my notes in the General Work for March, April and May for particulars regarding stopping, thinning and other operations. These tasks are the same for late as for early vines. You must be very careful about ventilation whatever the state of growth. The earliest vines will be approaching ripeness and must have a rather dry atmosphere. Excessive heat, however, is to be avoided. Late vines in unheated houses will require much more moisture in the atmosphere, which means that you must keep evaporating trays filled with water or thoroughly wet the paths two or three times a day. If red spider should appear, spray the foliage with clear water once or twice daily.

Up till this month outside borders usually need little or no watering, but from now on they should be watched closely and watered freely if they show signs of getting really dry. In order to conserve moisture it is a good plan to spread an 8-cm (3-in) mulch of strawy horse manure over the border after watering.

The earliest grapes will be ready for cutting some time during the month, and once you have done this you can spray the rods and leaves with water freely several times a day.

FIRST WEEK

Plant Tender Bedding Plants. The few tender bedding plants that I advised you to omit from May planting (see May, Fourth Week) may now go outdoors into their flowering quarters. These plants include dahlias, begonias, scarlet salvias, heliotropes and cannas, also a few choice foliage plants, such as abutilons, cordylines, ricinus, *Zea mays* and *Leucophyta* (*Calocephalus*) *brownii*. Details for planting are exactly as for those plants put out in May.

Sow Perennials and Biennials. Most perennials and biennials, if sown out of doors now, will make good sturdy plants for placing in flowering quarters in the autumn. I make exception only with forget-me-nots and Brompton stocks, which I find are better sown rather later as they get too big if sown now, tending to flower before the winter; this is always a bad point. The most useful biennials are Canterbury bells, various verbascums and *Coreopsis grandiflora*. Perennials which are almost invariably treated as biennials are wallflowers, *Cheiranthus allionii*, foxgloves, sweet Williams, double daisies, Iceland poppies and *Campanula pyramidalis*. These may also be sown now. Among the easiest perennials to raise from seed are aquilegias, lupins, oriental poppies, hollyhocks and delphiniums, also easy rock plants such as aubrietas, *Alyssum saxatile* and *Campanula carpatica*; but there are many other things that you can try if you can obtain the seeds. Sow thinly in drills 15 to 20 cm (6 to 8 in) apart and cover with from 0·5 to 2·5 cm ($\frac{1}{4}$ to 1 in) of soil, according to the size of the seeds. Violas, pansies, primroses and polyanthuses may also be sown now outdoors, but it is preferable to choose a rather shady place for these.

Sow St Brigid Anemones. Anemones of the St Brigid and de Caen types can also be raised quite readily from seed sown outdoors now and will flower next summer. Choose a sunny, sheltered position and sow the seed very thinly indeed in drills 1 cm ($\frac{1}{2}$ in) deep and 23 cm (9 in) apart. The reason that I stress the importance of thin sowing is that then no transplanting will be necessary and the plants can grow on unchecked in the seed bed until they have flowered next year.

Plunge Pot Shrubs and Roses Outdoors. From this time until the end of September, all the shrubs and roses that have been grown in pots for early flowering, and are either still in the greenhouse or have been removed to shelters and frames, will be much better in a sunny but not too scorchingly hot position outdoors. This also applies to greenhouse heaths, Indian azaleas, camellias and acacias. The ideal method is to prepare a deep bed of sifted ashes or coarse sand, and to plunge the pots up to their rims in this. Watering will be considerably reduced by this means and the soil in the pots will be maintained at a more even temperature. Do not on any account choose a position that is exposed to cutting draughts, as, for example, near an alleyway between buildings. Spray daily with clear water throughout the summer to ward off attacks by red spider mite. This is particularly necessary with Indian azaleas.

Prick off Cinerarias. Cinerarias sown early in May must be pricked off 5 cm (2 in) apart each way in seed boxes filled with the compost recommended for seed sowing. Stand in a frame and ventilate freely.

Place Chrysanthemums in Summer Quarters. Exhibition and decorative chrysanthemums grown in pots will be better out in the open from now onwards. If you have many of these plants I advise you to make a special standing ground for them in an out-of-the-way place. The soil should be well covered with ashes or gravel to give good drainage. The plants are then arranged in straight rows at least 75 cm (2½ ft) apart, so that you can move between them easily for watering, tying and bud taking. Drive a good strong stake into the ground at each end of each row, stretch a couple of wires between the pairs of stakes and then attach each bamboo cane to the wires. This is the ideal method with exhibition chrysanthemums grown to a single stem. With big decorative plants the horizontal wires get in the way.

Stop Exhibition Chrysanthemums. A few varieties of chrysanthemum grown for exhibition in November will need to be stopped now. (See catalogues of chrysanthemum specialists.)

Standing Out Chrysanthemums. Chrysanthemums grown in pots for decoration can be stood out on gravel or ash beds during the summer months

Thin out Vegetable Seedlings. Various vegetable seedlings from April and May sowings will be in need of thinning (see May, General Work).

Plant Outdoor Tomatoes. Tomatoes that have been well hardened off in frames may be planted outdoors in a sunny, sheltered position. A border at the foot of a fence or wall with a southerly aspect is the best possible place for the plants, which should be 38 cm (15 in) apart. If you have more than one row, space them 75 cm (2½ ft) apart. The soil should be in good condition, but not too richly manured, as it is wise to let tomatoes set a few fruits and then to feed regularly with any reliable tomato fertilizer.

Plant Out Aubergines and Capsicums. Plants that have been properly hardened off can now be planted outdoors in the

158

sunniest and warmest place available and in fairly rich soil. Space plants 30 to 38 cm (12 to 15 in) apart and, if there is more than one row, leave 60 cm (2 ft) between rows. Place a good cane for support to each plant.

Plant Vegetable Marrows and Ridge Cucumbers. Vegetable marrows and ridge cucumbers raised under glass and properly hardened off may be planted out on a prepared bed (see May, Fourth Week). If the weather is cold and nights tend to be slightly frosty, keep some big flower pots at hand and invert one over each plant every evening, removing it in good time the next morning. The plants should be at least 1 m (3 ft) apart each way in the beds. Pinch out the tip of each plant when it has made about six or seven leaves; then train the laterals that form evenly around the plant to fill the bed and pinch the tip out of each as soon as it reaches the edge of the bed.

Plant Runner Beans. Runner beans which were raised in boxes under glass in April will be ready for planting out in double lines 25 cm (10 in) apart, allowing 20 cm (8 in) from plant to plant in the rows. If you have more than one row of beans they should be at least 2 m (6 ft) apart, because when they grow up they cast a considerable amount of shade. For this same reason it is an advantage if all the rows can run north and south, as then each row does stand a chance to get some direct sunshine.

You must provide a stout stake for each plant. These stakes should be at least 2·5 m (8 ft) long and must be thrust as firmly as possible into the ground. There are many ways of finishing the task, but none that is simpler than to cross the sticks at the top and then place other sticks horizontally in the forks so made. Bind all the sticks together where they meet and you will have a support for your beans that will stand any amount of wind.

If you cannot obtain stakes for all your runner beans you can grow some of them as bush plants by the simple process of pinching out the growing points of the shoots from time to time. Quite a good crop of beans can be obtained in this manner,

Planting Runner Beans. This method of staking runner beans is the most effective and the most widely used

though, of course, it will not be so heavy, nor will the beans be quite so fine, as those from plants grown in the more usual way on stakes.

Plant Celery. You can also plant out celery with safety and without the necessity for any protection. Details of work are the same as for the earliest crop (see May, Second Week). Set out all plants that are 8 cm (3 in) high or more. Backward seedlings and those from late sowings may wait for a few weeks yet. Water in freely.

Pinch Broad Beans. The earliest broad beans should now have set about three clusters of pods each, and it is wise to stop them growing any taller by pinching out the tip of each plant. This may prevent an attack by black fly, because this pest invariably goes for the young growing tips, and if there is no soft growth it will seek food elsewhere. Incidentally, the stopping will hasten the development of the pods.

SECOND WEEK

Repot Auriculas. If you grow auriculas in pots now is the time to repot them. Shake the old soil from the roots and make certain that these have no woolly aphid upon them. This, by the way, is the same pest that causes the white woolly patches on apples, and is often known as American blight. If it should be present wash the roots in a solution of derris or HCH. Then repot either in 9- or 10-cm (3½- or 4-in) pots, reducing the size of the plants if necessary and using a compost of four parts of loam, one part of dried cow manure, one part of leafmould, and one part of mixed sand and crushed oyster shell. Pot firmly, water freely and place in a frame or a sheltered place outdoors. You can remove offsets with roots if you wish and pot them separately.

Divide Auriculas, Polyanthuses and Primroses. Auriculas, polyanthuses and coloured primroses growing in the open may be lifted and carefully divided if they are particularly good selected varieties. With ordinary mixed strains, however, it is better to raise a new stock each year from seed, as the old plants tend to get weakened by attacks from greenfly, red spider mite and other pests.

Lift Anemones in Frames. Anemones of the St Brigid and de Caen types, grown in frames for winter and spring flowering, will have completed their growth by this time and should be lifted. Shake the tubers clear of soil and place them in trays, surrounding them with a little dry peat moss. Then stand the trays in a cool dry place. The corms will keep safely under these conditions until you wish to plant them again.

Dig Early Potatoes. The earliest potatoes planted at the end of February will probably be ready for digging. Lift one or two roots and see what kind of a crop there is. There is no point in waiting for the tubers to mature. So long as they are big enough to be used, lift them, but only as you actually require them for use. It is a great mistake to dig too many early potatoes at once for they lose quality rapidly when taken out of the ground.

Thin Chicory. Chicory sown last month (see May, Second Week) will require thinning. Leave the seedlings 23 cm (9 in) apart.

Sow Stump-rooted Carrots. Make a last sowing of stump-rooted carrots outdoors (see March, Third Week). These will come in at about the same time as the maincrop carrots and will be more tender and delicately flavoured for immediate use. The maincrop is principally of value for storing for winter use.

Sow and Thin Chinese Cabbage. If this vegetable was sown in May (see May, second Week) thin seedlings now to 20 cm (8 in). Make a further sowing for succession.

Sow Parsley for Succession. Make a third small sowing of parsley for succession (see February, Fourth Week, and April, Third Week).

Expose Shallot Bulbs. Shallots will now be approaching their ripening period and you should draw the soil away from the bulbs a little in order to allow them to swell freely and get the full benefit of sunlight.

Start to thin Apples and Pears. You will now be able to see how many fruits have been formed on your apple and pear trees. It is no use leaving too many, or they will only get misshapen, small and poor in quality. Usually one per spur is enough, and two should be regarded as the maximum. If there are more than this the weakest or least satisfactory will have to be removed, and you can begin to do this now, but do not complete the work yet for there is usually a fairly heavy natural fall later in the month. Be content at the moment to thin the fruits to about four per cluster, removing any that are noticeably poor, badly shaped, or spotted. You will find a pair of pointed vine scissors most serviceable for this work.

Start to Summer-prune Gooseberries and Currants. You can save yourself a great deal of winter work, and incidentally improve the yield of your gooseberry and currant bushes by summer pruning. Start this now, but do not attempt to complete it all at once. The ideal is to spread the work over a period of about six weeks. Then the bushes will not suffer any check from sudden loss of foliage. Summer pruning, by the way, does not apply to black currants but only to the red and white kinds. It consists in cutting off the ends of all side shoots when they are about 15 cm (6 in) long. Shorten them to about 8 cm (3 in).

THIRD WEEK

Prune Flowering Shrubs. Any shrubs that flowered during May or early June can be pruned now, but this is not to say that pruning is always necessary. Much depends upon the purpose for which the shrub is being grown and the amount of space that you can spare it. For example, evergreen ceanothuses must be pruned annually when grown against a wall, but there is no necessity to prune them at all if they are cultivated as bushes in the open. The method against walls is to cut back to within 2·5 cm (1 in) or so of the main branches all laterals that are growing away from the wall.

Brooms may become very straggly if they are not pruned annually. You must never cut back into very hard, old wood, but it is quite safe to clip the bushes lightly now, shortening the young flowering shoots to within an inch or so of the older branches. Lilacs, rhododendrons and azaleas need no regular pruning of a severe nature, but it is a great advantage to cut off the faded flower trusses and so prevent the formation of seed. *Clematis montana* may be cut back sufficiently to keep it within bounds. The popular *Chaenomeles speciosa* (*Cydonia japonica*) must be pruned when grown against a wall. The best method is to shorten laterals a few at a time, spreading the work over a period of several weeks.

Take Pink Pipings. Now is the time to propagate pinks by means of cuttings. Select healthy-looking, non-flowering shoots

163

10 to 13 cm (4 to 5 in) in length and pull them out at a joint. This is known as taking a 'piping.' Insert these pipings firmly, 5 cm (2 in) deep and about 10 cm (4 in) apart each way, in sandy soil, preferably in a frame, but failing this in a shady border outdoors, and keep well watered. If in a frame shade from direct sunlight.

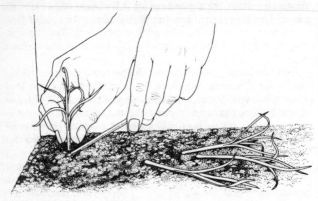

Taking Pink Pipings. Cuttings of pinks are taken in the form of 'pipings' – 10- to 13-cm (4- to 5-in) lengths of stem pulled out from a joint. These are inserted in frames of sandy soil

They should be well rooted and ready for planting out by the end of September.

Cut back Aubrietas, Arabis and Perennial Candytuft. Aubrietas, arabis and perennial candytufts may be cut back quite considerably as soon as they have finished flowering if you wish to prevent the plants from spreading very far. In any case, it is a good plan to remove the faded flowers before seed pods form. The work can be done very quickly with a large pair of scissors, or, where large clumps are concerned, with garden shears.

Pot Cyclamen into Flowering Pots. About this time cyclamen seedlings that were potted individually in April (see April, First Week) will be ready for their final potting into 13-cm (5-in) pots. Use a similar compost to that mentioned before, but add a little well-rotted manure to it if possible. As before, be careful not to bury the corm. After potting, arrange the plants in an unheated frame and shade from sunshine for a few days. After this the plants may have more light, but should always be shaded from very hot sunshine and must be ventilated freely, indeed the lights may be removed altogether most of the time and only replaced when the weather is stormy or cold.

Sow Cinerarias and Primulas for Succession. To provide a succession of flowers after those from the May sowing (see May, First Week) you should now make a second sowing of cinerarias. The seeds are treated in exactly the same way as before, except that now no artificial heat will be needed to effect germination. You can even place the seed pans in a frame if you are short of space in the greenhouse.

It is also an excellent plan to make a second sowing of *Primula sinensis* and its variety *stellata* to flower after the earliest plants (see April, Fourth Week). *P. malacoides* may be sown now for the first time. It grows more rapidly than the others, and there is nothing to be gained by sowing earlier.

Sow Greenhouse Calceolarias. Sow the large hybrid greenhouse calceolarias now. Seed should be sown in well-drained seed boxes and given the lightest possible covering of fine sand, for it is very small. Cover the boxes with brown paper and place the seeds in a frame to germinate. This is better than a greenhouse as it can be ventilated more freely. There is nothing more likely to harm greenhouse calceolarias then excessive heat.

Sow French Beans. Make one more sowing of French beans in a sheltered place outdoors in exactly the same way as advised in the notes for May, First Week. This will provide you with plants that will crop in September and continue until the first sharp frosts.

165

Stop Cutting Asparagus. It is most unwise to cut asparagus after the third week in June. Allow the plants to make foliage now so that new crowns may be formed for next year. Give the bed a small dressing of any good compound fertilizer. If you prefer to make your own mixtures, use three parts of super-phosphate of lime, two parts of sulphate of ammonia and one part of sulphate of potash at the rate of 55 g per square metre (2 oz per square yard).

Spray Apples against Codling Moth. If in former years grubs have been found feeding inside apples during July and August it is probable that the codling moth is responsible, and steps should be taken now to prevent further damage. Spray all apple trees at once with derris, carbaryl, fenitrothion or malathion making sure that the fruitlets are covered. It would be advisable to spray again in about 3 weeks' time, to catch any later-hatching grubs. This pest is easily confused with apple sawfly (see May, Fourth Week).

FOURTH WEEK

Sow Brompton Stocks and Forget-me-nots. This is a good time to sow Brompton stocks to stand the winter and flower outdoors next May and June. It is possible to germinate the seeds in the open, but I find it better to sow in boxes and place these in a frame. Here the seeds can be shaded from strong sunshine and protected from rain storms until they germinate. Cover the seeds very lightly with sandy soil and water moderately. Forget-me-nots may be sown at the same time, but these germinate freely enough in a shady place in the open. Sow in drills 1 cm ($\frac{1}{2}$ in) deep and 15 cm (6 in) apart.

Divide Mossy Saxifrages. Old clumps of mossy saxifrage may be divided, and this is a good policy if they are tending to get brown in the centre. Discard the brown pieces altogether, and replant the green clumps in a semi-shady place in soil that contains plenty of leafmould or moss peat. Water freely for a few weeks.

Lift and Divide June-flowering Irises. This is the ideal time for lifting and dividing all the May- and June-flowering flag irises, as most of the plants will be starting to make new roots. Of course, it is not wise to lift and divide the clumps every year, but after four or five years they tend to get overcrowded and to exhaust the soil. Then you should dig them up carefully with a fork, cut off the old central portions of bare rhizome, discarding them altogether, and replant the healthy outer growths with 8 to 10 cm (3 to 4 in) of rhizome attached to each. Plant in well-prepared soil which has been dusted with superphosphate of lime at the rate of 55 g per square metre (2 oz per square yard). If you use animal manure, work it in rather deeply, so that it does not come in contact with the rhizomes. These, by the way, should only just be covered with soil.

Start to Bud Roses. It is usually possible to start budding rose stocks at about this time, though much depends on the weather. If June is very dry, one may have to wait until well on into July, whereas if the weather is wet it is sometimes possible to start budding even earlier than this. The test is to make an incision in the stock and then attempt to lift the bark away from the wood. If it comes easily and cleanly budding can proceed at once, but if it drags away unwillingly it is better to wait awhile. The buds chosen should be from firm young shoots. A good test is to break off the thorns. If they come off easily, but leave moist-looking green scars, the wood is just right; if the scars are dry the wood is too ripe; but if the thorns refuse to break off easily, tearing instead, it is immature. Usually the tip of each shoot will have to be discarded as too young. Flowering stems can be used.

Pot Cinerarias. The first batch of cinerarias, sown early in May, will do better singly in pots now. Use John Innes potting compost No. 1 or a soilless equivalent and return the plants to a frame after potting. Ventilate very freely.

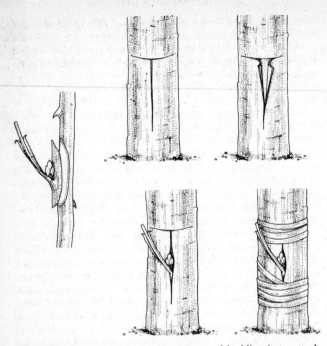

Rose Budding. As in grafting, the purpose of budding is to attach tissue of one plant to the roots of another – it is most frequently practised with roses. A 'T'-shaped slit is made in the bark of the stock and the bark is gently eased away. A bud is cut from a stem of scion material and the sliver of wood at the back is removed. The bud is then inserted into the cut and tied in place with budding tape. Bush roses are budded just below the level of the surrounding soil and standards at a height of 1·10 m (3 ft 6 in) on the bases of young side shoots, unless *Rosa rugosa* is used as a stock, in which case they are budded direct on to the main stem

168

Examine Grafted Fruit Trees. It is a good plan to examine any fruit trees that you grafted in March or April to make quite sure that all is in order. If the stock appears to have swollen a good deal, remove the grafting wax and make sure that the raffia tie is not strangling the scion.

FLOWERS, VEGETABLES AND FRUITS IN SEASON DURING JUNE

Herbaceous Plants: *Achillea millefolium* vars., *A. ptarmica* and vars., *A. taygetea, Aconitum napellus praecox, Anchusa italica* and vars., *Anthemis cupaniana, Anthericum liliago, Aquilegia canadensis, A. chrysantha, A. longissima, A. skinneri, A. vulgaris* vars., aquilegia hybrids (long spurred), *Armeria latifolia* and vars., *Aruncus sylvester, Asphodeline lutea, Asphodelus ramosus, Aster subcaeruleus, Astrantia carniolica, A. major, A. minor, Borago laxiflora, Campanula aucheri, C. glomerata* vars., *C. lactiflora, C. latifolia, C. latiloba, C. persicifolia* and vars., *C. rapunculoides, C. rhomboidalis, C. trachelium, C. vanhouttei, Centaurea dealbata, C. macrocephala, C. montana* and vars., *Centranthus ruber, Chrysanthemum leucanthemum* vars., *Cichorium intybus, Coreopsis grandiflora* and vars., *C. lanceolata* and vars., *Crambe cordifolia, Delphinium formosum,* delphiniums in var. (large-flowered hybrids), *Dianthus allwoodii, D. plumarius* (common pink), *Dicentra eximia, D. spectabilis, Dictamnus albus, Digitalis grandiflora, Dracocephalum ruyschiana, Eomecon chionantha, Eremurus elwesii, E. himalaicus, E. olgae, E. robustus, E. stenophyllus, Erigeron aurantiacus, E. philadelphicus, E. speciosus* and vars., erigeron hybrids, *Filipendula hexapetala flore pleno,* gaillardias, *Galega officinalis* and vars., *Gaura lindheimeri, Geranium dalmaticum, G. endressii, G. grandiflorum, G. ibericum, G. macrorrhizum, G. phaeum, G. pratense* and vars., *G. psilostemon, G. renardii, G. sylvaticum, Geum chiloense* vars., *Helenium hoopesii,*

Hemerocallis dumortieri, H. flava, H. middendorffii, hemerocallis hybrids, *Heuchera brizoides, H. sanguinea* and vars., *Heucherella tiarelloides, Hosta sieboldiana, Incarvillea delavayi, I. mairei, Inula glandulosa, Iris bulleyana, I. chrysographes, I. fulva, I. germanica* and hybrids (flag or German iris), *I. graminea, I. longipetala, I. orientalis, I. pallida, I. setosa, I. sibirica, I. spuria, I. susiana, I. tectorum, I. variegata, I. versicolor, Kniphofia caulescens, K. praecox, K. tuckii, Libertia formosa, L. grandiflora, L. ixioides, Linaria dalmatica, Lindelofia longiflora, Linum narbonnense, L. perenne, Lupinus arboreus* (tree lupin), *L. polyphyllus* hybrids (lupin), *Lychnis coronaria, L. haageana, L. viscaria* and vars., *Macleaya cordata, M. microcarpa, Malva moschata, Meconopsis betonicifolia, M. cambrica* and vars., *M. dhwojii, M. integrifolia, M. napaulensis, M. regia, M. sheldonii, M. superba, Mertensia virginica, Nepeta faassenii, N. grandiflora, N. mussinii, Oenothera fruticosa* and vars., *Paeonia albiflora* and vars. (Chinese peony), *P. officinalis* and vars., *P. tenuifolia, P. wittmanniana, Papaver nudicaule* (Iceland poppy), *P. orientale* and vars. (oriental poppy), *Paradisea liliastrum, Phlox divaricata* vars., and hybrids, *P. suffruticosa* hybrids, *Polemonium caeruleum* and vars., *P. carneum, P. pulcherrimum, Polygonatum multiflorum* (Solomon's seal), *P. odoratum,* potentillas (hybrids), pyrethrums in var., *Ranunculus aconitifolius flore pleno, R. acris flore pleno, Salvia haematodes, Saxifraga umbrosa* (London pride), *Smilacina racemosa, Stachys macrantha, Thalictrum aquilegifolium* and vars., *T. glaucum, Thermopsis montana, Trollius europaeus* and vars., *T. ledebourii* and vars., *Tropaeolum polyphyllum, Uvularia grandiflora, Verbascum olympicum, V. phoeniceum, V. thapsiforme,* verbascum hybrids, *Veronica gentianoides,* violas (bedding), *Viola tricolor* (pansy).

Hardy Bulbs, Corms and Tubers: *Allium aflatunense, A. albopilosum, A. caeruleum, A. cernuum, A. moly, A. neapolitanum, A. ostrowskianum, A. pulchellum, A. roseum, Anemone coronaria* and vars., *Brodiaea californica, B. elegans,* calochortuses and camassias (as in May), *Convallaria majalis prolificans, Gladiolus byzantinus, G. nanus* hybrids, *Hippeastrum pratense* (shelter), *Iris xiphioides* (English iris), *I. xiphium* (Spanish iris), *Ixiolirion montanum, Lilium aurelianense, L. bulbiferum, L. cernuum, L. dauricum, L. hansonii, L. martagon* and vars., *L. nepalense, L. pomponium, L. pumilum, L. pyrenaicum, L. rubellum, L. szovitzianum, L. tenuifolium, L. testaceum, L. umbellatum* hybrids, *Nomocharis mairei, N. pardanthina, Ornithogalum arabicum, O. montanum,* ranunculus (turban and French), *Scilla peruviana.*

Rock Plants: *Acantholimon glumaceum, A. venustum, Achillea clavenae, A. rupestris, A. tomentosa, Aethionema coridifolium, A. grandiflorum, A. pulchellum, A.* Warley Rose, *Alyssum montanum, A. saxatile* and vars., *A. spinosum, Androsace lanuginosa* and vars., *A. sarmentosa* and vars., *Antennaria dioica, Anthyllis montana, Aquilegia alpina, A. caerulea, Arenaria montana, A. purpurascens, Armeria maritima* and vars., *Asperula suberosa, Aster farreri, Astilbe simplicifolia, Calamintha alpina, C. grandiflora, Calceolaria polyrrhiza, Campanula allionii, C. barbata, C. carpatica, C. cochlearifolia, C. elatines, C. garganica* and vars., *C. portenschlagiana, C. poscharskyana, C. pulla, C. pulloides, C. rotundifolia, C. tommasiniana, C. waldsteiniana, Cerastium biebersteinii, C. tomentosum, Chiastophyllum oppositifolium, Codonopsis ovata, Convolvulus mauritanicus, Coreopsis rosea, Corydalis cashmeriana, C. cheilanthifolia, C. lutea, Cymbalaria aequitriloba, C. muralis, C. pallida, Cypripedium acaule, C. calceolus, C. pubescens, C. spectabile, Cytisus decumbens, Daphne petraea, Delphinium nudicaule, Dianthus alpinus, D. deltoides* and vars., *D. gratianopolitanus* and vars., *D. knappii, D. neglectus, D. subacaulis, Dryas drummondii, D. octopetala, D. suendermannii, Erinus alpinus* and vars., *Erodium chamaedryoides, E. corsicum, Genista pilosa, G. sagittalis, Geranium cinereum, G. pylzowianum, G. sanguineum* and vars., *G. wallichianum, Geum borisii, G. montanum, Globularia bellidifolia, G.*

*cordifolia, G. incanescens, G. nudicaulis, Gypsophila cerastioides,
G. monstrosa, G. repens, Helianthemum lunulatum, H. nummularium* hybrids, *Hieracium aurantiacum, H. villosum, Helichrysum bellidioides, Houstonia caerulea, Hutchinsia alpina,
Hypericum coris, H. empetrifolium, H. fragile, H. olympicum,
H. polyphyllum, H. repens, H. reptans, Leontopodium alpinum,
Lewisia columbiana, L. cotyledon, L. heckneri, L. howellii, L.
tweedyi, Linnaea borealis, Linum alpinum, L. arboreum, L.
flavum, L. salsoloides, Lithospermum diffusum* and vars., *L.
purpureo-caeruleum, Lysimachia nummularia* and vars., *Mazus
pumilio, M. reptans, Myosotis rupicola, Oenothera acaulis, O.
caespitosa, O. missouriensis, Onosma albo-pilosum, O. tauricum,
Orchis elata, Ourisia alpina, O. elegans, O. macrophylla, Oxalis
adenophylla, O. enneaphylla, Papaver alpinum, Parochetus communis, Penstemon davidsonii, P. fruticosus, P. heterophyllus, P.
menziesii, P. rupicola, P. scouleri, Phlox douglasii, P. subulata*
and vars., *Phyteuma comosum, P. scheuchzeri, Polemonium
confertum, Potentilla aurea, P. cuneata, P. fragiformis, P.
nepalensis* and vars., *P. nitida, P. tonguei, Primula capitata,
P. farinosa, P. mooreana, P. nutans, P. sieboldii, P. viali, Prunella
incisa, Ramonda myconi, R. nathaliae, R. serbica, Ranunculus
alpestris, Rhodohypoxis baurii, Roscoea cautleoides, Rosa chinensis minima, Saponaria ocymoides, Saxifraga aizoon* and vars.,
S. cochlearis, S. cotyledon and vars., *S. longifolia, Scabiosa
graminifolia, Schizocodon soldanelloides, Silene acaulis* and vars.,
S. alpestris and vars., *Sisyrinchium angustifolium, S. bermudiana,
Stachys corsica, Thymus nitidus, T. serpyllum* and vars., *Trollius
pumilius, Tunica saxifraga, Veronica bidwillii, V. fruticans, V.
pectinata, V. prostrata, V. teucrium,* violas (as May), *Waldsteinia
ternata.*

Hardy Aquatic and Bog Plants: *Acorus calamus, Alisma
plantago, Butomus umbellatus,* dodecatheons (as May), *Filipendula ulmaria flore pleno, Geum rivale, Hottonia palustris,
Hydrocleys commersonii, Iris kaempferi* and vars., *I. laevigata,*

I. monnieri, I. ochroleuca, I. pseudacorus, I. sibirica, Lysimachia vulgaris, Menyanthes trifoliata, Mimulus cardinalis, M. cupreus, M. luteus, M. ringens, Myosotis palustris, Nymphoides peltata, Primula alpicola, P. beesiana, P. bulleyana, P. burmanica, P. cockburniana, P. florindae, P. helodoxa, P. involucrata, P. japonica, P. poissonii, P. pulverulenta, P. secundiflora, P. sikkimensis, P. waltonii, Ranunculus aquatilis, Rodgersia pinnata, R. podophylla, Veronica beccabunga.

Annuals: Hardy varieties (as list for March, Third Week).

Bedding Plants: Ageratums, antirrhinums (autumn sown), calceolarias, Canterbury bells, fuchsias, lobelias, marguerites and pelargoniums (zonal and ivy leaved).

Evergreen Shrubs: *Abelia floribunda, Andromeda polifolia, Carpenteria californica, Ceanothus burkwoodii, C. lobbianus, C. thyrsiflorus, C. veitchianus, Cistus albidus, C. corbariensis, C. crispus, C. cyprius, C. ladanifer, C. laurifolius, C. loretii, C. populifolius, C. purpureus, C. salvifolius, C.* Silver Pink, cotoneasters, *Crinodendron hookerianum, Daboecia azorica, D. cantabrica, Daphne arbuscula, Erica stuartii, E. tetralix, Gaultheria shallon, G. veitchiana, Hebe anomala, H. balfouriana, H. brachysiphon, H. buxifolia, H. cupressoides, H. hulkeana, H. macrantha, H. salicifolia, Helichrysum rosmarinifolium, Jasminum humile* and vars., *Jovellana violacea, Kalmia angustifolia, K. latifolia, Leptospermum scoparium, Leucothoe davisiae, Olearia macrodonta, Phlomis fruticosa,* pyracanthas, *Raphiolepis umbellata, Rhododendron catawbiense, R. dicroanthum, R. discolor* and hybrids, *R. ferrugineum, R. griersonianum* and hybrids, *R. hirsutum, R. lepidotum, R. ponticum* and hybrids, hardy hybrid rhododendrons, *Salvia grahamii, Stranvaesia davidiana, Telopea truncata, Viburnum rhytidophyllum, Vinca major, V. minor, Yucca whipplei.*

Deciduous Shrubs: *Abelia triflora, Abutilon vitifolium, Adenocarpus decorticans, Aesculus pavia,* hybrid deciduous azaleas, *Buddleia alternifolia, B. colvilei, B. globosa, Calycanthus fertilis,*

C. occidentalis, Chionanthus retusa, C. virginica, Colutea arborescens, Cornus capitata, C. kousa, Cytisus scoparius and vars., *Deutzia corymbosa, D. discolor, D. longifolia, D. purpurascens, D. scabra* and vars., *D. vilmoriniae, D. wilsonii, Fremontia californica, Genista cinerea, G. hispanica, G. radiata, G. virgata, Halimodendron halodendron, Hedysarum multijugum, Hydrangea aspera, Indigofera gerardiana, I. potaninii, Jamesia americana, Kolkwitzia amabilis, Lonicera chrysantha, L. syringantha, Magnolia obovata, M. sieboldii, M. sinensis, M. watsoni, M. wilsonii, Neillia longiracemosa, Paeonia delavayi,* philadelphus vars., *Potentilla fruticosa* vars., *Rhododendron calendulaceum, R. occidentale, Rhodotypos scandens, Robinia hispida, R. kelseyi, Rosa alba, R. bracteata, R. brunonii, R. carolina, R. eglanteria, R. farreri, R. filipes, R. helenae, R. hugonis, R. macrantha, R. moschata, R. moyesii, R. multibracteata, R. omeiensis, R. pimpinellifolia, R. rugosa, R. sericea, R. willmottiae, R. xanthina,* hybrid garden roses, *Rubus deliciosus, Sophora davidii, Spiraea canescens, S. cantoniensis, S. douglasii, S. menziesii, S. nipponica, S. sargentiana, S. trichocarpa, S. vanhouttei, S. veitchii, Styrax wilsonii, Syringa emodi, S. josiflexa, S. josikaea, S. microphylla, S. prestoniae* vars., *S. reflexa, S. reticulata, S. velutina, S. villosa, S. vulgaris* and vars. (lilac), *Viburnum dilatatum, V. opulus* vars., *V. pubescens, V. tomentosum* and vars., weigela (all kinds), *Zenobia pulverulenta.*

Evergreen Trees: *Embothrium coccineum* and vars., *Magnolia nitida, Michelia fuscata, Prunus lusitanica* (Portugal laurel).

Deciduous Trees: *Aesculus californica, A. carnea, A. indica, Castanea sativa, Crataego-mespilus grandiflora, Fraxinus mariesii, F. ornus, Laburnum alpinum, L. watereri* vars., *Magnolia acuminata, M. macrophylla, M. tripetala, Malus coronaria, M. hupehensis, M. ioensis, Robinia pseudoacacia* (false acacia), *Sorbus aria* (whitebeam), *S. aucuparia* (mountain ash), *Styrax japonica, S. obassia, Viburnum lantana* (wayfaring tree), *V. lentago.*

Hardy Climbing Plants: *Aristolochia heterophylla, A. macro-*

phylla, *A. moupinensis*, *A. tomentosa*, *Clematis durandii*, *C. florida* and vars., *C. lanuginosa* and vars., *C. patens* vars., many large-flowered hybrid clematis, *Hydrangea petiolaris*, *Jasminum officinale*, *J. stephanense*, *Lonicera brownii*, *L. caprifolium*, *L. giraldii*, *L. glaucescens*, *L. henryi*, *L. japonica* and vars., *L. periclymenum belgica* vars., *L. tellmanniana*, *L. tragophylla*, *Mutisia decurrens*, *M. oligodon*, *Passiflora caerulea* (passion flower), *Rosa arvensis*, *R. banksiae*, *R. laevigata*, hybrid climbing roses, *Wisteria floribunda*, *W. sinensis*, *W. venusta*.

Greenhouse Plants: *Acalypha hispida*, achimenes, *Agapanthus africanus*, *Allemanda cathartica*, annuals, hardy and half hardy (see February, Third Week, and March, First Week), *Aphelandra squarrosa* vars., *Asclepias curassavica*, balsam, begonias (tuberous rooted), *Begonia coccinea*, *Beloperone guttata*, *Billbergia nutans*, bougainvilleas, *Brunfelsia calycina*, callistemons, cannas, carnations (perpetual flowering and border), celosias, celsias, *Cestrum aurantiacum*, *C. purpureum*, chorizemas, *Clianthus formosus*, *C. puniceus*, *Coronilla glauca*, correas, *Crossandra mucronata*, *Cuphea ignea*, daturas, *Erythrina crista-galli*, *Euphorbia splendens*, *Francoa ramosa* (bridal wreath), fuchsias, gardenias, gerberas, gloxinias, *Haemanthus puniceus*, heliotrope, *Hibiscus rosa-sinensis*, hippeastrums, hydrangeas, *Impatiens walleriana*, ixoras, lantanas, *Lapageria rosea*, lilies in var., *Mandevilla suaveolens*, marguerites, *Medinilla magnifica*, passifloras, pelargoniums (regal, show, zonal and ivy leaved), *Plumbago capensis*, *Rehmannia angulata*, smithianthas, *Sprekelia formosissima*, *Stephanotis floribunda*, strelitzias, streptocarpus, *Streptosolen jamesonii*, *Tibouchina semidecandra*, *Trachelium caeruleum*, *Trachymene coerulea*, tropaeolums.

Vegetables in the Garden: Asparagus, broad beans, shorthorn carrots, cauliflower (sown September), lettuce, mustard and cress, spring onions, onions (sown August), peas (early vars.), potatoes (early vars.), radish, rhubarb, spinach, turnips (sown March).

Vegetables under Glass: French beans, cucumbers, mushrooms (cool cellars and sheds), tomatoes.

Fruits Outdoors: *Cherries:* Bigarreau de Schrecken (D), Early Rivers (D), Frogmore Early (D), Knight's Early Black (D), May Duke (D), Waterloo (D). *Gooseberries:* green kinds. *Raspberries:* Glen Clova, Lloyd George, Malling Enterprise, Malling Jewel, Malling Orion, Malling Promise. *Strawberries:* Cambridge Favourite, Cambridge Vigour, Grandee, Redgauntlet, Royal Sovereign, Talisman.

Fruits under Glass: *Grapes, Peaches and Nectarines:* early varieties started in January and forced steadily; see list, July, Fruits under Glass.

July

GENERAL WORK

Cut off Faded Flowers. From time to time during the month you should examine all the flowering plants in the garden and remove any blooms or flower spikes that are so faded as to be no longer decorative. This applies to roses, to early-flowering herbaceous plants, and also to bedding plants and annuals. The object is to prevent seed formation, which weakens the plant unnecessarily. Exception may be made if one wants some seeds of any special thing, but then the best plan is to reserve one particular plant of this variety for seed bearing.

Thin and Disbud Dahlias. If you want some extra fine dahlias for exhibition, you must thin out the plants and only allow them to bear a restricted number of flowers. A good strong plant of one of the large-flowered varieties may carry three stems, but no more. Remove others, keeping only the sturdiest. Then, when the flower buds appear, remove all except the central terminal one on each stem. Plants that are only grown for garden decoration do not need this drastic restriction and may be allowed to grow naturally. All will benefit from liberal soakings of weak liquid manure every few days.

It will also be necessary to continue the disbudding of roses as described in the notes for June, General Work.

Continue to Trim Hedges. You can continue to trim evergreen hedges and topiary specimens as necessary to keep them neat and tidy.

Take Cuttings of Shrubs and Alpines. A great many hardy shrubs, and also shrubby alpines, such as helianthemums and penstemons, can be increased during July and August by cuttings prepared from firm young sideshoots and the ends of non-flowering stems. Select pieces from 2·5 cm (1 in) to 10 cm (4 in) in length, according to the nature of the plant. Prepare them by cutting the base of each cleanly through just below a joint and removing the lower leaves. Then insert them firmly in a mixture of equal parts moss peat and sand.

The cuttings must be prevented from flagging either by keeping them in a very still, moist atmosphere or by spraying them with water frequently. This second method is the most used by nurserymen but it involves the use of special equipment to provide the overhead spraying as required. This may be electrically or hydraulically controlled and small mist propagation units, as they are called, are available for amateur use.

A close, moist atmosphere can be provided in a propagator, and many small models are available – some with electric soil warming which improves the speed and certainty of rooting. Alternatively many cuttings can be rooted very efficiently simply by inserting them in pots filled with the peat/sand mixture and slipping each pot inside a polythene bag which can then be sealed with one of the wire twist closures that are supplied with bags sold for deep freezing.

Continue to Bud Rose Stocks. You can continue to bud rose stocks throughout the month so long as the bark parts readily from the wood of the stock (see June, Fourth Week). Sometimes, if the weather gets very hot and dry, the stocks refuse to work properly and then the work should stop for the time being.

Continue to Spray against Pests and Diseases. Caterpillars, red spider mites, thrips and greenfly are still sources of danger. Take prompt measures to destroy these pests as soon as they put in an appearance (see June, General Work). Fungal diseases, such as mildew, rust and black spot, are likely to be on the increase as the weather gets warmer. Occasional spraying with Bordeaux mixture, benomyl, thiram, captan or some other good fungicide is the only certain method of keeping them down. It is wise to spray roses every fortnight or so as a precautionary measure, for it is much easier to prevent diseases than it is to cure them. Other good remedies for black spot of roses and rose mildew are captan and dinocap respectively which should be sprayed on the leaves according to the manufacturer's instructions.

Continue to Feed Plants in Growth. You should continue to feed all plants that are making rapid growth as I advised in my notes for May and June (see General Work, May and June). For winter green crops planted during May and June, nitrate of soda may well be used in place of a compound fertilizer. Give two applications, each of 14 g per square metre ($\frac{1}{2}$ oz per square yard), at an interval of about 3 weeks.

Remove Grass Box from Lawn Mower. During this month and August, when the weather is likely to be hot, it is an excellent plan to remove the grass box from the lawn mower and let the tiny clippings fall on to the lawn. They will act as a mulch and will protect the roots from scorching.

General Greenhouse Management. There is really little to add to my remarks in the June notes on this subject. Heating for all ordinary greenhouse plants will now be quite unnecessary.

Indeed, the problem usually will be to keep the house sufficiently cool by day. This is particularly so in very small houses, which must, in consequence, be ventilated freely and shaded carefully. Shading for a few hours each day may even be necessary for such a sun-loving crop as tomatoes. Occasional damping down of paths and walls will also help matters, but spraying of the plants must be done cautiously when the sun is shining brightly.

Pot on Zonal Pelargoniums and other Greenhouse Plants. Spring-struck cuttings of zonal pelargoniums required for autumn flowering in the greenhouse are almost sure to need potting on into 15-cm (6-in) pots during July. Similar remarks apply to other greenhouse plants raised from spring cuttings (see March, General Work), except that sometimes even bigger pots may be required. In this connexion I refer you to my general remarks on potting in the notes for April, General Work, and would remind you that it is rarely wise to shift plants into pots more than two sizes larger than those in which they are already growing. Use the same compost as before but coarser in texture, and press it more firmly around the roots.

Continue to Thin Seedlings. Various vegetables sown last month for succession must be thinned out before they become overcrowded (see June, General Work).

Cut Globe Artichokes. From now onwards you can cut the heads of globe artichokes as they become available. On no account leave any on the plants so long that they begin to flower. The ideal time to cut them is when they are nice and plump, but before the scales begin to open out too much.

Continue to Plant Winter Greens. Continue to plant out all manner of winter green crops as you clear ground of early crops, such as dwarf peas, early potatoes and the first sowings of turnips and salad vegetables. So far as possible, choose showery weather for this work, but do not delay long on this account. If July is persistently dry, push on with the planting and then water freely for a few days.

180

Cutting Globe Artichokes. The best time to cut is when the heads are nice and plump but before the scales have opened out too much

Plant March-sown Leeks. Leeks from the March sowing (see March, Third Week) may also be planted, as opportunity occurs, on similar ground to the winter greens. Plant with a large dibber in holes 23 cm (9 in) deep, dropping the leeks right down into these, but not refilling the holes with soil. Simply water in thoroughly. This deep planting will blanch the stems without need for earthing up. The leeks should be 30 cm (1 ft) apart in rows 45 cm (18 in) apart.

Continue to Blanch Leeks. The process of blanching leeks grown in trenches must be continued gradually, as explained in my notes for June, General Work.

Plant Celery for Succession. During the month you can make further plantings of celery as plants from late sowings become available. It is not wise to shift the plants to the trenches while they are very small. Wait until they are at least 8 cm (3 in) in height and can be lifted with a nice ball of roots (see June, First Week).

Make Successional Sowings. These are in the main the same as for last month (see June, General Work). Sow turnips for the last time about the middle of the month. You can be rather more generous with the seed, as this crop will supply roots for storing. One more sowing each of lettuce, endive and summer spinach should meet all requirements. It is necessary to choose a shady place for all these crops, for heat and drought will make them run to seed prematurely. Mustard and cress and radishes can be sown as before, also in a cool position.

Feed, Train and Fumigate Tomatoes. Outdoor tomatoes will be growing freely and forming their flower trusses. Keep each plant to a single stem and nip out all side shoots at the earliest opportunity. Water freely during dry weather and, as soon as the bottom truss is set and you can see the tiny fruits swelling, spread a 5-cm (2-in) layer of well-rotted manure round the plants. From that time onwards feed every week with small doses of any good tomato fertilizer.

There is really nothing to add to my remarks on indoor tomatoes last month (see June, General Work). Cut back more foliage as you clear the lower trusses of fruit. Free ventilation, steady feeding and ample watering are the all-important points to watch.

Feed and Train Cucumbers. Plants in frames will now be tending to take the place of those in greenhouses, though even the latter may be kept going for a surprising time by frequent removal of all side growths that have ceased to bear and their replacement by young growth. Spray and water constantly to keep up the necessary moisture in soil and air. Ventilate rather more freely, especially when the temperature shows signs of rising above 27°C (80°F), but do not allow the air to get dry on this account or you are sure to have trouble with red spider mite and thrips. Heavier shading will help to keep the temperature down. Continue to stop and train the plants in frames and on outside ridges, and regulate growth in such a manner that the beds are never overcrowded but you are continually getting a new supply of laterals with flowers. Be very careful to cut the cucumbers directly they are fit to use. If a few hang and ripen, the plants will soon stop bearing.

Management of Fruit Under Glass. Peaches, nectarines and apricots under glass must be treated according to their state of growth (see General Work, May and June). As trees are cleared of ripened fruits spraying with water should begin again on a daily or twice daily basis. Ventilate freely by day, but do not let the temperature fall below 55°F at night. Even July nights can be chilly occasionally.

Protect Vines from Mildew. Thinning of the fruits will now become general with outdoor vines, and as the process is exactly the same as for indoor varieties I refer you to my earlier notes on that subject (see March, General Work). A thick mulch of well-rotted manure spread over the border will help the vines a lot at this season. Indoor vines in various stages of growth will also require treatment as before (see General Work for April, May and June).

Mildew may become troublesome from now onwards, covering leaves and grapes with a white, mealy growth. If there is the slightest sign of this disease, give increased ventilation and dust foliage and fruits with flowers of sulphur. Make certain that the border is not short of water, for dry soil combined with a damp, unventilated atmosphere are sure causes of mildew.

Shanking sometimes occurs at this time of the year. This is a physiological disorder which causes the footstalks of the berries to die, with the result that the berries themselves suddenly collapse. It is caused by poverty of soil or a cold, wet subsoil, and remaking of the border the following autumn is the best remedy.

FIRST WEEK

Lift Tulips, Hyacinths and some other Bulbs. Tulips and hyacinths will now have completed their growth and may be lifted and cleaned. Lay the bulbs in shallow trays and stand them in a dry, cool, airy place, but not in full sun. Dead tops can be removed and the bulbs sorted out into two sizes, the biggest for flowering again next year (though do not rely on them for the most important beds) and the smaller ones to be planted in good soil in an out-of-the-way place to grow on. If your garden is only small it will be best to throw these small bulbs away, for they will scarcely be worth the space they take up. Anemones of the St Brigid and de Caen types, and also turban ranunculuses, are treated in much the same way, the tubers being lifted as soon as foliage has died down. Store in a dry, cool place until planting time. Crocuses can also be lifted now, but only if they are over-crowded or you need the ground for something else. If you do have them out, get them replanted quite soon; they gain nothing from being out of the ground.

Complete Stopping of Carnations. By this time you should complete all the second stopping of perpetual-flowering carnations (see May, General Work). If the plants are stopped later than this they will not start to flower until well on in the new year, and carnations are much in demand at Christmas and even before. Roughly speaking, five months must elapse before a stopped growth can produce any flowers.

Stand out Regal and Show Pelargoniums. Show and regal pelargoniums will have practically finished flowering by this time and will be better out of the greenhouse. Stand them in the open in any sunny, fairly sheltered place and gradually decrease the water supply, practically withholding it for the last fortnight in July. If it rains a lot, lay the pots on their sides. The object is to check and ripen growth and give the plants a rest.

Sow Carrots. A small sowing of stump-rooted or intermediate carrots made now is often amply justified, especially if the season happens to be a bad one for carrot fly. This fly does all its damage early in the summer, and seedlings from a July sowing usually escape. In any case, young carrots in the autumn are very welcome.

Spray Potatoes with Bordeaux Mixture. Do not wait until disease attacks your potatoes, but spray them now with Bordeaux mixture. The potato blight disease is common and some of your plants are likely to become infected unless you take this precaution, and in any case spraying is repaid because it lengthens the season of growth and so indirectly increases the weight of the crop. You can purchase Bordeaux mixture in powder or paste form from many dealers in horticultural sundries and it is only necessary to dissolve this in water at the strength stated on the package. When spraying, be very careful to cover the under as well as the upper sides of the leaves.

Make an Outdoor Mushroom Bed. In sheds or other suitable buildings mushrooms can be grown throughout the year, but unprotected outdoors they are only satisfactory in late summer and early autumn. Now is the time to make such a bed. First you will need to get a good quantity of fresh stable manure. This you must turn and shake with a fork two or three times, at intervals of a day or so, until the first heat of fermentation has died down and the manure is decaying steadily. Then build it up into a ridge-shaped heap in the open, or a more or less flat-topped bank against a wall.

An alternative to stable manure is clean straw rotted with one of the special mushroom compost chemical preparations sold for the purpose. These must be used according to manufacturers' instructions.

Beds made against a north wall at this time of the year are usually very satisfactory. Tread the manure or compost firmly layer by layer as you build it up into the mound. When finished, the bed should be 75 cm (2½ ft) deep; it can be of any width, but

1 m (3 ft) is usual and convenient. Plunge a soil thermometer into the bed and, when the temperature falls to 21°C (70°F), insert sterilized mushroom spawn in small pieces at intervals of 25 cm (10 in) all over the bed. Simply make a hole about 2·5 cm (1 in) deep in the manure or compost, push a piece of spawn in, and cover it with manure. Then cover the whole bed with a 30-cm (1-ft)-thick layer of straw. After 2 or 3 weeks scrape away a little of the manure and see how things are getting on. If there are white filament-like growths penetrating the bed freely, the spawn is 'running' and the bed is ready for casing. This is done by covering the manure evenly with a 2·5-cm (1-in)-thick layer of loam, beaten smooth with the back of a spade. Then replace the clean dry straw to keep the bed at an even temperature. If the weather is dry, the bed must be watered occasionally with tepid water, but too much moisture is not desirable.

Start to Summer-prune Cherries and Plums. You can now begin to summer-prune cherries and plums growing on walls. It is not worth while trying to apply this method of pruning to large bushes and standards, for these are better allowed to grow rather freely. With the one exception of the Morello cherry, the method is the same for all varieties. Side shoots which have been growing during May and June should be shortened by about one-third each, but leaders terminating main branches are left unpruned. Do not do all the work on any one tree at once, but spread it over a period of about six weeks. In this way the trees will not suffer any check to growth. Morello cherries bear their best fruits on young wood, and so are disbudded just like peaches and nectarines. Side shoots growing on the fruiting laterals are gradually rubbed off or pinched back a few at a time with the exception of two per lateral, one near its base and one at its tip. The former will replace it after the winter pruning, while the latter serves to maintain a good flow of sap to swell and ripen the fruits.

Complete Thinning of Apples and Pears. It is now the time to complete the thinning of apples and pears (see June, Second Week). Reduce the fruits to one, or at most two, per spur.

Burn Straw on Strawberry Beds. If you have had any mildew or other disease on your strawberries or the plants have been badly attacked by greenfly and the beds have been covered with straw, set fire to the straw on the beds as soon as you have gathered all the fruits. This will burn up all the foliage and leave the bed looking very bare and sad for a week or so, but the crowns themselves will not be damaged and will soon produce healthy new growth. If the beds were not strawed the leaves can be cut off with shears or a sharp sickle, gathered up and burned. Of course, you must not do either of these things to any plants around which you intend to peg down runners (see below).

Peg Down Strawberry Runners. Strawberry plants tend to deteriorate after a few years, and so it is advisable to raise a few new plants every year to take the place of old, worn-out ones. To do this it is only necessary to peg down, at this time of the year, some of the plantlets that form on the runners. Each runner will form a number of plantlets if allowed to do so, but for propagation that nearest the parent plant is the best, and the tip of the runner may be pinched out beyond this. It is not usually wise to peg down more than three or four plantlets round each old plant. There are two methods of doing the work: one is simply to press the plantlet down on to the soil in the strawberry bed and hold it in position with a wooden or wire peg; and the other is to fill an 8-cm (3-in) flower pot with a mixture of loam, leafmould, and sand, plunge this into the strawberry bed at any convenient point, and peg the plantlet into it. The second method is the better of the two because, when the rooted runners are severed from their parent plant later on and are removed to a new bed, there need be no serious root disturbance. The pot, complete with roots, is simply lifted from the strawberry bed and the ball of soil tapped out intact. But rooting in pots does mean a little more watering. If you can get all the runners you

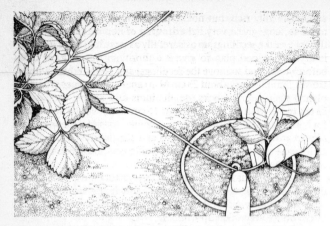

Pegging Down Strawberry Runners. The runners of strawberries are most conveniently propagated by pegging them down into pots of compost sunk into the ground. When rooted they are easily transplanted

require now, so much the better, for early rooting gives the best results, but if there are not enough runners at the moment you can continue to peg down throughout the month as the runners develop.

Cut off any runners you do not need, because they only weaken the plant. Continue to do this throughout the summer.

SECOND WEEK

Prick out Perennials and Biennials. Perennials and biennials sown in June (see June, First Week) will be in need of pricking out into a nursery bed. This should be in an open position except for violas, pansies, primroses and polyanthuses, which grow more quickly in partial shade. The ground must be well forked and reasonably rich, but not recently manured with dung. If it needs feeding, give a very light dressing of hop manure and fork this in. Get the seedlings up as carefully as possible (if the ground is dry it is a good plan to give it a thorough watering the day before you intend to move the seedlings) and replant them with a trowel. Plant in rows about 23 cm (9 in) apart. The bigger growing plants, such as hollyhocks, delphiniums and lupins, should be 23 cm (9 in) apart in the rows, but 15 cm (6 in) will be sufficient for plants such as wallflowers, double daisies, *Cheiranthus allionii* and primroses, while violas and pansies may be as close as 10 cm (4 in). Pinch out the tips of wallflowers and cheiranthuses to make them branch freely.

It is possible that Brompton stocks and forget-me-nots from the late June sowing may also be far enough advanced to prick out in the same manner. If they are not, the work should be done at the first favourable opportunity.

Prune Mock Oranges and Weigelas. Most mock oranges (Philadelphus) and weigelas (Diervilla) will have finished flowering by now, and you can prune them if you do not want the bushes to get very big. The method is to cut out all the stems that have just flowered, leaving younger shoots from lower down to take their place.

Gather Herbs for Winter Use. This is the time to gather most herbs for winter use. Do not delay until they have flowered or you will lose much of the flavour. Tie the stems into small bundles and suspend these head downwards from a beam or hook in a cool, dry and airy shed or room. When thoroughly dry the leaves can be stored in tightly stoppered jars or tins in any reasonably cool, dry place.

Start to Earth up Early Celery. If you want to have some sticks of celery for a late August show, you must start to earth up now. This is not a task that can be completed in one operation. At first content yourself by drawing 8 to 10 cm (3 to 4 in) of soil round the base of each plant. Remove basal offshoots as a pre-

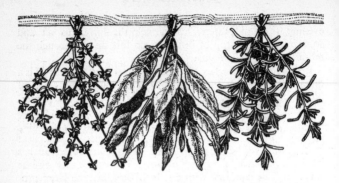

Drying Herbs. Annual herbs in particular can be harvested in summer and dried off for winter use

liminary, and tie the stems together with raffia so that soil does not find its way into the hearts of the plants. Then, about ten days later, draw up a further 10 cm (4 in) or so of soil, and keep on in this manner at short intervals until only the blades of the leaves can be seen. A further method of ensuring that the plants are kept clean and that soil does not percolate into their hearts is to tie brown paper collars round them before earthing up.

Sow and Thin Chinese Cabbage. Thin seedlings from the June sowing and make a further sowing for succession (see May, Second Week or June, Second Week).

Finish Planting Celery. All remaining celery seedlings should now be planted out in the trenches as soon as possible (see June, First Week). The last plants to be dealt with will be those from the April sowing in a frame (see April, Second Week).

Mulch and Spray Runner Beans. Runner beans will benefit from a fairly thick mulch of well-rotted manure spread on the ground for a distance of at least a couple of feet on either side of the row. When the plants begin to flower, spray them every evening with tepid water. This will help the flowers to 'set' and so ensure a good crop of beans. Keep this up all through the month and on into August.

Remove Plum Branches Attacked by Silver Leaf. Silver leaf is a disease caused by a fungus that actually infects the wood of plums and occasionally apples and pears. It cannot be counteracted by spraying, and the only method of preventing its spread is to cut off and burn affected branches, afterwards painting wounds with Stockholm tar. By law, wood killed by silver leaf must be removed before July 15. The leaves of diseased branches have a distinctive silvery appearance. The only other disease which may be confused with this is mildew, but the latter produces a white, mealy outgrowth on the leaves. With silver leaf there is no outward fungal growth until a later date, and then it is on the dead wood. At this time of the year there is just the telltale silvery sheen. The variety Victoria is particularly susceptible to attack, while Blaisdon Red, Yellow Pershore and River's Early Prolific are resistant to it.

Spray Apples against Codling Moth. Repeat application of one or other of the sprays recommended in June (see June, Third Week).

THIRD WEEK

Layer Border Carnations. Border carnations can be increased by cuttings like perpetual-flowering carnations, but it is much more satisfactory to increase them by layers. This means that you select young non-flowering shoots that can readily be bent down to soil level and make an incision with a sharp knife through a joint near the base of each. Then the slit portion of stem is bent down to open the slit, covered with fine sandy soil and is held firmly in position with a wooden or wire peg. If the layers are kept well watered, roots will soon be formed from the sides of the cut. In late August or early September the rooted layers can be cut completely from the parent plant and be planted elsewhere or potted up.

Summer-prune Wisterias. Wisterias that have filled their allotted space can be induced to flower freely year after year without making a lot of new growth by summer and winter pruning. Now is the time for the first of these operations. Shorten to about six leaves each all side growths formed on the main branches.

Summer-prune Roses. Bush and standard roses of the large-flowered type will pay for a light summer pruning now that the first flush of flowers is over. Cut back to about two leaves all stems that have flowered, but have no promising buds on them at the moment. Then give the beds a dusting of any good compound flower-garden fertilizer and hoe this in.

Prick Off and Pot Primulas, Calceolarias and Cinerarias. Greenhouse primulas sown in mid-June will now need pricking off exactly like the earlier batch (see June, First Week). These first primulas will also in all probability require a shift. Do not let them get crowded in their boxes or pans, but move them on singly into 8-cm (3-in) pots, using John Innes No. 1 or soilless potting compost. Return the plants to the frame after potting and give a little shade from strong, direct sunshine.

Calceolarias and cinerarias sown in June (see June, Third Week) are almost certain to be forward enough for pricking off in exactly the same manner as the primulas, except that the cinerarias should be spaced a good 5 cm (2 in) apart each way.

Sow Spring Cabbage. This is the time to make a first sowing of cabbages for use in the spring and early summer. Do not sow all the seed now, however, but keep some for a further sowing during the second week in August, as sometimes the later seedlings do best in the long run. Choose a suitable variety, such as April, Avoncrest, Durham Elf, Ellam's Early Dwarf, Flower of Spring or Harbinger. Scatter the seed thinly in a bed of finely broken soil and cover lightly. Water freely if the weather happens to be dry.

Lift and Store Autumn-sown Onions. Autumn-sown onions should now have completed their growth and ripened their bulbs, so you may just as well lift them and have the ground free for some other crop such as winter greens. Lift the onions carefully with a fork and lay them out in a sunny place for a few days to dry off. Then shake the soil from them and store in shallow boxes in a cool dry place.

Start to Summer-prune Apples and Pears. You can now start to shorten the laterals of apples and pears exactly as I described for cherries and plums earlier in the month (see First Week). The method is worth applying to all trained specimens, and also to small bushes, pyramids and half-standards, but involves too much labour with full standards or very big bushes.

Start to Pick Apples and Pears. A few of the earliest apples, such as Gladstone and Early Victoria, and also the pear Doyenné

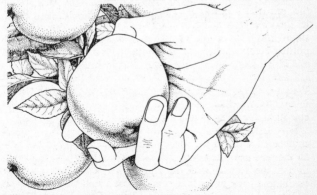

Picking Apples. If the fruits will part readily from the branches without tearing or wrenching they are ready for picking

193

d'Été, should be ripe by now, and you can begin to pick, but only as you actually require the fruits for use. These early varieties do not keep at all well off the tree, and no attempt must be made to store them. The test for ripeness with apples is to lift a typical fruit without actually wrenching or twisting it off its branch. If it comes away easily with its stalk it is ready for picking, but if it parts unwillingly, tearing off part of the spur or breaking in the middle of its stalk, it is not yet ripe. With pears the best test is to press one or two of the fruits very gently near the stalk; if yielding they are ready.

FOURTH WEEK

Plant Madonna Lilies. This is the ideal time to plant *Lilium candidum*, the Madonna lily. It differs from almost all other lilies in making quite a lot of new growth in late summer, and it should be planted before this starts. Another peculiarity is that the bulbs grow practically on the surface. You should plant them 20 cm (8 in) apart and only cover them with 5 cm (2 in) of soil. After a while they will probably work themselves out until they show; make no attempt to cover them again. This lily prefers a sunny position and reasonably good, but not freshly manured, ground.

Plant Colchicums, Autumn Crocuses and Sternbergias. You should also plant colchicums, autumn-flowering crocuses and sternbergias if you can obtain supplies. General bulb merchants rarely have them so early, but specialists will be able to supply. Plant the crocuses 8 cm (3 in) deep and 8 cm (3 in) apart; the colchicums and sternbergias 15 cm (6 in) deep and 10 cm (4 in) apart. All should be in well-drained soil and a rather sheltered but sunny position.

Lift Daffodils and Bulbous Irises. Daffodils and narcissi, also the various bulbous irises, will now have completed their growth and may be lifted and cleaned off if they are overgrown or you need the ground for something else. Otherwise leave them undisturbed for another year. They do not gain anything by annual lifting and drying, as do tulips and hyacinths. If you do lift them, get them replanted as soon as possible and certainly before the end of September.

Cut Back Helianthemums. Sun roses tend to get rather straggly if left to their own devices, but if cut back a little each year at about this time they can be kept quite neat and tidy. You can do the work with a large pair of scissors or even the garden shears.

Start to Feed Chrysanthemums. It is a mistake to begin to feed chrysanthemums of any type too early, but you can start now with safety. The more varied the feed the better. Give very small doses every five days or so mixed with plenty of water and used in place of the ordinary water. Liquid manure, made by steeping a small sack of cow, horse, or sheep droppings in a tub of water, can be varied with soot water and any good chemical fertilizer made especially for chrysanthemums and used strictly in accordance with manufacturer's instructions.

'Take' Early-flowering Chrysanthemum Buds. This term requires some explanation. It is virtually the chrysanthemum grower's equivalent to disbudding, for it means that the flower buds required for producing big blooms are retained, while all smaller buds or shoots surrounding or below them are rubbed out. It is only necessary to do this if you want big flowers borne singly on long stems. If your object is to have sprays of comparatively small flowers, let the plants grow on naturally. In any case you will not be able to complete all the disbudding at once, but look over the plants now, for some at least should be showing flower buds.

Sow Parsley for Autumn and Winter Use. Make a final sowing of parsley for autumn and winter use. If you sow the seeds in a very sheltered place, you can leave some of the plants undisturbed and keep on cutting from them as long as possible, but a portion of the seedlings will have to be transplanted into a frame in September if you wish to have a Christmas supply.

Sow Hardy Green Colewort. If you wish to have a really full supply of green vegetables right through the autumn months, make a small sowing of hardy green colewort (also known as collards) such as Wintergreen. Sow thinly in rows 30 cm (1 ft) apart where the plants are to mature. Coleworts are small, open-hearted cabbages.

Start to Bud Fruit Stocks. Stocks of various fruit trees, such as apples, pears, plums and cherries, can usually be budded at about this time. You can apply the same tests to the stocks as those suggested for rose stocks (see June, Fourth Week). Of course, there are no thorns by which you can test the shoots selected as scions, and as it is most important that they should be in just the right condition, you must examine them carefully. You should be able to peel the bark easily from the wood. If it tears, growth is either too young or too dry. The buds should be well developed and clearly visible. The actual details for budding are just the same as for roses, except that instead of inserting

Strawberries in Pots. Apart from normal plant pots, special strawberry pots can also be used

them as low down on the dwarf stocks as possible, they should be put in about 20 cm (8 in) above soil level. It is desirable that the union of rose stock and scion should be covered with soil, but this is not advisable with fruit trees, for the scions might then make roots of their own, which would upset the particular effect, dwarfing or otherwise, of the stock chosen.

Buds can only be inserted into stocks that have thin, supple bark. Some form of grafting in spring (see March, Fourth Week) must be used for old, hard-barked trees that are being reworked.

Strawberries in Pots. If you want to grow some early strawberries in the greenhouse lift a few of the most forward rooted runners now and pot them singly in 15-cm (6-in) pots in John Innes potting compost No. 2. The plants can stand in a frame or a cool position outdoors and must be watered regularly.

FLOWERS, VEGETABLES AND FRUITS IN SEASON DURING JULY

Herbaceous Plants: *Achillea filipendulina, A. millefolium* vars., *A. ptarmica* vars., *A. sibirica, A. taygetea, Aconitum cammarum, A. lycoctonum, A. napellus* vars., *Alstroemeria aurantiaca, A. chilensis, A. haemantha, A. ligtu, A. pelegrina, A. pulchella, Althaea rosea* vars. (hollyhock), *Anaphalis margaritacea, Anthemis cupaniana, A. nobilis, A. sancti-johannis, A. tinctoria* and vars., *Anthericum ramosum, Armeria latifolia* and vars., *Artemisia lactiflora, Aruncus sylvester, Asclepias tuberosa, Asphodeline lutea, Aster subcaeruleus* vars., *A. yunnanensis, Astilbe arendsii* hybrids, *Astrantia carniolica, A. major, Baptisia australis, Borago laxiflora, Buphthalmum salicifolium, Campanula alliariifolia, C. glomerata* vars., *C. lactiflora, C. latifolia, C. persicifolia* and vars., *C. rapunculoides, C. rhomboidalis, C. trachelium, Centaurea babylonica, C. dealbata, C. macrocephala, C. montana, C. ruthenica, Centranthus ruber, Cephalaria alpina, C. tartarica,*

Chrysanthemum leucanthemum vars., *C. maximum* vars., *Cimicifuga dahurica*, *C. racemosa*, *Clematis integrifolia*, *C. recta*, *Coreopsis grandiflora* vars., *C. lanceolata* vars., *Delphinium cardinale*, *D. formosum*, delphiniums in var. (large-flowered hybrids), *Dianthus allwoodii*, *D. barbatus* vars. (sweet William), *D. caryophyllus* vars. (border carnations), *Dicentra eximia*, *D. spectabilis*, *Dictamnus albus*, *Digitalis grandiflora*, *Dracocephalum grandiflorum*, *Echinacea purpurea* and vars., *Echinops bannaticus*, *E. ritro*, *E. sphaerocephalus*, *Erigeron aurantiacus*, *E. glaucus*, *E. speciosus* and vars., erigeron hybrids, *Eryngium alpinum*, *E. amethystinum*, *E. giganteum*, *E. oliverianum*, *E. planum*, *E. tripartitum*, *Euphorbia myrsinites*, *E. robbiae*, *Filipendula hexapetala flore pleno*, gaillardia hybrids, *Galega officinalis* and vars., *Gaura lindheimeri*, *Geranium endressii*, *G. grandiflorum*, *G. ibericum*, *G. pratense* vars., *G. sylvaticum*, *Geum chiloense* vars., *Gypsophila paniculata* and vars., *Helenium autumnale* and vars., *H. bigelovii* and vars., *Heliopsis scabra* vars., hemerocallis hybrids, *Heuchera brizoides*, *H. sanguinea* and vars., *Hosta fortunei*, *H. lancifolia*, *H. sieboldiana*, *Inula glandulosa*, *I. helenium*, *I. oculus-christi*, *I. royleana*, *Kniphofia caulescens*, *K. nelsonii*, *K. northiae*, *K. rufa*, *K. tuckii*, *K. uvaria* vars., *Lavatera olbia*, *Liatris pycnostachya*, *Limonium eximium*, *L. gmelinii*, *L. latifolium*, *Linaria dalmatica*, *L. purpurea*, *Linum narbonnense*, *L. perenne*, *Lychnis chalcedonica*, *L. coronaria*, *L. flos-jovis*, *L. haageana*, *L. viscaria* and vars., *Lupinus arboreus*, *Lysimachia clethroides*, *L. ephemerum*, *L. punctata*, *L. thyrsiflora*, *L. vulgaris*, *Lythrum salicaria* and vars., *L. virgatum* vars., *Macleaya cordata*, *M. microcarpa*, *Malva moschata*, *Meconopsis betonicifolia*, *M. cambrica* and vars., *M. napaulensis*, *M. paniculata*, *M. quintuplinervia*, *M. regia*, *Mertensia sibirica*, *Monarda didyma* and vars., *Morina longifolia*, *Nepeta faassenii*, *N. grandiflora*, *Oenothera biennis* vars., *O. fruticosa* and vars., *O. speciosa*, *O. tetragona* vars., *Papaver nudicaule* vars. (Iceland poppy), *Penstemon barbatus*, *P. gentianoides* hybrids (shelter in winter), *P. isophyllus*, *Phlox arendsii* hybrids, *P. decussata* hybrids, *P. maculata* vars., *P. suffruticosa* hybrids, *Phygelius capensis*, *Physostegia virginiana* and vars., *Platycodon grandiflorum*, *Polemonium caeruleum*, *P. carneum*, *P. lanatum*, *Polygonum amplexicaule*, *P. bistorta* vars., *P. campanulatum*, potentilla hybrids, *Romneya coulteri*, *R. trichocalyx*, rudbeckias, *Salvia sclarea* and vars., *Sanguisorba obtusa*, *S. tenuifolia*, *Scabiosa caucasica* and vars., *Sidalcea candida*, *S. malvaeflora* and hybrids, *Solidago virgaurea* vars., *Thalictrum adiantifolium*, *T. delavayi*, *T. dipterocarpum*, *T. speciosissimum*, *Tradescantia virginiana*, *Tropaeolum polyphyllum*, *Verbascum bombyciferum*, *V. chaixii*, *V. nigrum*, *V. olympicum*, *V. phoeniceum*, *V. thapsiforme*, *V. wiedemannianum*, verbascum hybrids, *Verbena bonariensis*, *V. rigida*, *Veronica longifolia* and vars., *V. spicata* and vars.

Hardy Bulbs, Corms and Tubers: *Allium albopilosum*, *A. beesianum*, *A. caeruleum*, *A. cernuum*, *A. moly*, *A. pulchellum*, *A. sphaerocephalum*, *Cardiocrinum giganteum*, *Crocosmia masonorum*, *Galtonia candicans*, gladiolus (early vars.), *Iris xiphioides* (English iris), *Lapeirousia cruenta*, *Lilium amabile*, *L. aurelianense*, *L. brownii*, *L. canadense*, *L. candidum* (Madonna lily), *L. chalcedonicum*, *L. columbianum*, *L. concolor*, *L. dauricum*, *L. duchartrei*, *L. humboldtii*, *L. japonicum*, *L. maculatum*, *L. martagon* and vars., *L. pardalinum*, *L. regale*, *L. superbum*, *Tigridia pavonia*.

Rock Plants: *Acantholimon glumaceum*, *Achillea ageratifolia*, *A. clavenae*, *A. tomentosa* and vars., *Androsace lanuginosa* and vars., *Antennaria dioica* and vars., *Armeria maritima* and vars., *Asperula suberosa*, *Astilbe simplicifolia*, *Calandrinia umbellata*, *Calceolaria polyrrhiza*, *Campanula carpatica* and vars., *C. cochlearifolia*, *C. garganica* and vars., *C. portenschlagiana*, *C. poscharskyana*, *C. pulla*, *C. pulloides*, *C. raddeana*, *C. raineri*, *C. rotundifolia*, *C. sarmatica*, *C. stansfieldii*, *C. tommasiniana*, *C. waldsteiniana*, *C. zoysii*, *Convolvulus althaeoides*, *C. cneorum*,

C. mauritanicus, Coreopsis rosea, Cymbalaria aequitriloba, C. muralis, C. pallida, Dianthus alpinus, D. deltoides and vars., *D. knappii, D. superbus, Epilobium fleischeri, Erodium chamae-dryoides, E. chrysanthemum, E. corsicum, E. guttatum, E. macradenum, E. manescavii, Frankenia laevis, Genista sagittalis, G. tinctoria plena, Gentiana asclepiadea, G. freyniana, G. graci-lipes, G. lagodechiana, G. septemfida, Geranium argenteum, G. cinereum, G. dalmaticum, G. pylzowianum, G. sanguineum* and vars., *Geum borisii, Globularia cordifolia, G. nudicaulis, Gypso-phila cerastioides, G. repens* and vars., *Helichrysum bellidioides, Hieracium aurantiacum, H. villosum, Hypericum coris, H. fragile, H. nummularium, H. olympicum, H. repens, H. reptans, Inula acaulis, I. ensifolia, Jasione jankae, J. perennis, Leontopodium alpinum, Linaria alpina, Linum alpinum, L. arboreum, L. flavum, L. monogynum, L. salsaloides, Lychnis lagascae, Lysimachia nummularia, Oenothera acaulis, O. missouriensis, Onosma albo-pilosum, O. tauricum, Othonnopsis cheirifolia, Papaver alpinum, Parochetus communis, Penstemon davidsonii, P. heterophyllus, Phuopsis stylosa, Phyteuma comosum, P. orbiculare, P. scheuch-zeri, Potentilla aurea, P. fragiformis, P. nepalensis* and vars., *P. nitida, P. tonguei, Primula capitata, P. mooreana, P. viali, Prunella incisa, Ranunculus alpestris, Rhodohypoxis baurii, Rosa chinensis minima, Scabiosa graminifolia, Sedum acre, S. album, S. anglicum, S. dasyphyllum, S. ellacombianum, S. ewersii, S. hispanicum, S. kamtschaticum, S. lydium, S. midden-dorffianum, S. pulchellum, S. reflexum, S. rupestre, S. spathuli-folium, S. spurium, Sempervivum allionii, S. arachnoideum* and vars., *S. calcaratum, S. funckii, S. globiferum, S. montanum, S. reginae-amaliae, S. tectorum, S. triste, Silene alpestris, S. schafta, Sisyrinchium angustifolium, Solidago virgaurea brachy-stachys, Stachys corsica, Thymus serpyllum* and vars., *Tunica saxifraga, Verbena peruviana, Veronica incana, V. prostrata, V. teucrium, Viola cornuta* and vars., *V. elegantula, V. gracilis* and vars., *V. hederacea.*

Hardy Aquatic and Bog Plants: *Acorus calamus, Alisma plantago, Aponogeton distachyus,* astilbes in vars., *Butomus umbellatus, Filipendula palmata, F. purpurea, F. rubra, F. r. venusta, F. ulmaria flore pleno, Hydrocleys commersonii, Iris aurea, I. fulva, I. kaempferi* and vars., *I. ochroleuca, I. sibirica* and vars., *Ligularia dentata, L. przewalskii, L. stenocephala, Lysimachia vulgaris, Menyanthes trifoliata, Mimulus cardinalis, M. cupreus, M. luteus* and vars., *M. ringens, Nuphar lutea,* nymphaeas in var., *Nymphaeoides peltata, Parnassia palustris, Pontederia cordata, Primula alpicola, Ranunculus lingua, Rodgersia aesculifolia, R. pinnata, R. podophylla, R. sambucifolia, R. tabularis, Sagittaria sagittifolia* and vars., *Stenanthium robustum, Stratiotes aloides, Typha angustifolia, T. latifolia, T. minima.*

Annuals: Hardy vars. (as June); half-hardy vars. (as list, February, Third Week).

Bedding Plants: As June, but also dahlias (bedding) and begonias (tuberous rooted and semperflorens).

Evergreen Shrubs: *Abelia grandiflora, Bupleurum fruticosum, Calluna vulgaris* and vars., *Carpenteria californica, Ceanothus burkwoodii,* cistus (as June), *Daboecia cantabrica, Daphne acutiloba, Desfontainea spinosa, Erica ciliaris* and vars., *E. cinerea* and vars., *E. tetralix, E. vagans* and vars., *E. watsonii, Escallonia edinensis, E. exoniensis, E. illinita, E. langleyensis, E. montevidensis, E. organensis, E. pterocladon, E. punctata, E. revoluta, E. viscosa,* escallonia hybrids, *Hebe anomala, H. balfouriana, H. brachysiphon, H. buxifolia, H. cupressoides, H. elliptica, H. franciscana, H. leiophylla, H. salicifolia,* hebe hybrids, *Helichrysum rosmarinifolium, Hypericum calycinum, Jasminum humile* vars., *Lavandula angustifolia* and vars., *L. dentata, L. latifolia* and vars., *L. stoechas, Magnolia grandiflora, Myrtus communis, Olearia haastii, O. nummularifolia, Osmanthus fragrans, Phlomis chrysophylla, P. fruticosa, Rhododendron auriculatum, R. diaprepes, R.* Polar Bear, *Salvia grahamii, Santolina chamaecyparissus, S. virens, Senecio greyi, S. laxi-*

folius, Teucrium fruticans, Ulex nanus, Vinca major, V. minor, Yucca filamentosa, Y. flaccida, Y. gloriosa.

Deciduous Shrubs: *Abutilon vitifolium, Aesculus parviflora, Buddleia alternifolia, B. davidii* and vars., *Calycanthus floridus, Ceanothus americanus, C. caeruleus* and hybrids, *Ceratostigma willmottianum, Clethra alnifolia, Colutea arborescens, Cotinus coggygria, Cytisus battandieri, C. leucanthus, C. nigricans, Deutzia scabra* and vars., *Escallonia virgata, Fremontia californica, Fuchsia magellanica* and vars., *F. riccartonii,* hardy hybrid fuchsias, *Genista aethnensis, G. cinerea, G. virgata, Halimodendron halodendron, Hedysarum multijugum, Hoheria lyallii, Holodiscus discolor, Hydrangea arborescens grandiflora, H. aspera, H. heteromalla bretschneideri, H. macrophylla* vars., *H. paniculata praecox, H. sargentiana, H. serrata, Hypericum beanii, H. calycinum, H. forrestii, H.* Hidcote, *H. patulum* and vars., *H.* Rowallane, *Indigofera gerardiana, Itea virginica, Jovellana violacea, Leycesteria formosa, Lyonia ligustrina, Magnolia sieboldii, Meliosma cuneifolia, Nandina domestica, Notospartium carmichaeliae,* philadelphuses (all), *Potentilla arbuscula, P. fruticosa* vars., *Robinia hartwigii, Rosa alba, R. bracteata, R. carolina, R. centifolia, R. damascena, R. filipes, R. gallica, R. moyesii, R. multibracteata, R. multiflora, R. rugosa, R. triphylla, R. wichuraiana,* hybrid garden roses, *Rubus odoratus, R. ulmifolius bellidiflorus, Sorbaria aitchisonii, S. arborea, S. assurgens, S. sorbifolia, Spartium junceum, Spiraea bumalda, S. japonica* and vars., *S. margaritae, S. menziesii* and vars., *S. veitchii,* stewartias (all), *Tamarix pentandra, Zenobia pulverulenta.*

Evergreen Trees: *Eucryphia cordifolia, E. intermedia, E. lucida, E. nymansensis, Magnolia grandiflora.*

Deciduous Trees: *Aesculus indica, Castanea sativa, Catalpa bignonioides, Cladrastis sinensis, Eucryphia glutinosa, Koelreuteria paniculata, Liriodendron tulipifera, Oxydendrum arboreum, Tilia cordata, T. euchlora, T. europaea, T. petiolaris, T. platyphyllos, T. tomentosa.*

Hardy Climbing Plants: *Berberidopsis corallina*, *Clematis durandii*, *C. fargesii*, *C. florida* and vars., *C. jackmanii* and vars., *C. lanuginosa* and vars., *C. viticella* and vars., *Jasminum officinale*, *J. stephanense*, *Lathyrus latifolius* and vars., *Lonicera americana*, *L. brownii*, *L. caprifolium*, *L. etrusca*, *L. heckrottii*, *L. japonica* and vars., *L. periclymenum* and vars., *L. sempervirens*, *L. tellmanniana*, *L. tragophylla*, *Passiflora caerulea*, *Periploca graeca*, *Polygonum baldschuanicum*, hybrid climbing roses, *Schizophragma hydrangeoides*, *Solanum crispum*, *S. jasminoides*, *Tibouchina semidecandra*, *Trachelospermum asiaticum*, *T. jasminoides*, *Tropaeolum speciosum*.

Greenhouse Plants: *Acalypha hispida*, achimenes, *Agapanthus umbellatus*, *Allemanda cathartica*, annuals as June, *Aphelandra squarrosa*, *Asclepias curassavica*, balsam, *Begonia coccinea*, begonias (tuberous rooted), *Beloperone guttata*, *Billbergia nutans*, bougainvilleas, *Brunfelsia calycina*, callistemons, *Campanula pyramidalis*, cannas, carnations (perpetual flowering and border), *Cassia corymbosa*, celosias, celsias, *Cestrum elegans*, *Clerodendrum speciosissimum*, *C. thomsonae*, *Clianthus formosus*, *C. puniceus*, *Cobaea scandens*, *Coronilla glauca*, correas, *Crassula falcata*, crinums, *Crossandra mucronata*, *Cuphea ignea*, daturas, *Didiscus caerulea*, dipladenias, *Eccremocarpus scaber*, *Erythrina crista-galli*, *Euphorbia splendens*, *Francoa ramosa*, fuchsias, gardenias, gerberas, gloriosas, gloxinias, heliotrope, *Hibiscus rosa-sinensis*, *Hoya bella*, *H. carnosa*, *Humea elegans*, *Hymenocallis calathina*, *Impatiens walleriana*, ipomoeas, ixoras, *Lagerstroemia indica*, lantanas, *Lapageria rosea*, *Lilium auratum*, *L. longiflorum*, *L. speciosum*, *Littonia modesta*, *Mandevilla suaveolens*, marguerites, *Maurandya barclaiana*, *Mimulus glutinosus*, *Mitraria coccinea*, myrtus, *Nerium oleander*, pancratiums, passifloras, pelargoniums (zonal and ivy leaved), *Plumbago capensis*, *Rehmannia angulata*, *Sandersonia aurantiaca*, smithianthas, stephanotis, streptocarpus, *Streptosolen jamesonii*, swainsonas, tecomas, trachelium, *Trachelospermum jasminoides*, trachymene, tropaeolums.

Vegetables in the Garden: Globe artichoke, beetroot, broad beans, French beans, runner beans, broccoli (calabrese vars.), shorthorn carrots, cauliflower, lettuce, vegetable marrow, mustard and cress, onions, peas, potatoes (early vars.), radish, spinach, turnips.

Vegetables under Glass: Cucumbers, mushrooms (cool cellars and sheds), tomatoes.

Fruits Outdoors: *Apples:* Beauty of Bath (D), Early Victoria or Emneth Early (C), Gladstone (D). *Blackberry:* Bedford Giant. *Cherries:* Archduke (D), Bedford Prolific (D), Bigarreau de Schrecken (D), Blackheart (D), Black Tartarian (D), Elton (D), Flemish Red (C), Frogmore Bigarreau (D), Governor Wood (D), Kentish Bigarreau (D), Kentish Red (C), Knight's Early Black (D), Merton Bigarreau (D), Noir de Guben (D), Peggy Rivers (D). *Currants, Black:* Blacksmith, Boskoop Giant, Davison's Eight, Laxton's Giant, Mendip Cross, Seabrook's Black, Wellington XXX. *Currants, Red:* Earliest of Fourlands, Fay's Prolific, Laxton's No. 1, Laxton's Perfection, Red Lake. *Currants, White:* White Dutch, White Versailles. *Gooseberries:* Careless, Golden Drop, Early Sulphur, Keepsake, Lancashire Lad, Langley Gage, Leveller, Whinham's Industry, Whitesmith. *Loganberry. Pears:* Doyenné d'Été (D), Early Market (D). *Plums:* Early Laxton (C), Rivers' Early Prolific (C). *Raspberries:* As June plus Malling Admiral and Norfolk Giant. *Strawberries:* As June plus Cambridge Late Pine, Gento and Hampshire Maid.

Fruits under Glass: *Apricots:* Blenheim, Frogmore Early, Moorpark, New Large Early. *Grapes:* Buckland's Sweetwater, Foster's Seedling, Royal Muscadine. *Nectarines:* Early Rivers, Elruge, Lord Napier. *Peaches:* Amsden's June, Duke of York, Hale's Early, Peregrine.

August

GENERAL WORK

Take Pelargonium Cuttings. You can take cuttings of both zonal and ivy-leaved bedding pelargoniums (geraniums) at any time during the month. Choose shoots, 10 to 13 cm (4 to 5 in) long, that are not carrying flowers. Sever them cleanly just below a joint and insert the cuttings around the edge of well-drained 10- to 13-cm (4- to 5-in) pots filled with sandy compost. The cuttings will root most rapidly if you stand them in a frame and shade them from direct sunshine, but they can also be rooted in any reasonably sheltered place indoors or out. Water moderately until the cuttings start to grow, after which they will need increasing supplies.

If you want a batch of greenhouse zonal pelargoniums for late spring and summer flowering, take a batch of cuttings now and treat them in exactly the same way as the bedding varieties.

Continue to Bud Fruit and Rose Stocks. You can continue to bud both fruit and rose stocks throughout the month provided the stocks work well (see note on Rose Budding, July, General Work). As a rule, however, it is wise to complete rose budding as early in the month as possible, as late buds do not give such good results.

Examine the early buds put in during June and July and loosen any ties that are cutting into the bark. It is advisable to replace such ties with new ones, as the buds may not yet have made a very secure union.

Continue to Remove Faded Flowers and Runners. Throughout the month continue to remove faded flowers from roses and bedding and herbaceous plants; also runners from violets. Disbud roses and dahlias if you require some big flowers (see June and July, General Work).

Complete Trimming of Hedges. Evergreen shrubs grown as hedges or topiary specimens can still be trimmed during August, but it is wise to complete the work for the season at the end of the month. Late trimming may result in soft autumn growth which will get damaged by frost.

Continue to Secure Shrub Cuttings. You can continue to take shrub cuttings during the month, as described in my notes for July (see July, General Work). Hydrangeas usually root very freely during this month, and do best if inserted singly in 6·5-cm (2½-in) pots, so that there need be no subsequent root disturbance. They must be kept in a shaded frame without ventilation until rooted and should be watered very freely.

Keep an eye on the cuttings of shrubs and other plants taken last month and as soon as these start to grow remove them very carefully from the frames or hand lights and pot them up separately in 6·5-cm (2½-in) pots, using the John Innes No. 1 or an equivalent soilless compost. Keep them in a frame or cool greenhouse for the time being, shading them from strong, direct sunshine and spraying them with tepid water every day. As they get hardened and root out into the new soil, accustom them to outdoor conditions, and eventually, after a few weeks, remove them to a plunge bed in a sheltered place outdoors. Plant them in a sheltered nursery bed in October or March.

Keep down Pests and Diseases. Most of my July notes on the subject of pests and diseases (see July, General Work) apply with equal force to August. One pest that is likely to be on the increase is the earwig. These can be trapped in small flower pots, filled with hay or straw and inverted on sticks among dahlias, chrysanthemums and other plants commonly attacked. Examine the traps every morning. Earwigs will hide in them by day, for they dislike the light. Another method is to poison the earwigs by dusting HCH or derris over and around their nests or watering them with trichlorphon.

'Take' Chrysanthemum Buds. Continue to 'take' early-flowering chrysanthemum buds – that is, to secure the good buds you need for flowering and to remove all shoots and buds

Trapping Earwigs. A simple yet effective means of catching earwigs is to invert a straw-filled plant pot on a cane among plants which are susceptible to attack. The pots are emptied daily and the pests destroyed

below them, as I explained in my notes for July, Fourth Week. A little later in the month exactly the same process must be applied to late-flowering chrysanthemums that are being grown for large blooms. Exhibition varieties are usually needed about the middle of November, and it is desirable that they should show their buds from the middle to the end of August. However, if some do show up early you must keep them now, for it is too late to remove them and wait for the next lot. Sometimes early buds can be retarded quite a bit by leaving the sideshoots to grow up around them for a week or so before pinching them out, but you must not overdo this, or you may starve the bud too much.

General Greenhouse Management. All the remarks in the June and July notes on this subject still apply with as much force as ever. Ventilation will be needed both day and night; top and side most days, but top only at night unless conditions are exceptional. Always be ready with shading at the first sign of scorched foliage, and damp down paths, stages and walls with increased freedom if red spider mite or thrips put in an appearance. August is generally the peak month for these drought-loving pests.

The earliest batches of achimenes, begonias and gloxinias will have finished flowering by this time, and their water supply should be very gradually reduced so that they ripen their growth and go to rest. Similar remarks apply to early hippeastrums, which will also be coming towards the close of their season of growth.

Make Successional Sowings. There are still a few successional sowings to be made. Mustard and cress and also radishes should be sown as before. A small sowing of stump-rooted carrots made early in the month in a very sheltered place will continue the supply of young roots well into the autumn, while endive and lettuce sown about the middle of the month, also in a sheltered border, will provide you with seedlings some of which can be left undisturbed, while others are transferred to a frame.

Start to Blanch Endive. By this month endive from the first sowing (see April, Fourth Week) should be ready for blanching. Only do a few plants at a time, however, as blanching stops growth. There are several ways of accomplishing this task, but none, I think, better than the very simple plan of covering each plant with an inverted plant pot or a saucer. If you use plant pots, you must be careful to cover the hole in the bottom of each to secure perfect blanching. It usually takes about a fortnight to get a complete blanch.

Continue to Blanch Leeks. This work must be continued as I have already described (see June, General Work) until a sufficient length of blanched stem – usually about 30 cm (1 ft) – is obtained.

Lift Second Early Potatoes as Required. When you come to the end of the first early potatoes make a start on the second early or mid-season varieties such as Catriona and Arran Banner, but only lift a few roots at a time as you require them.

Thin Vegetable Seedlings. Do not neglect to thin out seedlings of lettuce, spinach and other sowings made last month. Do the work as soon as you can conveniently handle the seedlings and water those you leave if the soil is dry.

Feed and Train Tomatoes. In the main, treatment of tomatoes this month is exactly the same as during July (see July, General Work). As soon as the outdoor plants have made four trusses of flowers, stop them from growing further by pinching out the tips of the main stems.

Clear out Spent Cucumbers. It is probable that the early cucumbers will not be worth keeping any longer, especially if you have a good supply of plants in frames. Clear them out when they cease to bear freely, and take the opportunity to give the house a thorough clean out and scrub down. If you have been troubled with thrips and red spider mite, fumigate with naphthalene or sulphur while the house is empty. Use one of the lamps specially manufactured for vaporizing these chemicals. They can be purchased from a dealer in horticultural sundries. If the house cannot be emptied use azobenzene in the form of a smoke canister. Specially prepared canisters can be purchased for this purpose. Other effective preparations, containing derris, can be used for dealing with red spider mite. Manufacturer's instructions should be followed.

Kill Woolly Aphid on Apples. This is a suitable time to take steps to destroy woolly aphid (sometimes known as American blight) on apples. This is an insect pest which infests cracks in the branches and twigs and protects itself with a white, cotton-wool-like covering. Go over the trees carefully and brush methylated spirits or a solution of HCH into the woolly patches. For larger attacks overall spraying with dimethoate or malathion may be carried out.

Pick and Summer-prune Apples and Pears. During this month and also throughout September you should continue to pick apples and pears as they ripen, applying the tests already described (see July, Third Week). You should also continue to summer-prune the trees (see July, Third Week), but strive to complete the work by the end of the month.

Management of Fruit Under Glass. There is nothing to add to my remarks on this subject in the notes for July, General Work, except that ventilation can be even freer and cleared trees sprayed with water more thoroughly than before.

Treat Vines according to Growth. Vines, both indoors and out, will be in various stages of growth, according in part to the time at which they were started and in part to the variety. Regarding actual treatment, there is nothing to be added to my former remarks (see notes on General Work, May, June and July). Early vines from which you have gathered the crop should be ventilated freely and sprayed with water fairly frequently if there is any sign of red spider on the leaves.

FIRST WEEK

Sow Stocks for the Greenhouse. Make sowings of both Beauty of Nice and Brompton stocks for flowering in pots in the greenhouse. The former will bloom from Christmas until February or March, while the Brompton stocks will follow on in late spring. Sow very thinly in well-drained pans or trays filled with John Innes seed compost or a soilless equivalent and germinate in a frame, shading until the seedlings appear, but thereafter giving full light and free ventilation. Prick off or pot the seedlings separately in 6·5-cm (2½-in) pots as soon as they have two true leaves each.

Pot Freesias for Early Flowering. Provided the corms are properly ripened, the earlier freesias can be potted the better. The beginning of August is usually about as soon as one can purchase the corms, so if you want a supply of flowers for Christmas, pot up some now in 13- to 15-cm (5- to 6-in) pots. You can place six corms in a 13-cm (5-in) pot or ten in a 15-cm (6-in) pot in John Innes No. 1 or a peat-based potting compost. Bury the corms 2·5 cm (1 in) deep in this and then stand the pots in a frame. Water moderately and shade from direct sunshine, but do not use the lights as yet. Old corms from last year that have been resting during the summer (see May, General Work) should also be shaken out and repotted now.

Pot Lachenalias. Lachenalias for winter flowering in the greenhouse should also be potted or be placed in hanging baskets, a very delightful method of growing these beautiful South African bulbs. The method of culture in pots is exactly the same as for freesias (see above). If to be grown in hanging baskets, the latter must be well lined with moss and then some of the bulbs should be placed at the bottom and around the sides of the basket, as well as on top. Use the same compost as for freesias in pots and cover the top bulbs to a depth of 1 cm (½ in). Hang the baskets up in a cool place for the time being and water moderately until

211

growth starts when the plants will need more to sustain them.

Repot and Start Arum Lilies. The arum lilies that have been resting during the summer (see May, General Work) should now be started into growth. If they have been more than one year in their present pots, repot them first. Shake the old compost off the tubers and place them in 15-, 20-, or 25-cm (6-, 8-, or 10-in) pots, according to their size. If they have made any sturdy offsets, these can be detached and potted separately in John Innes potting compost No. 1. Stand the pots in a sheltered place in the open and water very moderately at first, but gradually give more as growth proceeds.

Ripen off Onions. Onions from the January and March sowings will now be approaching ripeness, and you can hasten this by bending over the leaves just above the neck of each bulb.

Pot Winter-flowering Begonias. If you were able to root cuttings of winter-flowering begonias in late winter (see April, General Work) the plants should now be about ready for potting on into their flowering pots. These should be 13 to 15 cm (5 to 6 in) in diameter. Use John Innes potting compost No. 1. Place the plants on a shelf in the greenhouse and shade from direct sunshine.

Ripening Onions. Ripening will be hastened if the tops of onions are bent over, so exposing the tops of the bulbs to the sun

SECOND WEEK

Cut Back Violas and Pansies for Propagation. It is an excellent plan to cut back a few plants of any good violas and pansies one may have with a view to encouraging basal growth which will provide cuttings next month. Scissor off the present flowering shoots to within 2·5 cm (1 in) of the roots. Then scatter a little fine soil mixed with sand and sifted leafmould over the plants.

Pot Greenhouse Calceolarias and Cinerarias. As soon as green-house calceolarias begin to touch in the boxes in which they were pricked off last month (see July, Third Week) they must be pricked off a second time, leaving 8 cm (3 in) between plants, or, alternatively, potted up singly in 6·5-cm (2½-in) pots. For this use John Innes No. 1 or a soilless potting compost and return the plants to the frame, treating them as before and being very careful to keep them cool by free ventilation and shading. Also, keep a sharp eye on cinerarias in frames. The first batch sown in May (see May, First Week) is likely to require a move on into 13-cm (5-in) pots, while the later batch, pricked off last month (see July, Third Week) will certainly very soon require first pot-ting into 8-cm (3-in) pots. This I have already described in the notes for June, Fourth Week. Spray the plants daily with clear water.

Sow Cyclamen. It is possible to raise cyclamen from seed sown very early in the year and flower the plants the following winter, but very much better results are obtained by sowing about the middle of August and keeping the seedlings growing steadily, but slowly, throughout the following autumn, winter, spring, and summer so that they make fine big corms for flowering the following autumn and winter. Sow in well-drained pans in the usual seed compost and space the seeds individually 1 cm (½ in) apart each way. Cover with 0·5 cm (¼ in) of the same soil and then with a pane of glass and a sheet of brown paper, and germinate in any frame or greenhouse in which you can maintain a steady temperature of 16°C (60°F) or rather more. Very high temperatures are not necessary or advisable.

Restart Old Cyclamen Corms. Old cyclamen corms that have been resting in a shady frame since May (see May, Second Week) may now be repotted and started into growth. Clean off all the old foliage, shake most of the soil from the roots and repot in the smallest pots that will accommodate the roots comfortably, without any doubling up. Use John Innes potting compost No. 1. Return the plants to a shady frame for a few weeks, ventilate rather sparingly, water very moderately at first, but spray the corms daily with tepid water to encourage them to make new growth.

Cut Back Pelargoniums and Insert Cuttings. Show and regal pelargoniums that were stood outdoors last month (see July, First Week) should now be cut back. Shorten all growths to about 2·5 cm (1 in) and then begin to spray the plants daily with tepid water, continuing this daily throughout the month. The shoots that you cut off can be inserted as cuttings if you need some more plants. The method of preparing and rooting cuttings is exactly the same as for bedding geraniums (see General Work).

Sow Spring Cabbages. Make a second sowing of spring cabbages now in exactly the same way as described in the notes for July, Third Week. The reason for this is that in some seasons the earlier seedlings grow thin and spindly and eventually run to seed instead of forming hearts. If you also want to have some big red cabbages for pickling next year, sow a few seeds in exactly the same manner.

Lift Early Beetroot. Beetroots do not improve by getting very big, so lift the early globe varieties rather before they average the size of tennis balls – which will probably be about this time. Twist off the tops without injuring the skin of the beetroot in any way (bleeding is very easily caused and, if severe, may spoil the colour of the roots) and store them in any cool shed, cellar, or room. They will keep better if surrounded by sand that is just moist.

Storing Beetroot. The foliage is best twisted from the root to avoid 'bleeding' which will lead to discoloration of the roots

Prune Summer-fruiting Raspberries. By this time the summer-fruiting raspberries will have quite finished cropping, and the sooner they are pruned the better. Cut out, right to ground level, all the canes that have just fruited, and train in the young canes in their place. This treatment will also suit the variety Lloyd George, for though this raspberry is sometimes described as perpetual-fruiting, any late summer or autumn fruits it may carry will be on the current year's canes, not on last year's canes.

THIRD WEEK

Start Nerines. Give a little water to nerines that have been resting all the summer and increase the amount as soon as growth appears. The pots should stand on the staging in a sunny greenhouse. Ventilate freely and do not shade at all.

Sow Schizanthus for Spring Flowering. In order to have really large plants of schizanthus in 18- to 20-cm (7- to 8-in) pots for spring decorations in greenhouse and conservatory you should sow now. Sow seeds thinly in well-drained seed boxes, using a seed compost, and germinate in a frame. Keep the lights on and the frame shaded until the seedlings appear, then remove the shading and begin to give a little ventilation, increasing this until after a week or so the lights are only used to keep off heavy rain. The cooler the conditions under which the plants are grown the better, for schizanthus get drawn very easily.

Sow Winter Spinach and Spinach Beet. Choose a fairly sheltered place and make a sowing of prickly-seeded spinach to stand the winter. Sow the seed thinly in drills 2·5 cm (1 in) deep and 30 cm (1 ft) apart.

You can also make a sowing of spinach beet now for use in winter and spring. This useful variety of beetroot is grown solely for its leaves, which are used as a substitute for spinach. Sow the seeds in small groups 20 cm (8 in) apart, in drills 2·5 cm (1 in) deep, and make the drills 38 cm (15 in) apart. Later, you can single out the clusters of seedlings.

Start to Gather Mushrooms from Outdoor Beds. If you were able to make a mushroom bed in the open early in July (see July, First Week) you should examine it now for the first mushrooms. Gather the 'buttons' (young mushrooms) as they form. The bed should continue in bearing well on into the autumn.

Make New Strawberry Plantations. Strawberry runners that were pegged down early last month (see July, First Week) should now have made good roots and can be severed from their parent plants. A few days later you can lift them carefully and plant them in new beds. Choose a good open position and soil that has been deeply dug and well manured. Plant the strawberries 30 cm (1 ft) apart in rows 60 cm (2 ft) apart. After the first year alternate plants can be removed if the plantation has become overcrowded.

FOURTH WEEK

Pot Early Narcissus Bulbs. If you want narcissi by, or even before Christmas, pot tazetta hybrids such as Soleil d'Or and Scilly White now. Place the bulbs almost touching in pots of John Innes potting compost No. 1 and leave the tips of the bulbs exposed. Place the pots in a light greenhouse or frame but do not use any artificial heat yet.

Prune Hydrangeas. Most hydrangeas will have finished flowering and will benefit from a little pruning. Cut off each faded flower truss as far back as the first plump-looking growth bud, and remove any thin, weakly looking stems. Of course, if some of the branches are still producing good blooms leave these unpruned.

Lift Spring-sown Onions. Onions sown in January under glass and in March outdoors should now have completed their growth, and there is no point in leaving them in the ground any longer. Lift them carefully with a fork and spread them out on the surface to dry. After a few days you can shake any soil from the bulbs and store them, either on shelves or in shallow boxes in a dry, frost-proof shed or room, or else strung together in ropes.

Sow Onions. This is the time to sow onions, both for use as small salading in the spring and also to provide early bulbs before the spring-sown crop. For the former purpose White Lisbon is the best variety as it is very mild in flavour, but for bulb-making choose Reliance, Ailsa Craig, White Spanish, Express Yellow or some other variety known to do well when sown at this time. Select a fairly sheltered place and ground that has been well cultivated but not recently manured. Sow the seeds thinly in drills 1 cm ($\frac{1}{2}$ in) deep and 23 cm (9 in) apart.

Start to Earth up Maincrop Celery. It is now time to begin to earth up the maincrop celery. The process is exactly as described for early celery (see July, Second Week) except that with these bigger plants more soil will be required. It is quite a good plan

217

to draw the stems together with raffia or string before starting to earth up, so that one can have both hands free for working the soil around the plants.

Earthing Up Celery. The stems of celery are covered with soil so that they remain white and crisp

FLOWERS, VEGETABLES AND FRUITS IN SEASON DURING AUGUST

Herbaceous Plants: *Acanthus mollis*, *A. spinosus*, *Achillea filipendulina*, *A. millefolium* vars., *A. ptarmica* and vars., *A. sibirica*, *Aconitum cammarum* vars., *A. lycoctonum*, *A. napellus* vars., *Adenophora bulleyana*, *A. potaninii*, alstroemerias (as July), *Althaea rosea* vars. (hollyhocks), *Anaphalis margaritacea*, *A. nubigena*, *Anemone hupehensis* and vars., *A. hybrida* and vars., *A. vitifolia*, *Anthemis cupaniana*, *A. sancti-johannis*, *A. tinctoria* and vars., *Artemisia lactiflora*, *Asclepias incarnata*, *A. tuberosa*, *Aster acris*, *A. amellus* and vars., *A. frikartii*, *A. luteus*, *A. linosyris*, *A. thomsonii*, *Astilbe arendsii* hybrids, *Boltonia aster-*

oides, Buphthalmum salicifolium, Campanula alliariifolia, C. lactiflora, C. latifolia vars., *C. persicifolia* vars., *Catananche caerulea* and vars., *Centaurea dealbata, C. macrocephala, C. ruthenica, Chelone lyonii, C. obliqua, Chrysanthemum maximum* vars., *C. rubellum,* chrysanthemums (early-flowering hybrids), *Cimicifuga dahurica, C. foetida, C. racemosa, Clematis heracleifolia* and vars., *C. integrifolia, C. recta, Coreopsis grandiflora* and vars., *C. lanceolata* and vars., *Dianthus allwoodii* vars., *D. caryophyllus* vars. (border carnations), *Dierama pulcherrima, Dracocephalum ruyschiana, Echinacea purpurea* and vars., *Echinops bannaticus, E. humilis, E. ritro, E. sphaerocephalus,* erigerons (all), eryngiums (as July), *Filipendula hexapetala,* gaillardias, *Galega officinalis* and vars., *Gaura lindheimeri, Gentiana asclepiadea, Geum bulgaricum, G. chiloense* vars., *Gypsophila paniculata* and vars., *Helenium autumnale* and vars., *Helianthus decapetalus* vars., *H. laetiflorus* vars., *H. salicifolius, H. scaberrimus* vars., *Heliopsis helianthoides, H. scabra* and vars., *Hemerocallis aurantiaca, H. citrina, H. fulva* vars., *H. minor, H. multiflora, H. thunbergii,* hemerocallis hybrids, *Heuchera brizoides, H. sanguineum* and vars., *Heucherella tiarelloides, Hosta albomarginata, H. fortunei, H. lancifolia* and vars., *H. plantaginea, H. sieboldiana, Inula glandulosa, I. helenium, I. oculus-christi, I. royleana, Kniphofia erecta, K. galpinii, K. macowanii, K. nelsonii, K. rufa, K. uvaria* and vars. (red-hot poker), *Lactuca alpina, L. plumieri, Lavatera olbia, Liatris pycnostachya, L. spicata, Ligularia dentata, L. hessei, L. przewalskii, L. stenocephala, L. veitchiana,* limoniums (as July), *Linaria dalmatica, Linum narbonnense, L. perenne, Lobelia cardinalis, L. fulgens* and vars., *L. syphilitica* and hybrids, *Lychnis chalcedonica, L. coronaria, Lysimachia clethroides, L. ephemerum, L. leschenaultii, L. punctata, L. thyrsiflora, Lythrum salicaria* vars., *L. virgatum* vars., *Malva alcea* vars., *Monarda didyma* and vars., *Nepeta faassenii, N. grandiflora, N. mussinii, Oenothera biennis* vars. (evening primrose), *O. fruticosa, O. speciosa, O. tetragona,*

Papaver nudicaule and vars. (Iceland poppies), *Penstemon barbatus, P. gentianoides* hybrids (shelter in winter), *P. isophyllus, Phlox maculata* vars., *P. paniculata* hybrids, *Phygelius capensis, Physostegia virginiana* and vars., *Phytolacca decandra* (fruits), *Platycodon grandiflorum* and vars., *Polygonum amplexicaule, P. bistorta* vars., *P. campanulatum,* potentilla hybrids, *Romneya coulteri, R. trichocalyx, Rudbeckia fulgida* and vars., *R. laciniata* and vars., *R. maxima, R. nitida* vars., rudbeckia hybrids, *Salvia azurea, S. nemorosa* and vars., *S. sclarea* and vars., *S. uliginosa, Sanguisorba canadensis, S. obtusa, S. tenuifolia, Saponaria officinalis plena,* *Scabiosa caucasica* and vars., *Sedum maximum, Sidalcea malvaeflora* vars., *Silphium laciniatum, S. perfoliatum, Solidago canadensis, S. virgaurea* and vars. (golden rod), *Solidaster luteus, Stokesia cyanea, Thalictrum dipterocarpum, Tradescantia virginiana, Veratrum album, V. nigrum, V. viride,* verbascums (as July), *Verbena bonariensis, V. tenera, Veronica longifolia* and vars., *V. spicata* and vars., *V. virginica* and vars.

Hardy Bulbs, Corms and Tubers: *Allium beesianum, A. cernuum oxyphilum, A. ochroleucum, A. pulchellum, A. sphaerocephalum, Amaryllis belladonna* vars., *Anomatheca cruenta, Crinum bulbispermum* and vars., *C. moorei, C. powellii* and vars., *Crocosmia masonorum, Curtonus paniculatus, Cyclamen europaeum,* gladioli (large-flowered and primulinus vars.), *Lilium auratum, L. davidii* vars., *L. formosanum, L. henryi, L. philippinense, L. speciosum, L. sulphureum, L. superbum, L. tigrinum, L. wardii,* montbretias (hybrids), *Tigridia pavonia.*

Rock Plants: *Achillea clavenae, A. tomentosa* and vars., *Androsace lanuginosa* and vars., *Antirrhinum asarina, A. glutinosum, Astilbe simplicifolia, Calamintha alpina, Calandrinia umbellata, Campanula carpatica* and vars., *C. cochlearifolia, C. portenschlagiana, C. poscharskyana, C. tommasiniana, C. waldsteiniana, C. zoysii, Ceratostigma plumbaginoides, C. willmottianum, Chrysogonum virginianum, Convolvulus althaeoides,*

C. cneorum, C. mauritanicus, Corydalis cheilanthifolia, C. lutea, Cymbalaria aequitriloba, C. pallida, Erodium chamaedrioides and vars., *Genista tinctoria plena, Gentiana farreri, G. freyniana, G. lagodechiana, G. purdomii, G. septemfida* and vars., *Geranium argenteum, G. cinereum* and vars., *G. sanguineum* and vars., *Geum borisii, Gypsophila cerastioides, G. repens* and vars., *Hieracium aurantiacum, H. villosum, Hypericum coris, H. fragile, H. olympicum, H. repens, H. reptans, Hypsela reniformis, Inula acaulis, Limonium bellidifolium, Linaria alpina, Linum alpinum, L. arboreum, L. flavum, L. salsoloides, Lithospermum diffusum* and vars., *Nierembergia coerulea, N. repens, Oenothera acaulis, O. perennis, O. missouriensis, Onosma albopilosum, O. echioides, O. tauricum, Othonnopsis cheirifolia, Papaver alpinum, Parochetus communis, Penstemon heterophyllus, Phuopsis stylosa, Polygonum affine, P. vaccinifolium, Potentilla nepalensis* and vars., *P. nitida, P. tonguei, Rhodohypoxis baurii, Rosa chinensis minima, Scabiosa graminifolia, Sedum ewersii, S. kamtschaticum* and vars., *S. rupestre, S. spurium, Silene schafta, Solidago virgaurea brachystachys, Stachys corsica, Tunica saxifraga, Verbena peruviana, Viola cornuta* and vars., *Zauschneria californica, Z. cana.*

Hardy Aquatic and Bog Plants: *Alisma plantago, Anagallis tenella, Aponogeton distachyus, Cyperus longus, C. vegetus, Filipendula camtschatica, F. palmata, F. purpurea, F. rubra, F. ulmaria, Gentiana pneumonanthe, Hydrocleys commersonii, Lysimachia vulgaris, Lythrum salicaria* and vars., *Menyanthes trifoliata,* mimulus (as July), *Narthecium ossifragum,* nymphaeas (in var.), *Nymphoides peltatum, Orontium aquaticum, Parnassia palustris, Sagittaria sagittifolia* and vars., *Stenanthium robustum, Stratiotes aloides, Typha angustifolia, T. latifolia* (reed mace).

Annuals: Hardy vars. (as June, but sown April and early May), half-hardy vars. (as July), also asters.

Bedding Plants: As July, also dahlias of all types.

Evergreen Shrubs: *Abelia grandiflora, Bupleurum fruticosum,*

Calluna vulgaris and vars., *Cassia corymbosa, Ceanothus burk-woodii, Daboecia cantabrica, Erica ciliaris* and vars., *E. cinerea* and vars., *E. terminalis, E. tetralix* and vars., *E. vagans* and vars., *E. watsonii,* escallonias (as July), *Hebe* Autumn Glory, *H. franciscana* vars., *H. leiophylla, H. salicifolia, H. speciosa* and vars., hebe hybrids, hypericums (as July), *Itea ilicifolia,* lavandula (as July), *Myrtus communis, Olearia haastii, O. macrodonta, Osmanthus fragrans, Parasyringa sempervirens, Penstemon cordifolius, Phormium colensoi, P. tenax, Rhododendron auriculatum,* R. Polar Bear, *R. serotinum, Tamarix pentandra, Teucrium fruticans, Ulex gallii, U. nanus, Viburnum cylindricum, Vinca major, V. minor, Yucca filamentosa, Y. flaccida, Y. gloriosa, Y. recurvifolia.*

Deciduous Shrubs: *Abelia chinensis, A. schumannii, Aesculus parviflora, Amorpha canescens, Aralia chinensis, Buddleia davidii* vars., *Calycanthus fertilis, C. occidentalis, Caryopteris clandonensis, C. mastacanthus, Ceanothus caeruleus* and hybrids, *Ceratostigma willmottianum, Clerodendrum bungei, C. trichotomum, Clethra alnifolia, Colquhounia coccinea, Culutea arborescens, C. orientalis, Cyrilla racemiflora, Cytisus nigricans, Desfontainea spinosa, Escallonia virgata, Fuchsia magellanica* and vars., *F. riccartonii,* hardy hybrid fuchsias, *Genista aethnensis, Hedysarum multijugum, Hibiscus syriacus* and vars., *Hydrangea arborescens grandiflora, H. macrophylla* and vars., *H. paniculata grandiflora, H. sargentiana, H. serrata* vars., *H. villosa,* hypericums (as July), *Indigofera amblyantha, I. decora, I. gerardiana, I. hebepetala, I. potaninii, Itea virginica, Leptodermis kumaonensis, Leycesteria formosa, Lyonia ligustrina, Magnolia parviflora, Perovskia atriplicifolia, Potentilla arbuscula, P. fruticosa* and vars., roses, mainly garden hybrids, *Rubus odoratus, R. ulmifolius bellidiflorus,* sorbarias (as July), *Spartium junceum,* spiraeas (as July), stewartias, *Tripetaleia bracteata.*

Evergreen Trees: Eucryphias (as July), *Magnolia grandiflora* and vars.

Deciduous Trees: *Aesculus californica, Aralia chinensis, Eucryphia glutinosa, Evodia velutina, Koelreuteria apiculata, K. paniculata, Oxydendrum arboreum, Sophora japonica,* sorbus species (fruits, see Sept.), *Stewartia malacodendron, Tilia petiolaris, T. tomentosa.*

Hardy Climbing Plants: *Berberidopsis corallina, Campsis grandiflora, C. radicans, C. tagliabuana, Clematis durandii* and vars., *C. flammula, C. jackmanii* and vars., *C. jouiniana, C. lanuginosa* and vars., *C. orientalis, C. patens, C. rehderiana, C. tangutica, C. viticella* and vars., hybrid clematis, *Jasminum officinale, Lathyrus latifolius* and vars. (everlasting pea), *Lonicera alseuosmoides, L. brownii, L. japonica* and vars., *L. periclymenum* and vars., *Mutisia decurrens, M. oligodon, Periploca graeca, Polygonum baldschuanicum, Rosa bracteata* and hybrids, hybrid climbing roses, *Solanum crispum, S. jasminoides, Trachelospermum asiaticum, T. jasminoides, Tropaeolum speciosum.*

Greenhouse Plants: *Acalypha hispida,* achimenes, *Agapanthus africanus, Allemanda cathartica,* annuals (see June), *Aristolochia elegans, Asclepias curassavica,* balsam, begonias (tuberous rooted), *Begonia coccinea, Beloperone guttata, Billbergia nutans,* bougainvilleas, *Brunfelsia calycina, Campanula isophylla, C. pyramidalis,* campsis, cannas, carnations (perpetual flowering), *Cassia corymbosa,* celosias, celsias, *Clianthus formosus, C. puniceus, Cobaea scandens, Coronilla glauca, Crassula falcata, Clerodendrum speciosissimum, C. thomsonae,* crinums, *Cuphea ignea,* daturas, dipladenias, *Eccremocarpus scaber, Exacum affine, Erythrina crista-galli, Francoa ramosa,* fuchsias, gardenias, gerberas, gloxinias, hedychiums, heliotrope, *Hibiscus rosa-sinensis, Hoya bella, H. carnosa, Humea elegans, Hymenocallis calathina, H. ovata, Impatiens walleriana,* ipomoeas, ixoras, *Jacobinia carnea, Lagerstroemia indica, Lapageria rosea, Lilium longiflorum, L. speciosum* and vars., *Limonium profusum, Mandevilla suaveolens,* marguerites, *Maurandya barclaiana,* myrtus, *Nerium oleander,* pancratiums, passifloras, *Plumbago* *capensis, Rehmannia angulata, Saintpaulia ionantha,* smithianthas, *Stephanotis floribunda,* streptocarpus, swainsonias, *Tibouchina semidecandra, Trachelium caeruleum, Trachelospermum jasminoides, Trachymene coerulea,* tropaeolums (including double vars.), *Vallota purpurea.*

Vegetables in Store: Onions, shallots.

Vegetables in the Garden: Globe artichoke, broad beans, French beans, runner beans, beetroot, broccoli (calabrese vars.), cabbage, carrots, cauliflower, celery, ridge cucumbers, endive, kohl rabi, lettuce, vegetable marrow, mustard and cress, mushrooms, onions, peas, potatoes, radish, spinach, sweet corn, tomatoes, turnips.

Vegetables under Glass: Aubergines, capsicums, cucumbers, mushrooms (cool cellars and outhouses), tomatoes.

Fruits Outdoors: *Apples:* Beauty of Bath (D), Devonshire Quarrenden (D), Early Victoria (C), Ecklinville Seedling (C), George Cave (D), Grenadier (C), Irish Peach (D), Keswick Codlin (C), Lady Sudeley (D), Langley Pippin (D), Lord Grosvenor (C), Scarlet Pimpernel (D), St Everard (D), Tydeman's Early (D), White Transparent (C). *Blackberries:* Bedford Giant, Himalaya Giant, John Innes, Oregon Thornless, Parsleyleaved. *Cherries:* Emperor Francis (D), Florence (D), Géante d'Hedelfingen (D), Late Duke (CD), Merton Late (D), Morello (C), Napoleon Bigarreau (D), Tradescant's Heart or Noble (D), Turkey Heart (D). *Currants, Red:* Fay's Prolific, Laxton's No. 1, Laxton's Perfection, Red Dutch, Raby Castle, Red Lake, Rivers' Late Red. *Currants, White:* White Dutch, White Versailles. *Currants, Black:* Amos Black, Baldwin, Blacksmith, Cotswold Cross, Daniel's September, Davison's Eight, Seabrook's Black, Westwick Choice. *Gooseberries:* Careless, Cousen's Seedling, Keepsake, Lancer, Langley Gage, Lancashire Lad, Leveller, Warrington, Whinham's Industry, Whitesmith. *Grapes:* Gagarin Blue, Muscat de Saumur, Tereshkova Purple. *Loganberry. Melons. Mulberry. Pears:* Clapp's Favourite

(D), Doyenné d'Été (D), Jargonelle (D). *Plums:* Belle de Louvain (C), Black Prince (CD), Bountiful (D), Cambridge Greengage (D), Czar (CD), Denniston's Superb (D), Early Laxton (C), Early Transparent Gage (D), Evesham Wonder (C), Gisborne's Prolific (C), Green Gage (D), Laxton's Gage (D), Oullin's Golden Gage (CD), Purple Pershore (C), Rivers' Early Damson (C), Victoria (CD), Yellow Pershore (C).

Fruits under Glass: *Apricots:* Breda, Hemskirk, Moorpark, Shipley or Blenheim. *Figs. Grapes:* Black Hamburgh, Buckland's Sweetwater, Foster's Seedling, Madresfield Court, Royal Muscadine. *Melons. Nectarines:* Dryden, Elruge, Humboldt, Lord Napier. *Peaches:* Goshawk, Hale's Early, Peregrine, Rochester, Royal George.

September

GENERAL WORK

Plant Narcissi, Lilies, Bulbous Irises and other Bulbs and Corms. Narcissi (including the trumpet daffodils), crocuses, Spanish, English, and Dutch irises, snowdrops, muscari, scillas and also all lilies – with the exception of *Lilium candidum* (see July, Fourth Week) – can be planted with fair success at any time during the autumn, but the best results are obtained by early planting. If you can complete this work before September is out, so much the better. Tulips and hyacinths, however, may with advantage wait a little longer (see October, Fourth Week). All bulbs should be planted on fairly rich, well-worked soil, but preferably not ground that has been recently dressed with animal manure. Artificials of the right type are quite a different matter. A dusting of bonemeal, at 110 g per square metre (4 oz per square yard), makes an excellent finish to the preparation of any bulb bed. The actual depth of planting should vary a little according to the nature of the soil, being rather deeper on light than on heavy land, but a fair average is as follows:

Plant	Depth	Distance apart
chionodoxa	6·5 cm (2½ in)	8 cm (3 in)
crocus	5 cm (2 in)	8 cm (3 in)
crown imperial	15 cm (6 in)	30 cm (1 ft)
dog's tooth violet	5 cm (2 in)	15 cm (6 in)
hyacinth	15 cm (6 in)	20 cm (8 in)
iris, Dutch, English and Spanish	10 cm (4 in)	15 cm (6 in)
lilies (stem rooting)	20 cm (8 in)	30 cm (12 in)
lilies (not stem rooting)	15 cm (6 in)	30 cm (12 in)
muscari	8 cm (3 in)	10 cm (4 in)
narcissus	13 cm (5 in)	20 cm (8 in)
Scilla campanulata	10 cm (4 in)	10 cm (4 in)
Scilla sibirica	6·5 cm (2½ in)	5 cm (2 in)
snowdrop	8 cm (3 in)	8 cm (3 in)

Depths refer to the hole prepared and not to the soil actually covering the top of the bulb. On the important point of whether a lily is or is not stem rooting, the catalogue of any specialist will give you full information and is usually obtainable free for the asking. The list is too long to be printed here (see also note on pot lilies, p. 230).

Do all the planting with a trowel or spade rather than a dibber. The last-named tends to make a pointed hole in which the bulb hangs suspended, with a hole beneath it.

Sow Grass Seed. Grass seed will germinate well enough at any time during September, though, other things being suitable, the sooner it can be sown the better, for then it will be well established

Planting Bulbs in Grass. A special planting tool can be used to naturalize bulbs in grassy areas. The tool takes out a core of soil which is replaced when the bulb has been planted in the hole

before the winter. Details are exactly the same as for spring sowing (see April, First Week).

Take Cuttings of Evergreen Shrubs. Many hardy evergreen shrubs can be propagated quite readily from cuttings taken during September and rooted in a frame or even a sheltered border. The process is similar to that which I have described for summer cuttings (see July, General Work), except that, on the whole, larger shoots are selected. They may be from 15 to 23 cm (6 to 9 in) in length and should be pulled off with a 'heel' or cut closely beneath a joint. Insert them firmly 5 to 8 cm (2 to 3 in) deep in very sandy soil. If in a frame keep the light on, but only shade from very strong direct sunshine. Water sufficiently to keep the soil moist but not sodden. Privet, *Lonicera nitida*, laurel, aucuba, rosemary and lavender will all root readily in this way, and so will some herbs, such as thyme and sage.

Take Cuttings of Bedding Plants. Throughout September you can take cuttings of a variety of plants, notably bedding calceolarias and penstemons, verbenas, mesembryanthemums, violas and pansies (cut back last month), zonal geraniums (including the bedding varieties), antirrhinums and violets. With all except violets, violas and pansies the method is to prepare cuttings 8 to 10 cm (3 to 4 in) long from firm, non-flowering shoots. Violet cuttings are prepared from the ends of the runners; pieces about 8 cm (3 in) long are ideal. Viola and pansy cuttings are made from young, non-flowering shoots coming from the base of the plant or directly from the roots. Frequently these can be pulled out with a few young, white rootlets attached. Zonal pelargonium cuttings should be rooted in pots, as I have already described (see August, General Work), and must be accommodated in a frost-proof greenhouse from late September onwards, but the others are better inserted directly into a bed of sandy soil prepared in a frame. Dibble them in a few inches apart, water freely, and keep the lights on and shaded until the cuttings are rooted. Then ventilate freely throughout the winter, only keeping the frames closed when frost threatens and removing the lights altogether when the weather is mild.

Prevent Mildew. The disease most to be feared during this month is powdery mildew. It may appear on roses, culinary peas, delphiniums, chrysanthemums, gooseberries, plums and a variety of other plants and fruits. In all cases it covers leaves and stems with a whitish powdery growth. As a preventive, spray with benomyl or dinocap and repeat a fortnight later.

General Greenhouse Management. Nights now begin to get much colder and one must be watchful with ventilation. The aim should still be an average day temperature of close on 16°C (60°F), with a night minimum not much below 10°C (50°F). Side ventilators are not likely to be needed, and even the top ventilators should be closed early in the afternoon if the weather is cold. Shading can be washed off the glass about the middle of the month for all except the most shade-loving plants – some ferns, for example. Spraying and damping down should also be discontinued gradually. There will soon be too much moisture in the air for most greenhouse plants.

Continue the ripening of early hippeastrums, achimenes, begonias and gloxinias (see August, General Work). Some of the later batches will also need less water if they have finished flowering.

Pot Lilies for the Greenhouse. I have separated lilies from the other bulbs for the greenhouse because their treatment is rather different and also because it is not so essential to pot early. If you can buy all the bulbs you need early in September, by all means get them potted, because lilies gain nothing by being out of the ground. But a good many bulbs come from abroad – some from America and the Far East – and these do not usually arrive until later, so you may have to wait awhile if you need any of these (see January, General Work).

Lilies are best grown singly, in pots 15 to 18 cm (6 to 7 in) in diameter according to the size of the bulbs. Set the stem-rooting kinds (see p. 227) well down in the pots and only just cover them with soil now. Then, later on, as the stem grows, you can add top dressings of soil until the pot is almost full. Non-stem-rooting bulbs are potted nearer the surface and are not topdressed. Use John Innes compost No. 1. The pots are not plunged under ashes like narcissi but are stood in an unheated frame or greenhouse to form roots. Do not use any artificial heat until top growth is several inches in length.

Plant Bulbs in Ornamental Bowls. Hyacinths and narcissi that are to be grown in undrained ornamental bowls should be obtained as soon as possible. Special bulb fibre containing oyster shell and charcoal must be used for these. Put a few good lumps of charcoal in the bottom of the bowl, then spread a little fibre over it, set the bulbs firmly in position, allowing 2·5 cm (1 in) between each, and only just cover them with more fibre. Water freely and stand in a cool, dark place (a cupboard will serve admirably) until the shoots are about 2·5 cm (1 in) in length, when the bowls must be arranged in as light a place as possible. Keep the fibre moist throughout.

Make Successional Sowings. These can no longer be made outdoors as in former months – unless you live in a particularly mild district – but it is a good plan to make yet another sowing of lettuce and endive in unheated frames and also to sow radishes and mustard and cress in the same way.

Plant Spring Cabbage. Cabbages from the July sowing (see July, Third Week) will be ready for removal early in the month to the plot in which they will mature. You could not do better than follow them on after onions that have just been lifted or place them on the ground that has recently been cleared of potatoes. Rake it clean, give it a dusting of superphosphate of lime at the rate of 25 g per square metre (1 oz per square yard), and plant the cabbages about 30 cm (1 ft) apart in rows 45 cm (18 in) apart. Later in the month the seedlings from the August sowing (see August, Second Week) should be treated in the same way.

Continue to Earth up Celery and Leeks. From time to time during the month continue to draw more soil around celery plants and leeks, as described in the notes for May, First Week, July, Second Week and August, Fourth Week.

Continue to Blanch Endive. During the month you should continue to blanch a few endives as they reach a fair size (see August, General Work).

Treat Vines according to Growth. The same remarks as those I made in last month's notes still apply with equal force (see August, General Work).

Ripen Fruit Tree Growth Under Glass. Late peaches and nectarines may still be carrying fruits when the treatment recommended in earlier months must still be carried out, but the main effort during September is likely to be directed towards the thorough ripening of growth. This means plenty of ventilation when possible without lowering the temperature too much (13°C,

Blanching Endive. Endives are easily blanched by covering them with an inverted saucer or a plant pot with the hole covered

55°F, should be the day minimum, and it is as well that the thermometer should not fall lower than 10°C, 55°F, at night), the discontinuance of ordinary feeding, and a gradual reduction in water supply. If growth tends to be excessive give a dressing of sulphate of potash at 25 g per square metre (1 oz per square yard).

Ripen off Melons in Frames. Melons in the greenhouse are likely to be finished, or nearly so, by this time, but plants in frames should be ripening their fruits and the atmosphere must be kept dry. Do not spray the leaves with water at all and reduce the water supply to the roots, giving only sufficient to keep the leaves from flagging. Stand each fruit on an inverted flower pot to expose it to the sun as much as possible, and cover the frames at night with sacks or mats.

Continue to Pick Apples and Pears. Keep a sharp eye on apples and pears and continue to pick them as soon as they are ripe.

With certain varieties of pear, such as Beurré Hardy, Dr Jules Guyot and William's Bon Chretien, it is even advisable to pick a little before they are ripe and to complete the ripening process in a dry, fairly warm shed or room.

Complete Planting of Strawberries. There is still time to plant rooted strawberry runners in their fruit quarters, as I explained last month (see August, Third Week), but the sooner the work is completed the better. If for some reason you cannot get them all planted out in September, leave the rest of the plants undisturbed until March (see March, First Week).

FIRST WEEK

Sow Hardy Annuals. A number of hardy annuals may be sown outdoors now to stand the winter and flower in May and June next year. Sow them thinly where they are to flower and cover lightly with soil. Thin the seedlings out to 8 or 10 cm (3 or 4 in) apart as soon as they can be handled, but leave any further thinning until March or April. Among the best varieties for sowing in this manner are annual alyssum, calendula, candytuft, clarkia, annual coreopsis, cornflower, godetia, larkspur, nigella, Shirley and cardinal poppies, annual scabious and viscaria. Antirrhinums can also be sown now, but unless your garden is fairly sheltered I advise you to make this sowing in a frame. Give free ventilation, but use the lights to protect the seedlings against frost.

Sow Annuals for the Greenhouse. As I have already explained (see March, First Week), many annuals make first-rate pot plants for the cool greenhouse. If sown now they will start to flower in early spring and continue until May. Sow thinly in well-drained seed trays or pans and germinate in a frame or unheated greenhouse. Shade until the seedlings appear, but subsequently give them plenty of light and air.

Plant Anemones. Make a first planting of anemones of the St

Brigid and de Caen types. If these are put in in successional batches, it is possible to extend the flowering season. The tubers should be planted 8 cm (3 in) deep and 15 cm (6 in) apart. If you wish you can also make a similar planting in a frame, as by this means you can get even earlier blooms – with a bit of luck by January. Place the lights in position, but ventilate moderately when the weather is mild.

Pot More Freesias. Make a further potting of freesia corms as described in the notes for August, First Week. If these are placed in a frame, and are protected from frost with lights but no attempt is made to force them, they can be introduced to the warm greenhouse a few at a time from November onwards and will supply a succession of flowers in winter and early spring.

Pot on Primulas and Calceolarias. There may be quite a lot of potting on to be done if growth during August has been fairly good. Greenhouse primulas from the April sowing (see April, Fourth Week) should be about ready for their final pots, 13 cm (5 in) in diameter, while the June-sown primulas (see June, Third Week) are also likely to need potting singly into 8-cm (3-in) pots of John Innes potting compost No. 1. After potting, the plants can go back into the frame for a few weeks, but will not need much shading now, and they must be ventilated more sparingly.

Greenhouse calceolarias which were given more space in August (see August, Second Week) must also be moved along before they get starved. They can now go into 9-cm (3½-in) pots, other particulars being the same as for primulas.

Pot Hippeastrums. Pot specially prepared 'Christmas flowering' hippeastrums, one bulb in a 10- or 13-cm (4- or 5-in) pot of John Innes potting compost No. 1 or a peat-based equivalent and place the pots in a light room or greenhouse.

Sow Cauliflowers. In a sheltered place make a small sowing of cauliflowers. Scatter the seed thinly, broadcast and cover with 1 cm (½ in) of fine soil.

Thin Coleworts. If coleworts were sown in July (see July,

Fourth Week) thin the seedlings now to 15 cm (6 in) apart.

Make a Mushroom Bed under Cover. As I explained in the July notes (see July, First Week), mushrooms can be grown at any time of the year but are easier to manage at certain seasons. Just as July is the ideal time for making outdoor beds, so early September is the best for beds in frames and outhouses or sheds.

These beds will start to crop about the middle of October, just as the outdoor mushrooms are coming to an end, and with a little care will continue well into the winter. The method of forming the beds is exactly the same as before, except that in frames the whole area is covered with manure to a depth of 60 cm (2 ft). Also it is particularly important to cover frame beds with an extra thick layer of straw. The frame lights may also be covered with thick mats or sacking, for mushrooms do best in the dark, and the extra covering will help to keep the bed at an even temperature.

SECOND WEEK

Prune Rambler Roses. Most rambler roses will have finished flowering and may be pruned. If they have made a great deal of new growth, much of it from near ground level, you can cut out all the old canes that have just borne flowers, but if there is not much young wood you will have to keep the best of the old and simply remove that which is obviously worn out or diseased. If you have to do this you must be careful to cut back all faded flower trusses, together with any heps they may be bearing. Weeping standard roses are pruned at the same time and in a similar manner. After pruning, train the long shoots round the umbrella-shaped training frames, which should be securely fastened to the stakes supporting the plants.

Lift Maincrop Carrots. Lift the maincrop carrots sown in April (see April, Second Week). If they are left in the ground any longer the roots are liable to crack. Dig them up carefully with a

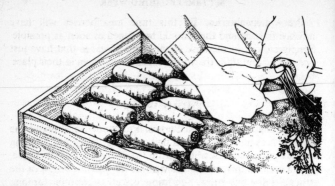

Storing Carrots. Carrots will keep best if they are stored in boxes of dry sand. In this way they are less likely to shrivel

fork, cut off the tops and store the roots in a heap in any shed, cellar, or other frost-proof place. They will keep better and be less likely to shrivel if they are covered with sand or sifted ashes.

Lift Maincrop Beetroot. The main crop of long beetroot sown in May should also be lifted and stored at about this time (and, in any case, before the roots get old and coarse) as described for early beet in the notes for August, Second Week.

Fix Grease Bands. Now is the time to fix grease bands around fruit trees. They are particularly serviceable on apples, but it is advisable to have them on all the bigger fruits just for safety. These grease bands are actually strips of grease-proof paper tied round the trunk or main branches, and also any stakes, at least a couple of feet above ground level and covered with a tacky substance. You can buy both paper strips and tacky compound from your local dealer in horticultural sundries. Keep the bands sticky until next March. They will catch all manner of insects that try to crawl over them, and are particularly serviceable against the winter moth, March moth and woolly aphid.

Prune Loganberries. By this time loganberries will have finished fruiting and they should be pruned as soon as possible. Simply cut out to the base of the plant all canes that have just borne fruit and train the young canes to the wires in their place.

THIRD WEEK

Start to Plant Evergreen Shrubs. From now until about the second week in October is usually the ideal time for planting hardy evergreen shrubs lifted from the open ground. Of course, you cannot do this work if the weather happens to be hot or the ground is dry, but neither condition is likely to continue for long at this time of the year. Plant very firmly and stake all big specimens at once. Later on, if winds are very cold and drying, erect temporary shelters of hurdles, evergreen boughs, or sacking strained between stakes to protect the shrubs, particularly on the north and east sides.

Plant Violets in Frames. Violets that have been growing outdoors since April (see April, Second Week) should now be removed to frames for winter flowering. The frames must stand in a sunny and fairly sheltered position and be filled with good loamy soil to within 20 cm (8 in) of the glass.

Plant the violet clumps almost touching one another. Water them in freely, but do not close the frames as yet. Later on, if frost threatens, put the lights on; but throughout the winter give the plants free ventilation whenever the weather is mild.

Plant Rooted Carnation Layers. Carnation layers pegged down towards the end of July (see July, Third Week) should be well rooted by this time. Scrape away a little of the soil and see how things are. If there are plenty of fibrous roots around the cut area sever the layers from the parent plants and, a few days later, lift them – each with a good ball of soil – and transfer them to their flowering quarters or, alternatively, pot them in 10- to

13-cm (4- to 5-in) pots, place them in a frame, and plant them out in March (see March, Fourth Week). The soil should be good and loamy, with a liberal addition of crushed mortar rubble and a sprinkling of bonemeal.

Prick off Schizanthus. Schizanthus seedlings from last month's sowing (see August, Third Week) will be in need of pricking off. This should be done at the earliest possible moment so that they have no chance of becoming leggy. Prick off the seedlings 5 cm (2 in) apart each way into deep, well-drained seed trays filled with the same compost as that used for seed sowing.

Pick all Tomatoes. Outdoor tomatoes are not likely to ripen any more on the plants now, so it is as well to pick all the fruits that are showing some trace of colour and stand them in a sunny window to ripen. Absolutely green fruits can be made into tomato chutney. The summer crop of tomatoes under glass will also be coming to an end and, in view of the fact that every inch of greenhouse space is likely to be required in the next few weeks, it will be as well to clear these also, treating them in the same way as the outdoor fruits.

Lift Potatoes for Storing. The exact date at which maincrop and late potatoes should be fit for storing cannot be decided entirely by the calendar as it depends to some extent upon disease and also the weather. If much disease appears, it is wise to lift the tubers at once, before they get badly affected. Similarly, if August is very dry at first, and then wet, later tubers may begin to make second growth and must be lifted before they have dissipated themselves in a multiplicity of small potatoes. But, given average weather and freedom from disease, lifting commonly becomes general about this time. There is no necessity to wait until haulm dies down if the tubers are a good size and the skin holds really firmly to them. You can easily satisfy yourself on these two points by lifting a sample root. If you decide to lift the whole crop, put aside any damaged tubers for immediate use and store the rest in a frost-proof shed or cellar. An alternative is to make a clamp in the open. This is done by placing a layer of dry straw on the ground, heaping the potatoes on it in a steep-sided bank, covering with more straw and then a good coating of soil beaten down with the back of a spade. It is a wise precaution to draw a few wisps of straw through the soil at intervals along the ridge to allow warm, damp air to escape.

Thin out Vegetable Seedlings. Spinach beet, winter spinach, lettuce and endive, from the sowings made last month (see August, Third Week and General Work), will need thinning out. Leave the plants of spinach beet about 38 cm (15 in) apart and the spinach itself about 10 cm (4 in) apart. The lettuces should be from 20 to 30 cm (8 in to 1 ft) apart, according to variety, and the endive 30 cm (1 ft) apart. The seedlings of endive and lettuce can be transplanted carefully, either to a very sheltered border or, better still, to a frame. Water them in freely and they will provide a succession to those plants left undisturbed. An alternative method with endive is to thin out the plants now to about 10 cm (4 in) apart and then lift the bigger plants at the end of October and transfer to a frame. They stand transplanting much better than lettuce, and by means of this late shifting one can sometimes make use of a frame that is filled with cucumbers or melons at the moment.

FOURTH WEEK

Pot and Box Bulbs for Early Flowering. Lose no time in potting or boxing all the hyacinths, tulips, narcissi, ixias, gladioli of the *Gladiolus nanus* type, and bulbous irises including those suitable for forcing, such as Wedgwood, that are required for flowering in the greenhouse or house during winter and spring. If the containers are provided with drainage holes use either John Innes potting compost No. 1 or a peat-based potting compost. If they are undrained bowls use special bulb fibre consisting of peat, crushed shell and crushed charcoal. This can be purchased ready for use. Place the bulbs of tulips and narcissi almost touching one another and barely covered with compost. Space the smaller bulbs and corms about 2·5 cm (1 in) apart and cover to a depth of 1 to 2 cm ($\frac{1}{2}$ to $\frac{3}{4}$ in). Then stand all the containers in the coolest place available. This can be outdoors at the foot of a north-facing wall if the containers are drained, but undrained containers must be kept under cover or they may be flooded by rain. Outdoors it helps to cover the pots with an 8- to 10-cm (3- to 4-in) layer of moist peat, sand, or well-weathered boiler ashes as this helps to keep the temperature below 9°C (48°F) which is what is required for the first eight to twelve weeks.

Pot Cyclamen Seedlings. Cyclamen seedlings from the sowing made in August (see August, Second Week) should be ready for pricking off or potting. Often the seed germinates very irregularly, so, if some of the seedlings are too backward for potting at the moment, leave them in the seed pans, lifting the more forward ones with a sharpened wooden label. The ideal time for potting is when the seedlings have two or three leaves each. Pot singly in 5-cm (2-in) pots, using John Innes potting compost No. 1. Keep the tiny corms well up on the surface of the soil. After potting, stand the pots on a shelf or staging in the greenhouse, giving them a good light place but shading them for a while from any very strong direct sunshine. Maintain an average day temperature of 13°C (55°F) and 7°C (45°F) at night. Similar remarks apply if you decide to prick off in boxes instead of potting singly.

House Late-flowering Chrysanthemums. It is wise to bring in all chrysanthemums that are to flower in the greenhouse now before frost damages their tender buds. Pot plants should be carried in and set on a hard bottom of ashes or gravel, or be arranged on staging, while plants that have been grown outdoors for lifting (see May, Fourth Week) must be dug up with as much soil as possible and either be planted in the greenhouse borders or else be dropped into suitable boxes and tubs. Give the plants sufficient room for air to circulate between them and light to reach their leaves, otherwise you are certain to have trouble with mildew. Ventilate very freely while the weather is mild, but at any threat of frost close the house early in the afternoon and even use a little artificial heat if necessary.

Shelter Tender Plants. It will also be necessary to give some shelter to all tender greenhouse plants that have been outdoors during the summer months. This includes pelargoniums of various kinds (not forgetting the cuttings that have been rooted in pots), marguerites, perennial mesembryanthemums, fuchsias, double tropaeolums, hydrangeas, heliotropes, Indian azaleas, camellias, genistas, arum lilies and agapanthus (blue Kaffir lily). Any of these that have been used for summer bedding should also be lifted and potted if you wish to save them for another year.

Placing Tender Plants in Frames. As the weather becomes colder move tender garden plants into cold frames

241

The blue *Salvia patens* and dahlias and begonias used for bedding may be left outdoors until frost first blackens their foliage. If you have no room for the other bedding plants as they are, you can cut back growth severely so that they do not take up so much space.

A good frame will provide sufficient protection for all these plants for a while if you cover the lights with sacks on frosty nights, but by the end of October it will be safer to have most of them inside the greenhouse, where you can use a little artificial heat to exclude frost.

Perpetual-flowering carnations that have been stood out for the summer should also be brought into shelter before they are injured by frost. Stand them in a light greenhouse with plenty of ventilation and just enough artificial heat to keep out frost and prevent the atmosphere from becoming damp and stagnant.

Transplant Parsley to a Frame. Lift some of the parsley seedlings from the July sowing (see July, Fourth Week) and transplant them carefully into a frame filled with good soil with which you have mixed some leafmould and a little old manure. Set the plants about 15 cm (6 in) apart each way and water them in freely. They will provide a crop throughout the winter if you use the lights just for frost protection.

Sow French Beans for Forcing. French beans are easier than most vegetables to force, and, if you have space at your disposal in a greenhouse that can be heated to a temperature of about 16°C (60°F), you may make a sowing now for a winter crop. The method is exactly the same as for early spring crops (see January, Fourth Week).

FLOWERS, VEGETABLES AND FRUITS
IN SEASON DURING SEPTEMBER

Herbaceous Plants: *Achillea filipendulina*, *A. ptarmica* and vars., *Aconitum cammarum* Spark's Var., *A. carmichaelii*, *A. napellus pyramidale*, *Actaea spicata* (fruits), anemones (as August), *Artemisia lactiflora*, *Aster acris*, *A. amellus* and vars., *A. cordifolius* and vars., *A. ericoides* and vars., *A. frikartii* and vars., *A. novae-angliae* and vars. (Michaelmas daisies), *A. novi-belgii* and vars. (Michaelmas daisies), *Boltonia asteroides*, *Buphthalmum salicifolium*, *Catananche caerulea* and vars., *Chrysanthemum rubellum*, *C. uliginosum*, chrysanthemums (early-flowering Japanese vars.), *Cimicifuga japonica*, *C. racemosa*, *C. simplex*, *Coreopsis grandiflora* and vars., *Echinacea purpurea* and vars., *Eupatorium purpureum*, gaillardias (hybrids), *Galega officinalis* and vars., *Gentiana asclepiadea*, *Geum coccineum* vars., *Gypsophila paniculata* and vars., *Helenium autumnale* and vars., *Helianthus atrorubens*, *H. decapetalus* and vars., *H. mollis*, *H. salicifolius*, *H. scaberrimus*, *Heliopsis scabra* and vars., *Hosta lancifolia*, *H. plantaginea*, *H. tardiflora*, *Inula hookeri*, *I. royleana*, *Kniphofia erecta*, *K. galpini*, *K. nelsonii*, *K. uvaria* and vars., *Lavatera olbia*, limoniums (as July), *Liriope muscari*, *L. spicata*, *Lobelia cardinalis*, *L. fulgens* and vars., *L. syphilitica* and hybrids, *Lysimachia clethroides*, *Monarda didyma* and vars., *Oenothera biennis* and vars., *Papaver nudicaule* and vars. (Iceland poppies), *Penstemon barbatus*, *P. isophyllus*, *P. gentianoides* hybrids, *Phlox paniculata* hybrids, *Phygelius capensis*, physalis in var. for fruits, *Podophyllum emodi* (fruits), *Polygonum amplexicaule*, *P. campanulatum*, *Romneya coulteri*, *R. trichocalyx*, *Rudbeckia fulgida* and vars., *R. laciniata* and vars., *R. maxima*, *Salvia azurea*, *S. sclarea*, *S. uliginosa*, *Sanguisorba canadensis*, *Saponaria officinalis plena*, *Scabiosa caucasica* and vars., *Schizostylis coccinea* and vars., *Sedum spectabile* and hybrids, *Silphium per-*

243

foliatum, Solidago virgaurea and vars., *Solidaster luteus, Stokesia cyanea, Tradescantia virginiana, Verbena bonariensis, V. rigida, Veronica longifolia* and vars., *V. virginica*.

Hardy Bulbs, Corms and Tubers: *Amaryllis belladonna* (shelter), *Colchicum agrippinum, C. autumnale* and vars., *C. byzantinum, C. speciosum* and vars., *Crinum bulbispermum* and vars., *C. powellii* and vars., *Crocus cancellatus, C. pulchellus, C. speciosus, C. zonatus, Cyclamen africanum, C. europaeum, C. graecum, C. neapolitanum, Leucojum autumnale, Lilium auratum, L. formosanum, L. henryi, L. speciosum* and vars., *L. sulphureum, L. tigrinum, Merendera montana,* montbretias (hybrids), *Nerine bowdenii, Oxalis lobata, Schizostylis coccinea* and vars., *Scilla autumnalis*.

Rock Plants: *Androsace lanuginosa* and vars., *Antirrhinum asarina, Astilbe chinensis pumila, Ceratostigma plumbaginoides, C. willmottianum, Convolvulus mauritanicus, Gaultheria procumbens* (fruits), *Gentiana farreri, G. macaulayi, G. sino-ornata, Nertera depressa* (fruits), *Oenothera missouriensis, Penstemon heterophyllus, Polygonum affine, P. vaccinifolium, Pyrola rotundifolia, Sedum cauticola, S. ewersii, S. kamtschaticum, Silene schafta, Solidago virgaurea brachystachys, Verbena peruviana, Viola cornuta* and vars., *Zauschneria californica*.

Hardy Aquatic and Bog Plants: *Butomus umbellatus, Gentiana pneumonanthe, Kirengeshoma palmata, Parnassia palustris, Typha angustifolia, T. latifolia* (reed mace).

Annuals: Hardy vars. (as June, but sown in May), half-hardy vars. (as July).

Bedding Plants: As July.

Evergreen Shrubs: *Abelia grandiflora, Bupleurum fruticosum, Ceanothus burkwoodii, Daboecia cantabrica,* ericas (as August), *Hebe* Autumn Glory, *H. speciosa* and vars., *Hypericum calycinum, H.* Hidcote, *Osmanthus heterophyllus, O. fortunei, O. fragrans, Parasyringa sempervirens, Phormium colensoi, P. tenax, Rhododendron serotinum, Teucrium fruticans, Ulex gallii,*

U. minor, Viburnum cylindricum, Vinca major, V. minor, Yucca gloriosa, Y. recurvifolia.

Deciduous Shrubs: *Abelia chinensis, A. schumannii, Amorpha canescens, Buddleia paniculata, B. variabilis* and vars., *Calycanthus occidentalis, Caryopteris clandonensis, C. mastacanthus, Cassia marylandica, Ceanothus azureus* and hybrids, *Ceratostigma willmottianum, Clerodendrum trichotomum, C. t. fargesii, Clethra alnifolia, Colletia armata, C. cruciata, Colquhounia coccinea, Colutea arborescens, C. orientalis, Cyrilla racemiflora, Desfontainea spinosa* (shelter), *Desmodium spicatum, Fuchsia magellanica* and vars., *F. riccartonii,* hardy hybrid fuchsias, *Hibiscus syriacus* and vars., *Hydrangea arborescens grandiflora, H. macrophylla* and vars., *H. paniculata* and vars., *H. serrata* and vars., *Hypericum augustinii, H.* Hidcote, *H. hircinum, H. hookerianum, H. moserianum, Indigofera amblyantha, I. gerardiana, I. hebepetala, I. potaninii, Itea ilicifolia, Leptodermis kumaonensis, Leycesteria formosa, Perovskia atriplicifolia, Potentilla fruticosa* and vars., hybrid roses, *Spartium junceum, Spiraea menziesii* and vars., *Tamarix pentandra, Tripetaleia bracteata, Vitex agnus-castus* (shelter).

Evergreen Trees: *Magnolia grandiflora* and vars.

Deciduous Trees: *Alnus nitida, Aralia chinensis, Laburnum anagyroides autumnale, Oxydendrum arboreum, Sophora japonica.*

Hardy Climbing Plants: *Campsis grandiflora, C. radicans, C. tagliabuana, Clematis durandii* and vars., *C. flammula, C. jackmanii* and vars., *C. jouiniana, C. lanuginosa* and vars., *C. orientalis, C. rehderiana, C. tangutica, C. viticella* and vars., *Jasminum officinale, Lonicera alseuosmoides, L. brownii, L. heckrottii, L. japonica* and vars., *L. periclymenum serotina* (late Dutch honeysuckle), *Pileostegia viburnoides, Polygonum baldschuanicum, Rosa bracteata* and hybrids, hybrid climbing roses, *Solanum crispum autumnalis, S. jasminoides, Tropaeolum speciosum.*

Fruiting Trees, Shrubs and Climbers: *Berberis aggregata, B.*

aristata, *B. concinna*, *B. darwinii*, *B. dictyophylla*, *B. gagnepainii*, *B. hookeri*, *B. jamesiana*, *B. koreana*, *B. lycium*, *B. polyantha*, *B. prattii*, *B. pruinosa*, *B. rubrostilla*, *B. sieboldii*, *B. vulgaris*, *B. wilsoniae*, *B. yunnanensis*, *Callicarpa bodinieri*, *C. dichotoma*, *C. japonica*, *Celastrus orbiculatus*, *Clematis flammula*, *C. orientalis*, *C. tangutica*, *C. vitalba*, *Coriaria japonica*, *C. terminalis*, *Cotoneaster adpressus*, *C. bullatus*, *C. buxifolius*, *C. congestus*, *C. conspicuus* and vars., *C. dammeri*, *C. dielsianus*, *C. divaricatus*, *C. franchetii*, *C. frigidus*, *C. henryanus*, *C. horizontalis*, *C. lucidus*, *C. microphyllus*, *C. rotundifolius*, *C. salicifolius* and vars., *C. simonsii*, *Crataegus altaica*, *C. arnoldiana*, *C. coccinioides*, *C. crus-galli*, *C. douglasii*, *C. durobrivensis*, *C. lavallei*, *C. macrantha*, *C. mollis*, *C. monogyna* (hawthorn), *C. orientalis*, *C. oxyacantha* (hawthorn), *C. phaenopyrum*, *C. prunifolia*, *Euonymus europaeus* (spindle), *E. latifolius*, *Hippophae rhamnoides* (unisexual), *Lycium chinense* and vars., *Malus arnoldiana*, *M. baccata*, *M.* Dartmouth, *M.* Golden Hornet, *M.* John Downie, *M. prunifolia*, *M.* Red Jade, *M. robusta*, *M. toringoides*, *Pernettya mucronata*, *Pyracantha angustifolia*, *P. atalantioides*, *P. coccinea* and vars., *P. crenato-serrata*, *P. rogersiana*, *P. watereri*, *Rhaphithamnus spinosus*, *Rosa highdownensis*, *R. moyesii*, *R. multibracteata*, *R. multiflora*, *R. rubrifolia*, *R. rugosa* vars. and hybrids such as Frau Dagmar Hastrup and *scabrosa*, *R. webbiana*, *Sambucus canadensis*, *S. nigra* and vars., *Skimmia reevesiana*, *S. japonica* (unisexual), *Sorbus aria*, *S. aucuparia*, *S. domestica*, *S. esserteauana*, *S. hupehensis*, *S.* Joseph Rock, *S. pohuashanensis*, *S. sargentiana*, *S. scopulina*, *S. vilmorinii*, *Symphoricarpus albus*, *S. orbiculatus*, *Viburnum betulifolium*, *V. davidii*, *V. henryi*, *V. lantana* (wayfaring tree), *V. molle*, *V. opulus*, *V. prunifolium*, *V. rhytidophyllum*, *Vitis heterophylla*, *V. vinifera purpurea*.

Greenhouse Plants: Achimenes, *Agapanthus africanus*, *Allemanda cathartica*, *Asclepias curassavica*, begonias (tuberous rooted), *Beloperone guttata*, *Begonia coccinea*, bougainvilleas, bouvardias, *Browallia speciosa major* (sown March), *Brunfelsia* *calycina*, *Campanula isophylla*, cannas, carnations (perpetual flowering), *Cassia corymbosa*, celsias, cestrums, *Cobaea scandens*, *Coronilla glauca*, *Cuphea ignea*, daturas, *Eccremocarpus scaber*, *Exacum affine*, *Francoa ramosa*, fuchsias, gardenias, gerberas, gloxinias, heliotropes, *Hibiscus rosa-sinensis*, *Humea elegans*, ipomoeas, *Jacobinia carnea*, *Lagerstroemia indica*, lantanas, *Lilium longiflorum*, *L. speciosum* and vars., *Limonium profusum*, *Luculia gratlssima*, marguerites, *Maurandya barclaiana*, nerines, petunias, *Saintpaulia ionantha*, streptocarpus, *Tibouchina semidecandra*, *Trachelium caeruleum*, *Vallota purpurea*.

Vegetables in Store: Beetroot, onions, shallots.

Vegetables in the Garden: Globe artichoke, French beans, runner beans, beetroot, broccoli, cabbage, carrots, cauliflower, celeriac, celery, ridge cucumbers, endive, kohl rabi, leeks, lettuce, vegetable marrow, mushrooms, mustard and cress, parsnips, peas, potatoes, radish, spinach, sweet corn, tomatoes, turnips.

Vegetables under Glass: Aubergines, capsicums, cucumbers, mushrooms (cool cellars and outhouses).

Fruits Outdoors: *Apples:* Ellison's Orange (D), Epicure (D), Exquisite (D), Fortune (D), Gascoyne's Scarlet (D), Golden Noble (C), Golden Spire (C), Grenadier (C), James Grieve (D), Lady Sudeley (D), Langley Pippin (D), Lord Grosvenor (C), Lord Suffield (C), Peasgood's Nonsuch (CD), St Edmund's Russet (D), St Everard (CD), Stirling Castle (C), S. T. Wright (C), Worcester Pearmain (D). *Apricots:* Moorpark. *Blackberries:* Himalayan Giant, John Innes, Parsley-leaved. *Cherries:* Morello (C) (north wall). *Currants, Black:* Baldwin, Daniel's September, Westwick Choice. *Figs. Grapes:* Brandt, Golden Chasselas, Miller's Burgundy, Muscat Hamburgh, Reine Olga, Riesling Sylvaner, Royal Muscadine, Schuyler. *Melons. Nectarines:* as August. *Peaches:* as August. *Pears:* Beurré d'Amanlis (D), Clapp's Favourite (D), Dr Jules Guyot (D), Gorham (D),

Marguerite Marillat (D), Merton Pride (D), Souvenir de Congress (D), Triomphe de Vienne (D), William's Bon Chrétien (D). *Plums:* Belle de Louvain (C), Bradley's King (Damson) (CD), Bryanston Gage (D), Cambridge Gage (D), Coe's Golden Drop (D), Comte d'Althan's Gage (D), Delicious (D), Farleigh's Prolific Damson (C), Giant Prune (C), Green Gage (D), Jefferson's Gage (D), Kirke's Blue (D), Late Transparent Gage (D), Merryweather Damson (CD), Monarch (CD), Pond's Seedling (C), Severn Cross (CD), Shropshire Damson (CD), Victoria (CD), Warwickshire Drooper (C), White Bullace (CD), White Magnum Bonum (D). *Raspberries:* September.

Fruits under Glass: *Apricots:* Moorpark. *Figs. Grapes:* Black Hamburgh, Black Prince, Foster's Seedling, Madresfield Court, Royal Muscadine. *Melons. Nectarines:* Humboldt, Pine Apple, Rivers' Orange, *Peaches:* Barrington, Bellegarde, Dymond, Goshawk, Sea Eagle.

October

GENERAL WORK

Use Slow-acting Fertilizers. October is a good month during which to use such slow-acting fertilizers as basic slag, bonemeal and kainit. The first supplies phosphates and lime, the second mainly phosphates and the third mainly potash. Most fruit trees will benefit from a topdressing of basic slag and kainit applied now, the former at 170 g per square metre (6 oz per square yard) and the latter at 85 g per square metre (3 oz per square yard). The herbaceous border may have bonemeal at 110 g per square metre (4 oz per square yard), and this will also do a lot of good to bulb beds and to bulbs that are naturalized in grass. Lime can also be applied now. All parts of the vegetable garden can do with a dose every third or fourth year, unless the ground happens to be naturally impregnated with lime or chalk. Use about 225 g per square metre (8 oz per square yard) of hydrated (air-slaked) lime. On light sandy soils ground chalk is really better, but must be given more freely – about 900 g per square metre (2 lb per square yard). In all cases the fertilizers or lime need only be scattered over the ground. Rain will wash them in, and if the ground is to be dug or forked later on this will further incorporate them with the soil.

Gather Fallen Leaves. Be careful to sweep up all fallen leaves from time to time during the month. They are a particular source of danger in the rock garden, for if they lie thickly upon the plants they may kill them. All healthy leaves can be built up into a heap in some out-of-the-way corner and left to rot. Similar remarks also apply to any other soft refuse – old pea and potato haulm for example, and the tops of carrots, beetroots and other vegetable crops. But if there has been any disease in the plants from which leaves or refuse have come, do not keep them in this way but burn them without delay.

Turf and Repair Lawns. This is an excellent time to lay new lawns from turf or to repair worn patches in old ones. Cut out the turf from the worn places with an edging tool and lift with a sharp spade or special turf-lifting tool, making all sides straight. It is a well-nigh impossible task to fit a patch neatly into a curved hole. When laying a number of turves side by side, stagger them like the bricks in a wall so that the joints do not come together in both directions. This will give a better 'bind' until such time as the turves have rooted into their new soil (see March, General Work, for further particulars).

If your lawn has been used a lot for games during the summer, it will also benefit from a thorough aeration, either with a spiked roller or a fork thrust in at frequent intervals. Then mowing will not be necessary anything like so frequently from early October onwards. An occasional raking with a spring-toothed grass rake will remove moss, and you should also use a birch broom frequently to distribute worm casts. If these are allowed to lie on the grass, they will kill it in small patches.

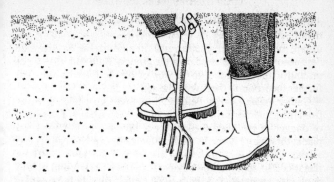

Aerating a Lawn. A garden fork or hollow-tined aerator can be used to advantage at this time of year to relieve compaction on lawns – particularly those which have been used for games

Prepare Rose Beds, Fruit Sites and Vacant Ground. You should get all new rose beds, also the site for new fruit trees and deciduous trees and shrubs of all kinds, prepared as early in October as possible. The ideal time for planting all these things is in November (see November, General Work), and it is all to the good if the ground can have a few weeks in which to settle between digging and planting. Dig the ground at least 60 cm (2 ft) deep, and, unless it is already very rich, work in plenty of well-rotted animal manure or decayed vegetable refuse in the second spit, but keep it away from the surface for it will do no good to freshly planted roots. Finish off with a surface dusting of basic slag at the rate of 170 g per square metre (6 oz per square yard). This is most useful, for it sweetens the soil and also adds phosphates to it. If you can also dig or trench any other vacant ground during October so much the better, for, though this work can be done at any time during the summer or winter when the ground is not very sticky, considerable advantage is gained by early soil cultivation. Leave the surface quite rough so that a large area is exposed to the weather.

Lift Begonias, Dahlias and Other Half-hardy Plants. Begonias, dahlias, cannas and *Salvia patens* that have been growing out of doors during the summer months must be removed to a frost-proof store just as soon as their foliage is blackened by frost. Precisely when this will happen no one can say. Very often it is early in October, but there have been seasons when these plants have continued unharmed until November. So keep a sharp look-out and be ready to dig the tubers up as soon as frost puts a stop to their display. Cut off the dead growth just above the tubers and store the latter in trays and boxes according to their size. It is a good plan to pack them round with dry moss peat as this is a protection and keeps them from drying out too much. Do not water at all, but place the boxes in any dry, fairly cool, but frost-proof place. A good outhouse or garden shed will do well – or a cupboard, so long as it is not alongside a fireplace.

Plant Spring Bedding. As soon as you are able to clear beds of their temporary summer occupants, such as geraniums, marguerites, scarlet salvias, begonias and dahlias (see September, Fourth Week, and also notes on begonias, dahlias, etc., above), and have cleared out all annuals that have finished flowering, lose no time in planting the spring occupants of the beds. These may include wallflowers, *Cheiranthus allionii*, forget-me-nots, double daisies, polyanthuses and coloured primroses, together with various bulbs, particularly tulips and hyacinths. May-flowering tulips can be planted together with forget-me-nots or wallflowers, but the early-flowering tulips and hyacinths are not sufficiently tall to stand above these and so, if you wish to have a groundwork beneath them, use double daisies, arabis or aubrietas. Wallflowers and cheiranthuses should be planted from 23 to 30 cm (9 to 12 in) apart, according to the size of the plants; forget-me-nots, double daisies and polyanthuses, 15 to 20 cm (6 to 8 in) apart. I have given distances for bulbs by themselves on pages 227 and 261, but if they are planted with a ground-work of other plants they may be spaced out more: 30 to 38 cm (12 to 15 in) apart will be a good average. The only preparation that the ground will need is a dressing of hop manure at the rate of a double handful per square metre (per square yard), well forked in, and a topdressing of bonemeal at 110 g per square metre (4 oz per square yard).

Plant Herbaceous Perennials. On light, well-drained soils, October is quite a good month for planting most herbaceous perennials, but it is better to do the work in spring (see March, General Work) on all heavy or wet soils. Details of planting are exactly the same in either case. Perennials and biennials raised from seed in June (see June, First Week) may also be planted now.

Insert Hardwood Cuttings. Many shrubby plants, both ornamental and useful, including gooseberries, currants and rambler roses, can be increased at this time of the year by means of what the gardener calls 'hardwood cuttings'. These differ from summer cuttings (see July, General Work) in being prepared from much riper and firmer wood. Select shoots of the current year's growth from 15 to 30 cm (6 to 12 in) in length according to the nature of the plant. They can either be cut immediately below a joint, exactly like the summer cuttings, or else pulled off the parent plant with a thin strip of older wood (gardeners call these heel cuttings, but many amateurs refer to them as slips). If you adopt the latter method, and it is a good one, trim off the thin piece of bark close to the knob of wood at the base of the cutting. In the case of gooseberries nick out all the lower growth buds to prevent sucker shoots from being formed below the soil. Insert the cuttings to a depth of 8 to 10 cm (3 to 4 in) in sandy soil, in a sheltered place outdoors. These hardwood cuttings root slowly and will not be ready for removal to their permanent quarters until the following autumn.

If desired all these cuttings can be treated with a root-forming

Inserting Hardwood Cuttings. This is the time of year to insert cuttings made from the firmer, riper wood of shrubs and fruit bushes. The cuttings are prepared 15 to 30 cm (6 to 12 in) long and inserted in trenches in a sheltered spot outdoors

hormone powder or solution as described on page 58.

General Greenhouse Management. Nights are now likely to be sufficiently cold to necessitate the use of artificial heat for the majority of favourite greenhouse plants. The ideal temperatures to be aimed at are about 13°C (55°F) by day, rising to 18 to 21°C (65 to 70°F) with direct sun heat and never falling below 7°C (45°F) even on the chilliest nights. Damping down and spraying with water are not likely to be needed, except for hothouse plants in temperatures over 18°C (65°F). Supply water to plants in growth in sufficient quantity to keep the soil moist right through, but avoid splashing unnecessarily and be careful to keep water off the leaves and crowns of primulas. Air should be admitted through top ventilators rather than those at the side, and it is unlikely that any ventilation will be needed at night for most of the plants. Chrysanthemums, however, must be kept as hardy as possible or they may contract mildew. If this disease does appear, dust the leaves with flowers of sulphur, space the plants out as much as possible to let in light and air, and use a little artificial heat to dry the atmosphere.

Rest Begonias, Gloxinias, Achimenes and Hippeastrums. Tuberous-rooted begonias, gloxinias, achimenes and hippeastrums will be going to rest and can be finally dried off during this month, after which the begonias may be shaken out of their soil and stored in dry coconut fibre or peat moss. Gloxinias are sometimes treated in the same way, but are really better in the soil in which they have been growing. Tap the dry balls of compost out of the pots, heap them together, and cover them with sacks. Of course, both these and the begonias must be in a dry, frost-proof place, but a high temperature is not desirable. Something around 10°C (50°F) is ideal.

Hippeastrums are allowed to get dry in their pots, after which they can stand in any out-of-the-way place – piled up on their sides if that is more convenient. Similar remarks apply to cannas which are grown in pots.

Vallotas are never dried off to quite this extent, but their water supply is greatly reduced during the winter. It is quite sufficient to keep the soil just slightly moist. Reduce the temperature to about 7°C (45°F) if possible. Similar remarks apply to clivias. This is a good time to purchase and pot new bulbs of both these plants. Use the ordinary potting compost and the smallest pots that will hold the bulbs comfortably.

Pot Hardy Plants for the Greenhouse. Several hardy perennial plants commonly grown out of doors also make good pot plants for the greenhouse. They include herbaceous astilbes in a great number of varieties, Solomon's seal and *Dicentra spectabilis*. Pot these now in the smallest pots that will accommodate the roots and then stand them in a frame or plunge them in ashes or sand in a sheltered place outdoors until you need them. They can be brought into the greenhouse in successive batches from

January onwards, and if kept in a temperature of about 16°C (60°F) will grow rapidly and soon come into flower.

Disbud Perpetual-flowering Carnations. Young plants of perpetual-flowering carnations rooted as cuttings in the winter should now be forming flower buds, and to get the best results these must be thinned out. Leave only the central terminal bud on each flower stem and remove all others at as early a stage of development as possible. See that the long, slender stems are properly staked. There is nothing better for this purpose than the circular galvanized wire supports made specially for the purpose.

Protect Cauliflowers. The white hearts (curds) of cauliflowers are liable to be damaged by frost, so look over the bed occasionally and bend some of the outer leaves over any hearts that are forming. This will give them all the protection they need.

Continue to Blanch Endive. Similar instructions to those given in my August and September General notes still apply.

Ripen Fruit Growth Under Glass. Your aim should still be to ripen any soft green growth that remains on peaches, nectarines and apricots under glass. Keep the air as dry as possible by free ventilation and, if possible, the occasional use of artificial heat if the air outside is very damp and stagnant; do not spray with water at all unless red spider is still about, and maintain a temperature of 7 to 10°C (45 to 50°F).

Similar remarks apply to vines. With late vines that are still carrying bunches it is a good plan to remove some of the foliage so that berries are exposed to the light and relieved from the danger of drips of water from the leaves.

FIRST WEEK

Protect Outdoor Chrysanthemums. If any of the early-flowering border chrysanthemums are still flowering well, it will be advisable to rig up some kind of temporary shelter over them. Quite an effective method is to drive a few stout stakes, about 1·5 m (5 ft) in length, into the bed at convenient points, join them across the top with a few horizontal bars nailed or tied in position, and then throw some sacking over them on frosty nights, making it secure at the corners with string. It does not take much to keep off the light frosts that are quite capable of ruining all the chrysanthemum flowers and buds.

Protect Outdoor Chrysanthemums. Early flowering chrysanthemums which are still bearing blooms are best given some protection from frost

Pot on Cinerarias and Stocks. Cinerarias sown during the third week in June are likely to be in need of a move into larger containers. Give them 13-cm (5-in) pots and the same compost as before, but rather coarser in texture. You can still keep them in a frame for a few weeks if you are very careful to close it up early in the afternoon and cover with sacks on cold nights, but they will soon have to go into the greenhouse.

Precisely similar remarks apply to stocks intended for winter flowering (see August, First Week).

Pot a Last Batch of Freesias. This is the time to make a last potting of freesias to flower in the spring. Details are as before (see August, First Week), except that now you will have to use the lights considerably more, especially at night, for there will be increasing danger of frost from now on.

Bring Early Arums, Freesias and Lachenalias into the Greenhouse. If you want to have some arums to cut for Christmas, you must bring a batch of plants into the greenhouse now. Arrange them in a light place not too far removed from the glass and maintain a night temperature of 13°C (55°F), rising to 18°C (65°F) by day. Water freely.

You may also bring in some more freesias (see August, First Week). Arrange them on the staging and maintain a temperature of 16°C (60°F) by day and 10°C (50°F) by night. Lachenalias in pots and boxes (see August, First Week) may also be brought into the greenhouse now. There is no need to hurry them at all unless you want early flowers. Any temperature above freezing point will serve for them. Both plants like plenty of light and air.

Plant Spring Cabbage. Plant as many as possible of the spring cabbages from the August sowing (see August, Second Week). Any seedlings that remain in the seed beds after the middle of the month are best left undisturbed until February (see February, Second Week).

Complete Earthing up of Late Celery and Leeks. Complete all earthing up of celery as soon as possible. I have already given full particulars in the notes for July, Second Week and August, Fourth Week. Sometimes rust appears on the leaves at this time of the year. Prompt removal of affected plants, followed by immediate spraying with Bordeaux mixture, will check it.

Leeks should also be earthed up for the last time. The longer the length of fully blanched stem obtained, the better.

SECOND WEEK

Sow Sweet Peas. The best exhibition sweet peas are obtained from sowings made at this time of the year. Some growers sow outdoors where the plants are to bloom, but a far better method in most districts is to sow in pots – about five seeds in an 8-cm (3-in) pot – and to germinate them in an unheated frame. Once the seedlings are up they can be ventilated very freely – indeed, the lights will only be needed in very frosty or windy weather. The great advantage of this method is that the seedlings are much more under control and can be protected from excessive cold or wet if necessary.

Prick off Cauliflowers. Cauliflowers sown last month (see September, First Week) must now be transferred to a frame. Prepare a bed of finely broken soil in this and dibble the seedlings straight into it 8 cm (3 in) apart each way. Ventilate freely and only use the lights when there is danger of frost.

Gather all Remaining Apples and Pears. At this time it is wise to complete the gathering of all apples and pears. It is not advisable to let them hang once the weather gets really wintry. Bring all into store. Apples keep very well if carefully packed in boxes deep enough to hold three or four layers. These should be stood in a cool but frostproof place preferably with a slightly moist atmosphere. A shed with an earthen floor is ideal, because there is usually a little moisture arising from the floor. Pears, however, keep more satisfactorily in a rather dry atmosphere; indeed, with them it is really a slow ripening process rather than keeping. Lay them out thinly in a room or cellar with an average temperature of about 10°C (50°F). Never pile them one on top of the other. Watch carefully for the ripening period as pears spoil quickly.

THIRD WEEK

Lift Gladioli and Montbretias. All gladiolus corms will be better out of the ground now. Dig them up carefully with a fork, cut the leaves off just above the corms and place the latter in shallow boxes, in which they can be stored in any dry, cool but frost-proof place. Remove any small corms and keep these for growing on a reserve bed. They may not flower next year, but they can be fattened up for the following season. Tiny cormels (spawn) can also be kept and grown on, but this is more of a specialist's job, and is only worth carrying out with new and expensive kinds. Pull off and throw away the old, shrivelled corms that adhere to the bottoms of the new ones.

Choice montbretias are also better out of the ground for the winter, but there is no need to move the old common kinds, for these are hardy enough to look after themselves. Some people store the choice varieties exactly like gladioli, but I prefer to replant them, close together, in a frame and keep them nearly but not quite dry until March, when they can be started into growth once more. The lights can be kept on most of the time, but it is a good plan to remove them occasionally for a few hours on mild days, just to give the frame an airing.

Stop Feeding Chrysanthemums. It is rarely wise to continue the feeding of exhibition chrysanthemums after this date. Experience proves that, if feeding is carried on too long, buds tend to decay in the centre. From now on supply them with plain water only.

Lift and Store Turnips. Lift a good supply of turnips of reasonable size and store them in a frost-proof place for the winter. They will keep quite well in a heap in any dry shed or outhouse, but are all the better for a light covering of dry sand or ashes. Cut off the tops first. If you leave some of the roots in the ground they will supply a useful crop of turnip tops in late winter and spring.

Cut back Asparagus and Globe Artichokes. The growth of asparagus will have turned yellow and the sooner it is removed the better. Do this with a pair of garden shears and cut off all the tops close to the soil. All rubbish should then be raked together and burned.

The yellowing leaves and stems of globe artichokes should also be cut down. Then fork between the plants lightly and cover the crowns with some sharp dry ashes or a thin layer of leaves as a protection against frost.

FOURTH WEEK

Plant Tulips and Hyacinths. Unlike many other hardy bulbs, tulips and hyacinths do benefit from a thorough drying off and ripening out of the ground, and there is nothing to be gained by planting before late October. This is also convenient, because they can then be planted in the beds just cleared of summer bedding plants and annuals. Give the soil a dusting of bonemeal at the rate of 110 g per square metre (4 oz per square yard), fork this in and then plant the bulbs: the hyacinths 15 cm (6 in) deep and 20 cm (8 in) apart, early tulips 8 cm (3 in) deep and 20 cm (8 in) apart, May-flowering tulips 10 cm (4 in) deep and 20 cm (8 in) apart.

Pot on Greenhouse Plants. Right at the end of October it is a good plan to finish off any greenhouse potting there may be to do before getting really busy with outdoor planting. It is probable that June-sown primulas and calceolarias will be ready for a move into 10- to 13-cm (4- to 5-in) pots, while the early cinerarias, sown at the beginning of May, will require their last shift into the 18- to 20-cm (7- to 8-in) pots in which they will flower. John Innes potting compost No. 1 will do admirably, but may be rather coarser in texture for the cinerarias than for the other plants. It is no longer really safe to have any of these plants in frames, and you should remove them to a light airy greenhouse in which you can maintain an average temperature of 13°C (55°F).

Roses and deciduous pot shrubs such as lilacs, deutzias, forsythias and cherries, that are to be flowered early in the greenhouse, may also be repotted now if they need it; but do this work with as little root disturbance as possible. Simply transfer the unbroken root ball to a larger receptacle and work some fresh compost such as John Innes potting compost No. 2 around it. After this treatment return the plants to a frame or to a plunge bed in a sheltered position outdoors.

Pot Annuals for the Greenhouse. Annuals sown in September for flowering in the greenhouse in spring should now be ready for potting singly in 8-cm (3-in) pots. Use John Innes potting compost No. 1 or a peat-based equivalent, and after potting arrange the plants in a frame or cool greenhouse. Water moderately and ventilate freely whenever the weather is mild, but be careful to exclude all frost. Pinch out the points of clarkias to make the plants branch.

Precisely similar remarks apply to schizanthus seedlings pricked off in September (see September, Third Week). Pinch out the growing tip of each plant, as advised for clarkias.

With certain annuals grown for greenhouse display, a better effect is obtained by placing three or four plants in a pot than by potting singly. Examples are leptosyne, limnanthes, mignonette, nemophila, phlox and saponaria.

Lift and Box Mint. A supply of young mint shoots is usually very welcome at Christmas and after, and can be obtained very easily by lifting a few roots now, laying them thinly on any fairly light compost spread in deep seed trays, covering them with a further inch of the same compost and bringing them into a warm greenhouse. Any temperature over 10°C (50°F) will secure growth – the higher it is the quicker the roots will grow. Keep just moist at first, but when shoots begin to appear, water more freely.

Make Lily of the Valley Beds. This is a good time at which to make new lily of the valley beds. Choose a cool, semi-shady place and good rich soil with plenty of humus. Plant the crowns separately, 8 cm (3 in) apart in rows 15 cm (6 in) apart. The simplest method is to nick out shallow trenches with a spade, lay the roots in these, and just cover the crowns.

FLOWERS, VEGETABLES AND FRUITS
IN SEASON DURING OCTOBER

Herbaceous Plants: *Aconitum carmichaelii, Anemone hupehensis, A. hybrida, A. japonica, A. vitifolia, Aster cordifolius* and vars., *A. ericoides* and vars., *A. grandiflorus, A. novae-angliae* vars., *A. novi-belgii* vars. *A. ptarmicoides, Boltonia asteroides,* gaillardias, geums, *Helianthus atrorubens, H. decapetalus* vars., *H. scaberrimus* vars., *Kniphofia uvaria, Liriope muscari, L. spicata, Lobelia fulgens* vars., *Physalis alkekengi* (fruits), *Podophyllum emodi* (fruits), *Scabiosa caucasia* and vars., *Schizostylis coccinea* and vars., *Sedum spectabile* and hybrids, *S. telephium, Solidago virgaurea* vars., *Stokesia cyanea, Verbena bonariensis, V. rigida.*

Hardy Bulbs, Corms and Tubers: *Colchicum autumnale, C. byzantinum, C. decaisnei, C. giganteum, C. speciosum* vars., *Crocus asturicus, C. cancellatus, C. kotschyanus, C. longiflorus, C. ochroleucus, C. pulchellus, C. salzmannii, C. sativus, C. speciosus, Cyclamen africanum, C. neapolitanum, Galanthus nivalis reginae-olgae, Merendera montana, Nerine bowdenii, Sternbergia clusiana, S. lutea.*

Rock Plants: *Ceratostigma plumbaginoides, C. willmottianum, Gaultheria procumbens* (fruits), *Gentiana farreri, G. macaulayi, G. sino-ornata, Lithospermum diffusum* vars., *Nertera depressa* (fruits), *Polygonum vaccinifolium, Verbena peruviana, Zauschneria californica.*

263

Evergreen Shrubs: *Abelia grandiflora*, *Buddleia asiatica*, *Calluna vulgaris* and vars., *Elaeagnus macrophylla*, *E. pungens*, *Erica carnea* vars., *E. ciliaris* and vars., *E. darleyensis*, *E. tetralix* and vars., *E. vagans* and vars., *E. watsonii*, *Fatsia japonica*, *Hebe* Autumn Glory, *H. speciosa* hybrids, *Mahonia fortunei*, *Olearia paniculata*.

Deciduous Shrubs: *Abelia schumannii*, *Buddleia auriculata*, *Ceratostigma willmottianum*, *Disanthus cercidifolius*, *Fuchsia magellanica* vars., *F. riccartonii*, hardy hybrid fuchsias, *Hamamelis virginiana*, *Hypericum augustinii*, *Hydrangea paniculata* (some forms), *Osmanthus heterophyllus*, *Perovskia atriplicifolia*, roses (garden hybrids), *Salix bockii*, *Teucrium fruticans*, *Vitex agnus-castus*.

Evergreen Trees: *Arbutus andrachnoides*, *A. unedo*.

Deciduous Trees: *Alnus nitida*.

Hardy Climbing Plants: *Clematis flammula*, *C. jackmanii* hybrids, *C. jouiniana*, *C. lanuginosa* hybrids, *C. lasiandra*, *Lonicera alseuosmoides*, *Pileostegia viburnoides*, roses (climbing hybrids).

Fruiting Trees, Shrubs and Climbers: Mainly as September, though birds may strip some varieties.

Greenhouse Plants: Abutilons, *Begonia coccinea*, bouvardias, *Browallia speciosa major*, *Brunfelsia calycina*, carnations (perpetual-flowering), *Cassia corymbosa*, celsias, chrysanthemums, *Cobaea scandens*, *Coronilla glauca*, *Eccremocarpus scaber*, *Erica gracilis*, *Eupatorium ligustrinum*, *Exacum affine*, gardenias, *Humea elegans*, ipomoeas, *Jacobinia pauciflora*, *Luculia gratissima*, manettias, marguerites, *Maurandya barclaiana*, nerines, *pelargoniums* (zonal and ivy leaved), *Saintpaulia ionantha*, streptocarpus, *Tibouchina semidecandra*, *Trachelium caeruleum*.

Vegetables in Store: Beetroot, carrots, onions, potatoes, shallots.

Vegetables in the Garden: Jerusalem artichokes, broccoli, cabbage, carrots, cauliflower, celeriac, celery, coleworts, endive, kohl rabi, leeks, lettuce, mushrooms, parsnips, peas, spinach, turnips.

Vegetables under Glass: French beans, cucumbers, mushrooms, mustard and cress, radish, tomatoes.

Fruits Outdoors: *Apples:* Allington Pippin (D), American Mother (D), Arthur Turner (C), Charles Ross (D), Cornish Aromatic (D), Cornish Gillyflower (D), Cox's Pomona (CD), Ecklinville Seedling (C), Egremont Russet (D), Ellison's Orange (D), Emperor Alexander (CD), Exquisite (D), Fortune (D), Gascoyne's Scarlet (D), Golden Noble (C), Golden Spire (C), Gravenstein (CD), Lord Derby (C), Herring's Pippin (CD), Howgate Wonder (C), James Grieve (D), King of the Pippins (D), Lord Derby (C), Lord Lambourne (D), McIntosh Red (CD), Peasgood's Nonsuch (CD), Rev. W. Wilks (C), Rival (CD), Royal Jubilee (C), Schoolmaster (C), St Edmund's Pippin (D), Stirling Castle (C), S. T. Wright (C), Wealthy (D), Worcester Pearmain (D). *Figs* (shelter). *Grapes:* Brandt, Golden Chasselas, Royal Muscadine. *Medlars. Pears:* Beurré Bedford (D), Beurré Diel (D), Beurré Hardy (D), Beurré Superfin (D), Bristol Cross (D), Conference (D), Durondeau (D), Emile d'Heyst (D), Fertility (CD), Fondante d'Automne (D), Hessle (D), Jersey Gratioli (D), Louise Bonne (D), Marguerite Marillat (D), Marie Louise (D), Packham's Triumph (D), Pitmaston Duchess (D), Thompson's (D). *Plums:* Golden Transparent Gage (D), Langley Bullace (C), Late Orange (CD), Marjorie's Seedling (CD), Merryweather Damson (C), President (C), Reine Claude de Bavay Gage (D), White Bullace (CD), *Quinces. Raspberries:* September.

Hardy Nuts: Cobnuts, filberts, walnuts.

Fruits under Glass: *Figs. Grapes:* Alicante, Black Hamburgh, Gros Maroc, Lady Hastings, Muscat Hamburgh.

November

GENERAL WORK

Tidy up Herbaceous Borders. By this time most herbaceous perennials will have finished flowering, and the borders may be tidied up for the winter. Cut off all dead or dying stems and leaves, but leave evergreen leaves such as those of kniphofias. Give the ground a dusting of bonemeal if you have not already done this (see October, General Work), and prick over the surface of the border with a fork, but be careful not to disturb roots or to dig up bulbs accidentally. It is really wise to mark the positions of the latter clearly when planting.

Dig all Available Ground. As I have already explained (see October, General Work), the earlier in the autumn ground can be turned over roughly the better. By this time a great deal of the vegetable garden should be free for digging or trenching. The latter is simply deep digging to a depth of two or even three

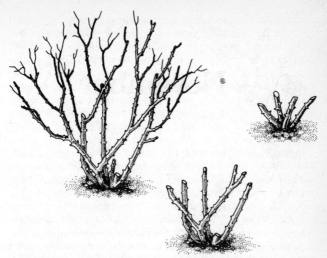

Pruning Large-flowered Roses. Large-flowered (hybrid tea) roses can be pruned now. On established bushes (left) the procedure is as follows: all dead and diseased wood is removed altogether as are any shoots which are weak or which cross through the centre of the bush. A well-spaced framework should be left and new growths cut back to a length of 15 or 23 cm, 6 or 9 in, (centre). Roses being grown to produce exhibition blooms can have their new shoots cut back to 5 cm (2 in), newly planted roses can be reduced to a height of 5 or 8 cm, 2 or 3 in, (right)

spades (almost 1 m, 3 ft). Very deep trenching can only be practised on rather good soil, but there are few gardens that would not benefit from periodic trenching two spades deep, especially if care is taken to keep the first and second spits (a spit is the depth of a spade) in the same relation one to the other as formerly, and not bring the lower and less fertile soil to the top.

Do as much of this work as you can now, and make no attempt to break up the surface as yet. The rougher it is left the greater will be the surface exposed to the beneficial action of wind and frost. Manure or garden compost can be worked in at the same time if required, or alternatively you can apply slow-acting fertilizers or lime, if not already given (see October, General Work). It is not usually wise to apply manure and lime at the same time, as the latter liberates and wastes ammonia from the manure, but they can be used at a few weeks' interval, one way or the other, without ill effect.

Prune Roses. The pruning of almost all bush and standard roses can begin as soon as all leaves have fallen and be continued as convenient until March. If the roses are only required for garden display cut back all strong young growths made last year to a length of about 15 to 23 cm (6 to 9 in). Weaker shoots should be cut back to a couple of inches, while really thin, spindly wood is best removed altogether. If the roses are required for exhibition, they should be pruned rather more severely, strong shoots being cut back to 5 or 8 cm (2 or 3 in), weaker ones removed. Of course, all dead or damaged growth must be removed first of all.

Newly planted roses should all be pruned in the same way as those required for exhibition. Climbing roses, as distinct from ramblers (any catalogue will put you right on this), are also pruned now. Usually it is sufficient to shorten strong growths by about one-third and weaker ones from a half to two-thirds, but occasionally, if a plant has not been making satisfactory progress, rather harder pruning should be carried out.

Cluster-flowered roses vary more in their growth and some may be treated like large-flowered kinds while others will thrive with a little thinning only and shortening of young growth by about one-third.

Prune Deciduous Hedges. All deciduous hedges, such as quick (hawthorn), blackthorn, myrobalan plum, sweet briar, beech and tamarisk, may be pruned during November, and this is a good time to do any hard cutting that may be necessary to keep growth within bounds. The base of a hawthorn or sweet briar hedge sometimes gets bare, but can be kept well furnished with growth by bending down a few long branches and pegging them into position. If the hawthorn branches refuse to bend, half-slit them near the base with a billhook.

Gather Rose Heps. If you have made any special rose crosses and wish to try your hand at seed raising, gather the heps now. Lay them thinly in seed trays, cover with a little silver sand, and place outdoors in an exposed position for the winter. The more the heps get frozen the better, because this will break them up and prepare the seeds for germination (see March, Second Week). The process is known as stratification, and can be applied to any berries or haws.

Plant Trees, Shrubs, Roses and Climbers Lifted from Open Ground. This is the great month of the year for planting all deciduous trees, shrubs and climbers, both ornamental and fruiting, when lifted from the open ground. The sooner the work

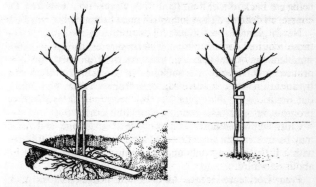

Tree Planting. Always plant trees at the correct depth and provide a strong stake and good tree-ties

269

can be completed once the leaves have fallen the better, but if you have much to do it will almost inevitably be necessary to spread the planting over several weeks, because it is not possible to work either when the ground is frozen or when it is very wet. However, if you cannot finish it all by the first or second week in December, I advise you to postpone the remainder until early February (see February, General Work) rather than to do it when the ground is very cold and wet.

In almost all cases the details of planting are the same. Protect the roots from sun and drying winds until you are quite ready to plant them. Prepare a hole wide enough to accommodate all the roots spread out in a perfectly natural manner and deep enough to permit the uppermost to be covered with a clear 8 to 10 cm (3 to 4 in) of soil. Cut off any broken or bruised root ends, hold the tree or bush in position in the middle of the hole (it is all to the good if you have someone to help you in this), and throw back the soil a little at a time, gently jerking the plant up and down meanwhile, so that the fine particles of soil work down between the roots. When the hole is almost full, tread the soil down really firmly. Then return the rest of the soil, but leave this loose and level on the surface. All standard trees and large bushes should be made secure to strong stakes driven firmly into the soil immediately before planting, while trained fruit trees must also be tied to their supports without delay. There is nothing that will delay rooting so much as constant disturbance by wind.

Deciduous climbing plants such as honeysuckles, clematises, *Polygonum baldschuanicum*, jasmines and ornamental vines are usually supplied in pots, and this is a great advantage, as it means that one is practically certain to get the roots intact and un-injured. If they are at all dry on arrival, soak them in a bucket of tepid water for a few minutes, then stand them out to drain for an hour or so. When you are ready to plant, carefully tap the plant out of its pot, loosen the roots in the pot ball a little and work some of the new soil around them. Be sure to make them really firm in their new surroundings and to tie the shoots up to a support at once.

Bush apples, pears, plums and cherries should be planted 4·5 m (15 ft) apart, but standards of these same trees must be allowed from 7·5 to 9 m (25 to 30 ft) each. Espalier-trained apples and pears and fan-trained plums, cherries, peaches, nectarines and apricots must be about 3·75 m (12 ft) apart. Cordon apples and pears are planted 60 cm (2 ft) apart, and, if there is more than one row, the rows must be at least 2 m (6 ft) apart and should run north and south for preference. Bush currants and gooseberries must be at least 1·25 m (4 ft) apart each way – it is really wise to allow blackcurrants 1·5 m (5 ft), as they grow very vigorously. Raspberry canes should be 38 cm (15 in) apart in rows 2 m (6 ft) apart, while loganberries, blackberries and other vigorous bramble fruits need nearly twice that amount of space.

For ornamental trees and shrubs, no hard and fast rules for distance can be given, as they differ greatly in growth, but as a general guide I would suggest that most of the smaller shrubs should be planted 1 m (3 ft) apart and the bigger kinds 1·5 to 2 m (5 to 6 ft) apart, and that no trees should be closer than 4·5 m (15 ft). Most climbing plants, including roses, should be at least 2 m (6 ft) apart. Bush roses must be from 45 to 60 cm (1½ to 2 ft) apart each way, while standards should be at least 1·25 m (4 ft) apart.

General Greenhouse Management. During November lack of light and a damp coldness in the atmosphere are two of the principal obstacles that one usually has to overcome in the greenhouse. If the glass is at all dirty, wash it thoroughly, both inside and out. Ventilate very cautiously. Open the top ventilators a little for a few hours during the day when the weather is mild and reasonably clear, but keep them shut if it is very cold or foggy. If you have ample artificial heat at your disposal the problem of ventilation is greatly simplified, for the air within the greenhouse can be warmed, dried and made to rise steadily through the ventilators even when the atmosphere outside is heavy and cold with moisture.

Keep a sharp look-out for decayed leaves or bracts and remove these at once. Dust the plants with flowers of sulphur to prevent the disease from spreading. Avoid splashing water about. Damping down and spraying with water will only be required by a few exceptional things, such as tropical foliage plants and winter cucumbers, and as these also require a much higher temperature than the general run of greenhouse plants, they must be grown by themselves. In the mixed greenhouse, where such plants as primulas, cinerarias, calceolarias and cyclamens are growing together with pelargoniums, marguerites and other stored bedding plants, a day temperature of 13°C (55°F) will serve now, but it should not be allowed to fall below 7°C (45°F) at night.

Attend to Plants in Frames. From now on until the early spring plants in frames will require very careful handling. Some, such as rooted viola, pansy and violet cuttings, sweet pea seedlings and also violet clumps, are quite hardy and only in need of protection from hard frost or heavy rains, which might disturb the small cuttings and seedlings or prevent the clumps from flowering. These need very free ventilation. Lights may be removed altogether during the day when the weather is mild, but should be placed on the frames again before the sun sets. Cauliflowers, antirrhinums from late summer cuttings and seeds, bedding calceolarias and penstemons need just a little more protection, but are almost hardy. They should always be fully exposed on warm, sunny days and ventilated freely whenever there is no frost or very cold wind. Others again, such as pelargoniums, marguerites and choice fuchsias, are liable to be damaged severely by even a few degrees of frost, and must be well protected with sacks at night. Ventilate the frames on favourable days, but be careful to get the lights back in time to trap heat against the night.

In all cases, take advantage of a warm day now and then to

have the lights off and examine all plants carefully. Remove and burn any decayed or yellowing leaves. Also stir the surface of the soil with a pointed stick to aerate it.

Water sufficiently to prevent the soil from getting dry, but reduce the amount during frosty weather, especially for the tender plants.

Pot Shrubs for the Greenhouse. November is a good month during which to purchase and pot many deciduous shrubs for early flowering in the greenhouse. Hydrangeas, lilacs, brooms, deutzias and roses are all suitable. After potting, stand the hydrangeas in a frame and protect from frost, but plunge the others to the pot rims in a sunny, sheltered place outdoors. Make no attempt to force these shrubs in a high temperature the first winter, but you can bring them into a cool greenhouse in December or January to get flowers a few weeks ahead of the normal season. You can also purchase Indian azaleas in bud now, either in pots or with their roots wrapped in hessian, and these latter have only to be potted up in a suitable compost to be ready for mild forcing.

Cut back Chrysanthemums. As chrysanthemums in the greenhouse finish flowering, cut them back to within 5 or 8 cm (2 or 3 in) of ground level. This will make more room in the house and will also encourage the roots to throw up sucker shoots which will make the ideal cuttings later on (see December, Third Week).

Successional Sowings. The only successional sowings to be made are mustard and cress and radishes, all in a warm greenhouse or frame with soil-warming cables. A temperature of 10 to 16°C (50 to 60°F) is necessary to ensure germination and quick growth. If it is 5°C (10°F) higher, so much the better for them.

Protect Cauliflowers from Frost. The curds of the early cauliflowers will be forming now and it is as well to protect them by bending some of the outer leaves over them.

Forcing Chicory. Roots of chicory can be lifted from the ground and brought into a warm, dark place for forcing. Place the roots quite close together in pots or boxes of moist peat and cut the shoots or 'chicons' when they are 15 cm (6 in) high

Blanch Endive in Frames. Most, if not all, endive plants will be in frames, and you can blanch them as previously described (see August, General Work), or, if you want a lot at once, by the even simpler process of covering a whole frame so thickly with sacks that all light is excluded.

Lift and Blanch Chicory. Dig up roots of chicory as required, pack them quite close together in pots or boxes filled with moist peat and bring them into a warm, dark place. New growth will be made quickly and can be cut when 15 cm (6 in) high for use as salad.

Prune Fruit Trees. November is the best month for doing any hard pruning of fruit trees and bushes that may be necessary. However, if you have followed out a system of summer pruning as I have advised (see June, Second Week, and July, First and Third Weeks), there will not be a great deal to do now. Shorten all the laterals (side shoots) of summer-pruned apples, pears, plums, sweet cherries, apricots, gooseberries and red and white currants to about two, or at most three, dormant growth buds each, unless, with fan-trained trees, there is room to tie in a few at full length. Leading shoots that are going to extend main branches or be the foundation of new branches should be shortened by about one-third of their length, while the central leaders of espalier-trained trees are shortened to about 38 cm (15 in) if another pair of horizontal arms is required, or cut off altogether if the tree already has sufficient arms. In all these instances I am referring to the shoots actually formed during the past summer. In estimating the length of any stem that is to be pruned there is no need to take into account any of the old wood formed in previous years. In the case of big trees that were not summer pruned, this hard winter pruning is not desirable. Instead content yourself with the removal or shortening of thin, weak, or badly placed stems and the removal of all dead or diseased wood. The purpose of this pruning should be to keep the trees reasonably open to light and air.

Peaches, nectarines and Morello cherries that have been disbudded during the spring and summer (see April, Fourth Week and July, First Week) are pruned differently. Each old fruiting lateral is cut right out and the new lateral retained at its base for the purpose of replacement is trained in its place. If there is no suitable basal shoot prune to the best young growth available.

Blackcurrants, though not summer pruned, are now treated in somewhat the same way as these peaches. That is to say, you must cut out as much as possible of the old growth that has just borne fruit to make way for strong young stems. Many of the best may come right from the base of the bush.

Ventilate and Prune Fruit Trees Under Glass. All the fruit trees under glass must now be pruned in exactly the same way as those outdoors. No artificial heat will be required unless some growth is still unripened (see October, General Work), and ventilation can be really free through both top and side ventilators, the house only being closed completely when the thermometer falls much below freezing point.

Ventilate Vines according to Growth. The latest-fruiting vines may still be carrying bunches of grapes and will need very careful ventilation and heating. The latter will be used to keep the air dry rather than to maintain a high temperature; 10°C (50°F) will be a sufficient average. Ventilation must be given with the same object. In a damp, stagnant, cold atmosphere berries will crack and mould will appear on them. All fallen leaves must be swept up and removed daily. Vines that have finished fruiting are much easier to manage. They can be ventilated freely and will need no artificial heat while they remain dormant.

FIRST WEEK

Place Glass over Alpines. Some choice alpines, and especially woolly-leaved plants such as many of the androsaces, suffer badly during the winter from excessive wet, which lodges in their leaves and makes them rot. Plants such as these can be completely protected by covering them now with pieces of glass supported well above the plants on notched sticks or bent pieces of wire. Make no attempt to close in the sides of the shelter. Free circulation of air is essential.

Lift Early-flowering Chrysanthemums. Border chrysanthemums are quite hardy in many gardens, but sometimes they rot off during the winter, so to be on the safe side it is advisable to lift a few plants of each variety now and place them close together in a frame, or in boxes which can be stood in a cool greenhouse. Simply pack a little light soil between them; that left over from seed trays will do well. Cut off the stems 5 to 8 cm (2 to 3 in) above soil level. No artificial heat will be necessary, and only enough water to keep the soil from drying out. Later on these 'stools', as they are called, will furnish plenty of good cuttings (see February, General Work).

Complete the Planting of Tulips and Hyacinths. There is still time to plant tulips and hyacinths (see October, Fourth Week), but the sooner the work is completed the better.

Bring Early Bulbs into the Greenhouse. Examine the bulbs that were boxed or potted in September and placed in a plunge bed (see September, Fourth Week). A few of the most forward may now be brought into a moderately heated greenhouse, but do not attempt to force them too fast at first. An average day temperature of 16°C (60°F), falling to 10°C (50°F) at night, will be ample to begin with, but may rise to 21°C (70°F) once the flower buds are well formed. Another important point is to make quite certain that the bulbs have made plenty of roots before bringing them into the greenhouse at all. You can tap one or two out of the pots carefully without disturbing them, or alternatively you can learn a lot by examining the drainage holes and slits in the bottoms of the pots and boxes. When the soil begins to get full of roots they will start to grow through these drainage openings.

From this time onwards it is advisable to keep an eye on the plunge bed and either to remove forward boxes and pots of bulbs to the greenhouse, or, if you are not ready for them, to place them in an unheated frame, preferably with a north aspect. Here growth can be retarded for weeks without harm to the bulbs.

Start to Force Indian Azaleas and other Shrubs. If you want some really early flowers on Indian azaleas, bring the plants into a slightly warmer temperature now – an average of 18 to 21°C (65 to 70°F) will do admirably – and spray them lightly every morning with slightly tepid water. Various other early-flowering shrubs, such as forsythias, ornamental cherries, *Viburnum carlesii*, *Jasminum primulinum*, and even lilac can also be brought into the greenhouse now, but do not subject them to temperatures above 16°C (60°F) unless they are really well established in pots.

Sow Broad Beans. There can be no doubt that the very best way to grow early broad beans is to sow seeds in boxes in February and germinate them in a warm greenhouse (see February, First Week). But if you have no glasshouse it is worth making an outdoor sowing now in a sheltered place. Choose a longpod variety and sow the seeds 10 cm (4 in) apart in drills 5 cm (2 in) deep and 45 cm (18 in) apart for dwarf, or 75 cm (30 in) apart for tall kinds.

SECOND WEEK

Sow Hardy Culinary Peas. Some people are very successful with culinary peas sown now outdoors where they are to mature. A rather sheltered position and well-drained soil are essentials to success, and you must also use an absolutely hardy variety, such as Pilot Improved or Meteor. Other details of sowing are the same as in the spring (see March, Second Week).

Lift Seakale for Forcing. The top growth of seakale should have died down by this time, and the roots will be ready for lifting in preparation for forcing. Dig them up carefully, cut off the side thongs and lay these in bundles in a sheltered position outdoors in readiness for planting out in March (see March, First Week). Then stand the stout central roots, each provided with a crown from which growth will come, against a shady wall or fence and heap ashes or sand around them until only the crowns are visible. They will keep safely like this all the winter, and you can pot up and force a few at a time as you require them. Pot three or four in a 15- or 18-cm (6- or 7-in) pot, using any old potting or seed compost, bring them into a warm greenhouse, and cover with another empty pot, blocking up the drainage hole in the bottom of this with a piece of slate or turf. The crowns must be in absolute darkness. Water moderately. In a temperature of about 16°C (60°F) growth will be rapid. When the blanched shoots are about 23 cm (9 in) long you can cut them. The forced roots are useless and should be thrown away.

Start to Force Rhubarb. Rhubarb may also be forced from now onwards throughout the winter. Roots started at once in a temperature of about 21°C (70°F) will give good sticks at Christmas. The method of forcing is different from that of sea-kale. Strong roots are lifted and allowed to lie on the ground unprotected for a day or so. If the weather is frosty so much the better; growth will be all the quicker for this exposure. Take the roots into a warm greenhouse, stand them quite close together in deep boxes or on the floor under the stages, pack soil between them and keep them absolutely dark by fixing up a screen of sacking, linoleum, or boards. Water moderately and maintain a temperature of 13 to 24°C (55 to 75°F). A few more roots should be brought in every fortnight or so.

THIRD WEEK

Lift and Store Jerusalem Artichokes, Parsnips, Horseradish and Salsify. Jerusalem artichokes will have completed their growth, so cut off all the tops and lift the tubers with a fork. Store the larger tubers in exactly the same way as potatoes (see September, Third Week), and put the smaller tubers on one side in a dry shed or room for planting later on.

Parsnips and horseradish are perfectly hardy, and will not suffer any harm if left in the ground all the winter; indeed, the parsnips are actually improved in flavour by frost, but as it is well-nigh impossible to lift these long roots when the ground is frozen hard, it is as well to dig up a few now and store them in a shed or cellar as a standby. Simply cut off the tops, pile up the roots, and cover them with a little dry sand, ashes or soil.

At least a portion of the crop of salsify should also be lifted and stored in exactly the same way as the parsnips and horse-radish. If you wish, however, you can leave a portion of the bed undisturbed, so that the roots may produce flowering stems in spring. These young shoots are boiled and eaten like asparagus.

FOURTH WEEK

Cut and Store Grapes. There is not much point in trying to keep the bunches of late grapes hanging on the vines any longer, especially if you have a cool, dark and dry room in which you can store them. Cut each bunch with 23 cm (9 in) or more of the ripened lateral from which it is hanging, insert the lower end of this into a bottle nearly filled with clean, soft water and containing a few pieces of charcoal, and then stand the bottle in a rack or on a shelf, tilting it sufficiently to prevent the berries from coming into contact with it, or, for that matter, anything else.

Prune Early and Maincrop Vines. By this time the leaves should have fallen from early and maincrop vines, and the sooner most of them are pruned the better. Outdoor vines may also be pruned. For both types pruned at this time the method is the same. Cut back every lateral (side) growth to within one, or at most two, dormant growth buds of the main rod or spur. Then rub or pull all loose shreds of bark from the main rods and paint the latter thoroughly with Gishurst compound. This is a proprietary preparation containing soap and sulphur which is used to kill mealy bug. Be particularly careful to work this in to all rough, gnarled places round the spur, where insects may be hiding. After pruning and cleaning, cut the ties holding the main rod and lower it on long pieces of cord so that it hangs more or less parallel with the floor. This will discourage sap from rushing up to the top when the vine is restarted and will ensure an even 'break' all over.

FLOWERS, VEGETABLES AND FRUITS IN SEASON DURING NOVEMBER

Herbaceous Plants: *Aster grandiflorus, Helianthus atrorubens, Helleborus niger altifolius, Hosta tardiflora, Iris unguicularis,*

Liriope muscari, *L. spicata*, physalis (fruits), *Podophyllum emodi* (fruits).

Hardy Bulbs, Corms and Tubers: *Colchicum decaisnei*, *Crocus cancellatus* and vars., *C. hyemalis* and vars., *C. longiflorus*, *C. medius*, *C. nudiflorus*, *Cyclamen africanum*, *C. neapolitanum*, *Galanthus nivalis*, *Schizostylis coccinea* and vars., *Sternbergia clusiana*.

Rock Plants: *Gentiana farreri*, *G. macaulayi*, *G. sino-ornata*.

Evergreen Shrubs: *Buddleia asiatica*, *Elaeagnus macrophylla*, *E. pungens*, *Erica carnea* vars., *E. darleyensis*, *Fatsia japonica*, *Hebe* Autumn Glory, *H. speciosa* vars., *Mahonia fortunei*, *Olearia paniculata*, *Viburnum tinus*.

Deciduous Shrubs: *Buddleia auriculata*, *Crataegus monogyna praecox*, *Hamamelis virginiana*, *Viburnum fragrans*.

Evergreen Trees: *Arbutus andrachnoides*, *A. unedo*.

Deciduous Trees: *Prunus subhirtella autumnalis*.

Hardy Climbing Plants: *Jasminum nudiflorum*, *Lardizabala biternata* (shelter).

Fruiting Trees, Shrubs and Climbers: Mainly as October, but most malus fruits will have fallen.

Greenhouse Plants: Abutilons, begonias (Gloire de Lorraine and Optima types), *Begonia venusta*, bouvardias, *Browallia speciosa major*, carnations (perpetual flowering), chrysanthemums, cinerarias, *Crossandra guineensis*, cyclamen, *Erica canaliculata*, *E. gracilis*, *E. hyemalis*, *Eriostemon buxifolia*, *Exacum affine*, freesias, *Jacobinia pauciflora*, *Kalanchoe blossfeldiana*, *Libonia floribunda*, manettias, *Oxalis versicolor*, pelargoniums (zonal), *Primula obconica*, *P. sinensis*, *Reinwardtia trigyna*, *Saintpaulia ionantha*, *Sparmannia africana*, *Tibouchina semidecandra*, *Trachelium caeruleum*.

Vegetables in Store: Beetroot, carrots, onions, parsnips, potatoes, shallots, turnips.

Vegetables in the Garden: Jerusalem artichoke, Brussels sprouts, cabbage, cauliflower, celeriac, celery, coleworts (sown

June), endive, kohl rabi, leeks, lettuce (shelter), parsnips, savoys, spinach.

Vegetables under Glass: French beans, cucumbers, endive, lettuce, mushrooms, mustard and cress, radish.

Fruits in Store: *Apples:* Allington Pippin (D), American Mother (D), Beauty of Kent (C), Bismarck (C), Blenheim Orange (D), Bramley's Seedling (C), Charles Ross (D), Cornish Gillyflower (D), Cox's Orange Pippin (D), Cox's Pomona (CD), Crimson Bramley (C), Crimson Cox (D), Cutler Grieve (D), Delicious (D), Egremont Russet (D), Emperor Alexander (CD), Gascoyne's Scarlet (D), Golden Noble (C), Gravenstein (CD), Herring's Pippin (CD), Howgate Warden (C), Joy Bells (D), King of the Pippins (D), Lane's Prince Albert (C), Laxton's Superb (D), Lord Derby (C), Lord Lambourne (D), Margil (D), McIntosh Red (CD), Norfolk Royal (D), Peasgood's Nonsuch (CD), Rev. W. Wilks (C), Ribston Pippin (D), Rival (CD), Roundway Magnum Bonum (D), Royal Jubilee (C), Salcote Pippin (D), Sunset (D), Warner's King (C), Wealthy (D), Wellington (C). *Medlars. Pears:* Belissime d'Hiver (C), Beurré Clairgeau (D), Beurré Diel (D), Beurré Six (D), Conference (D), Doyenné du Comice (D), Durondeau (D), Marie Louise (D), Packham's Triumph (D), Pitmaston Duchess (D), Seckle (D), Thompson's (D), Winter Nelis (D). *Quinces.*

Fruits under Glass: *Grapes:* Alicante, Appley Towers, Canon Hall Muscat, Gros Colmar, Gros Guillaume, Lady Downe's, Mrs Pince, Muscat of Alexandria, Prince of Wales.

Nuts in Store: Cobnuts, filberts, walnuts.

December

GENERAL WORK

Continue to Dig Vacant Ground. Digging and trenching can be continued throughout the month as opportunity offers, but it is not wise to do this work when there is much snow on the grown, nor when it is frozen or very wet.

Sterilize Infected Soil. This is a task which can be done at any time of the year, but as it is essential that the soil should have no plants growing in it and, where it has been sterilized by chemical means, that it should remain unused for a month or so after treatment, December is often the most convenient month for the work. The purpose of sterilization is to rid the soil of all harmful organisms, including insect pests and the spores of fungi, which cause diseases. There is no point in treating soil that is in good order, but if diseases or pests have been rampant, sterilization may be well repaid.

Sterilizing Soil. Chemical sterilization of soil is a relatively easy operation. The soil is spread out on a hard surface, such as concrete, the sterilant applied with a watering can and the pile is then covered with sacks or tarpaulin and left for the required time

Chemical sterilization is commonly carried out with either formaldehyde or cresylic acid. Formalin, which has a form-aldehyde content of 38–40%, is diluted with 49 times its own bulk of water and the soil is then soaked thoroughly with it. Soil can be treated *in situ*, but a more effective method is to spread it out on a hard floor, soak it, and then immediately draw it into a heap and cover with sacks to trap the fumes. You must not use the soil until it has lost all smell of the chemical.

Precisely similar methods are adopted with cresylic acid. This you can purchase in various strengths, but that known as 'pale straw-coloured carbolic acid' is most suitable. Dilute it with 39 times its own bulk of water.

Another method of sterilizing soil is by heat. Steam can be used for supplying this and is the best medium, since it will neither char the soil nor make it too wet. The amount of soil treated at any one time must be sufficiently small to allow the temperature to reach 100°C (212°F) in about 30 to 40 minutes.

This temperature is maintained for 10 minutes, when the soil is removed immediately and allowed to cool down rapidly by being spread out thinly. The soil, unlike that chemically treated, can be used for any purpose as soon as it has cooled, but as the treatment results in a reduction of fertility for a while, it is advisable to counteract this by adding suitable fertilizers as in the John Innes composts.

Small and large proprietary steam sterilizers can be obtained but it is also possible to sterilize soil in a saucepan using boiling water. The soil should be fairly dry to start with, and for 3·4-l (6-pt) saucepan 285 ml ($\frac{1}{2}$ pt) of water is sufficient. As soon as it boils, fill the saucepan with soil to within 1 cm ($\frac{1}{2}$ in) of the top and boil for 7 minutes with the lid on. Leave it to stand for 7 minutes more, and then spread it out to cool.

You should note that soil fumigation is a rather different matter from sterilization as it is directed solely at insect pests, for example, wireworms, leatherjackets and millepedes, and has no effect upon diseases. Flaked naphthalene is commonly used for the purpose, and is dug into any vacant ground at the rate of 110 g per square metre (4 oz per square yard). There are also a number of proprietary soil fumigants, many of them embodying naphthalene in some form or other, which must be used strictly in accordance with manufacturer's instructions.

Start to Propagate Carnations. Perpetual-flowering carnation cuttings may be taken from now until the end of March. They are best prepared from side shoots produced a little way up the flowering stems. Avoid those right at the base and right at the top. Shoots about 8 cm (3 in) in length are ideal and can be obtained by pulling gently away and down from the plant. The heel or small strip of skin that comes away from the old stem should be trimmed off close to the base of the cutting, which is then ready for insertion. Alternative methods are to cut the shoot just below a joint and not pull it away at the heel, or to pull it upwards so that it slips out of the joint. This last method is known as taking a piping. These cuttings are ready for insertion without further fuss. They should be inserted firmly 2·5 cm (1 in) deep in either pure silver sand or a mixture of good loam and silver sand in about equal parts. They root more quickly and reliably in the pure sand, but need considerably more attention as to watering, which is a nuisance if one has to be away from home most of the day. Carnation cuttings are rooted in a greenhouse maintained at a temperature of about 10°C (50°F), but it is an advantage to keep them close, preferably in a propagating box and to warm the soil to about 16°C (60°F).

Continue to Cut back Chrysanthemums. Throughout the month continue to cut back the later chrysanthemums as soon as they finish flowering (see November, General Work).

Prune Roses. Continue to prune bush and standard roses (see November, General Work).

Stop Sweet Peas. Autumn-sown sweet peas (see September, Second Week) should be pinched at some time during the winter. It does not matter when it is done, so long as it is before the plants have made shoots more than 8 cm (3 in) in length. Stopping here means that the top of each seedling is pinched out.

Bring More Bulbs into the Greenhouse. Bring in further batches of bulbs to the greenhouse from the plunge bed and frame to ensure a succession of flowers later on (see November, First Week).

Continue to Force Seakale and Rhubarb. At intervals of about a fortnight bring in further roots of rhubarb and seakale and force them in the greenhouse (see November, Second Week).

Continue to Lift and Blanch Chicory. Further roots should be lifted and treated as already described (see November, General Work).

Continue to Protect Cauliflower. From time to time during the month you must continue to bend down leaves over the curds of cauliflower as they form (see November, General Work).

Successional Sowings. These are exactly the same as last month

– mustard and cress and radishes – all in a warm greenhouse or a frame equipped with soil-warming cables.

Continue to Prune Fruit Trees. Throughout the month you can proceed with the pruning of fruit trees and bushes of all kinds (see November, General Work). It is a mistaken notion that fruit trees must not be pruned when the weather is frosty.

Ventilate Greenhouses Containing Fruit Trees and Vines. There is really nothing of importance to add to my November notes on the management of these houses. Free ventilation should be the rule right up to the time at which vines and fruit trees are restarted into growth. If the weather is very cold, close up the houses in sufficient time in the afternoon to keep off the worst frost, but a few degrees of frost will do no harm at all.

FIRST WEEK

Protect Tender Plants, Christmas Roses and Celery. Very little damage is done by early autumn frosts to such slightly tender plants and shrubs as gunneras, eremuruses, escallonias, evergreen ceanothuses and crinodendrons, but as the winter sets in with greater rigour it is advisable to provide some protection for these if they happen to be growing in rather exposed places. Wall shrubs and climbers which are in any way tender can be protected efficiently and without difficulty by hanging sacking in front of them or fixing wattle hurdles close up to them and then stuffing any intervening space with straw or bracken. The plant must not be entirely shut off from air. Whatever form of protection you use, always leave the top open so that foul air and moisture may escape.

For slightly tender herbaceous plants, the crowns of which may be injured by frost, the best method of protection is to place a piece of fine-mesh galvanized wire-netting over each, heap dry leaves, straw, or bracken on this, and cover with another piece of netting pegged down at the corners.

Christmas roses (hellebores) are not in the least tender, but they will be forming their flower stems now and the blooms will benefit from a little protection to keep off heavy rain and mud splashes. Cover them with spare frame lights supported on bricks at the four corners, or with cloches.

Late celery may be injured by very hard frosts or heavy rain, so it is good policy to cover the ridges at this time with a little dry straw or bracken, held in position with some wire-netting pegged down to the soil, and also to dig a shallow trench on each side of the ridge to run off surplus surface water.

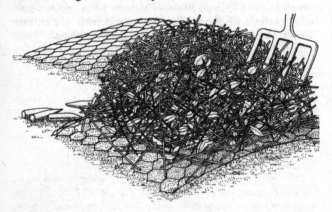

Protecting Tender Herbaceous Plants. Any herbaceous plants which are susceptible to frost damage can be protected by covering them with a layer of straw sandwiched between two layers of wire netting

SECOND WEEK

Prune Clematis jackmanii. Clematises of the *Jackmanii* and nearly allied *Viticella* classes may be pruned. It is not absolutely essential to do the work at once, so long as it is completed before the end of February, but in the interests of tidiness the sooner it is completed the better. There are two methods of pruning. One is to cut all growth back to within about 30 cm (1 ft) of the ground every year, so keeping the plants fairly small, and the other to allow a framework of main vines to form and then prune each side growth back to one joint.

THIRD WEEK

Start to Take Chrysanthemum Cuttings. Some growers start taking cuttings of chrysanthemums considerably earlier than this, but I do not think that the amateur gains anything by being in too much of a hurry. You should start on those varieties that

Taking Chrysanthemum Cuttings. Select short, sturdy cuttings, sever them just below ground level and insert them in pots, boxes or a frame of well-drained soil

are to be grown for second crown buds, and particularly on November incurves and singles.

The best shoots to select are those that come up through the soil direct from the roots. These should be severed just below soil level when they are a couple of inches or so in length. They are prepared by cutting off the lower leaves with a very sharp knife and trimming off the base cleanly just below a joint; then insert them about 1 cm ($\frac{1}{2}$ in) deep in sandy soil. It does not matter much whether they are in boxes, pots, or directly in a bed made up on the staging in the greenhouse so long as there is ample provision for drainage. The cuttings cannot be rooted out of doors at this time of the year. It is possible to manage them in a well-constructed frame, but it is much easier in a greenhouse with just a little artificial heat to keep out frost. Some growers keep the cuttings in a frame within the greenhouse, while others prefer to have them open on the staging. Both schemes work well, but using the latter method rather more watering is necessary, and it is advisable to spray every morning with slightly tepid water.

FOURTH WEEK

Remove Christmas Plants to Greenhouse. The sooner pot plants used in the house for decorations during the Christmas festivities can be returned to the greenhouse the better. They do not like the over-dry atmosphere and ever-changing temperature of living rooms at all, and quickly deteriorate as a result. Palms, aspidistras and dracaenas will benefit from a thorough sponging down with tepid water into which a few drops of milk have been stirred. After this they should be kept in a rather warm atmosphere for a few days and sprayed daily with clear water. Flowering plants such as cyclamens, primulas, cinerarias and heaths should be given as light a place as possible on the staging in a temperature of 13 to 16°C (55 to 60°F), and be watered very carefully, all excesses one way or the other being avoided. Remove any withered or mouldy leaves. Berried solanums should also be given plenty of light and a rather higher temperature.

FLOWERS, VEGETABLES AND FRUITS IN SEASON DURING DECEMBER

Herbaceous Plants: *Helleborus niger* and vars., *Iris unguicularis*, *Schizostylis coccinea* and vars.

Hardy Bulbs, Corms and Tubers: *Crocus imperati*, *C. laevigatus*, *Cyclamen coum*, *Galanthus cilicicus*, *G. nivalis*, *Merendera persica*, *Narcissus serotinus*, *Sternbergia lutea angustifolia*.

Evergreen Shrubs: *Buddleia asiatica* (shelter), *Erica carnea* vars., *E. darleyensis*, *Fatsia japonica*, *Mahonia japonica*, *Olearia forsteri* (shelter), *Rhododendron* Lee's Scarlet, *Viburnum tinus*.

Deciduous Shrubs: *Buddleia auriculata*, *Chimonanthus praecox*, *Daphne mezereum autumnalis*, *Hamamelis intermedia*, *H. japonica*, *H. mollis*, *Lonicera fragrantissima*, *L. standishii*, *Rhododendron mucronulatum*, *Viburnum fragrans*.

Evergreen Trees: *Arbutus unedo*.

Deciduous Trees: *Crataegus monogyna praecox*, *Prunus subhirtella autumnalis*.

Hardy Climbing Plants: *Jasminum nudiflorum*, *Lardizabala biternata*.

Fruiting Trees, Shrubs and Climbers: *Aucuba japonica*, *Berberis hookeri*, *Celastrus orbiculatus*, *C. scandens*, *Cotoneaster conspicuus*, *C. frigidus*, *C. horizontalis*, *C. microphyllus*, *C. rotundifolius*, *Crataegus crus-galli*, *C. lavallei*, *Hippophae rhamnoides*, *Ilex aquifolium* (holly), *Pyracantha angustifolia*, *P. atalantioides*, *P. coccinea*, *P. rogersiana*, *Rosa fargesii*, *R. moyesi*, *Sorbus* Joseph Rock, *Taxus baccata*. Some of the other varieties mentioned in October may continue, but those listed above are particularly reliable. Much depends upon birds.

Greenhouse Plants: Abutilons, azaleas, begonias (Gloire de Lorraine and Optima types), bouvardias, *Browallia speciosa major*, camellias, carnations (perpetual-flowering), chrysanthemums, cinerarias, *Correa speciosa*, cyclamen, *Erica gracilis* and vars., *E. hyemalis*, *Exacum affine*, freesias, hippeastrums, *Jacobinia pauciflora*, *Kalanchoe blossfeldiana*, *Primula kewensis*, *P. malacoides*, *P. obconica*, *P. sinensis* and vars., *Reinwardtia trigyna*, *Saintpaulia ionantha*, *Schlumbergera buckleyi*.

Vegetables in Store: As November.

Vegetables in the Garden: Jerusalem artichoke, Brussels sprouts, cauliflower, celeriac, celery, coleworts (sown July), endive, kale, leeks, lettuce (shelter), parsnips, savoys.

Vegetables under Glass: Chicory, endive, lettuce, mushrooms, mustard and cress, radish, rhubarb, seakale.

Fruits in Store: *Apples:* Adams' Pearmain (D), Allington Pippin (D), Annie Elizabeth (C), Barnack Beauty (CD), Belle de Boskoop (CD), Bismarck (C), Blenheim Orange (D), Bramley's Seedling (C), Claygate Pearmain (D), Cornish Aromatic (D), Cornish Gillyflower (D), Court Pendu Plat (D), Cox's Orange Pippin (D), Crawley Beauty (C), Crimson Bramley (C), Crimson Cox (D), Cutler Grieve (D), Delicious (D), Egremont Russet (D), Gascoyne's Scarlet (D), Golden Delicious (D), Golden Noble (C), Gravenstein (CD), Howgate Wonder (C), Joy Bells (D), King of Tompkin's County (D), King's Acre Pippin (D), Lane's Prince Albert (C), Laxton's Pearmain (D), Lord Derby (C), Lord Lambourne (D), Margil (D), Monarch (C), Newton Wonder (C), Norfolk Royal (D), Orleans Reinette (D), Ribston Pippin (D), Rival (CD), Rosemary Russet (D), Roundway Magnum Bonum (D), Saltcote Pippin (D), Sunset (D), Superb (D), Warner's King (C), Wellington (C), William Crump (D), Wyken Pippin (D). *Pears:* Bellissime d'Hiver (C), Beurré Clairgeau (D), Beurré Diel (D), Beurré Six (D), Blickling (D), Catillac (C), Glou Morceau (D), Joséphine de Malines (D), Santa Claus (D), Vicar of Winkfield (C), Winter Nelis (D).

Index

Note: d = line drawing

Abutilon:
  cuttings 57–8
  planting 156
  potting 88
Acacia: plunging 157
Achimenes:
  resting 208, 230, 255
  starting 37, 100, 139
Agapanthus: housing 241
Ageratum: sowing 40
alpines:
  cuttings 178
  in frames 17–18
  planting 84, 131–2
  protecting 276
  sowing 67–8
Alyssum:
  annual: sowing 71, 233
  saxatile: sowing 156
Amaranthus: sowing 41
American blight 161, 210
Anagallis: sowing 42
Anchusa:
  root cuttings 18
  sowing 62
Androsace: protecting 276
Anemone:
  in frame 17–18
  lifting 161–2, 184
  planting 39, 233–4
  sowing 156–7
annuals:
  dead-heading 177
  for greenhouse: potting
    36, 74, 262
  sowing 62, 233
  half-hardy: hardening off
    86, 107, 119
  planting 138
  sowing 41–2, 71, 109, 128
  hardy: sowing 70–1, 100,
    109, 128, 233

hardy annuals: *cont.*
  thinning 104–5, 104d
Antirrhinum:
  cuttings 229
  in frames 17–18, 272
  hardening off 56, 87
  planting 108
  sowing 24, 42, 233
aphicides 116
aphids (greenfly and blackfly)
    87, 116, 148, 179
apple blossom weevil 67
Apples:
  bark ringing 130
  budding 196–7
  diseases 103, 131, 140
  grafting 77–9, 78d
  greasebands 109–10
  pests 67, 140–1, 166
  picking fruit 193–4, 193d,
    210, 232–3, 259
  planting 271
  pruning 19, 274–5
    summer 193, 210
  reworking 20
  spraying 67, 103, 130–1,
    140, 166, 191
  thinning fruit 162–3, 186–7
Apricots:
  disbudding 34–5, 60, 110,
    127
  pollinating 34, 60
  pruning 19, 275
  ripening growth 256
  starting 45
  spraying 183
  thinning 127, 154
aquatics: planting 117–18,
    118d
Aquilegia: sowing 67–8, 156
Arabis:
  cutting back 165
  planting 252
  transplanting 84
Artichoke:
  Globe: cutting 180, 181d
    cutting back 261
    planting 97

Globe Artichoke: *cont.*
  sowing 97
  thinning 124
  Jerusalem: lifting 279
    planting 38–9, 38d
Arum Lily:
  housing 241, 258
  repotting 212
  resting 89, 120–1, 132
  starting 212
Asparagus:
  cutting 129, 130d, 166
  cutting back 261
  mulching 25
  planting 97–8, 98d
  sowing 97
  thinning 124
Asparagus fern: 62–4
Asparagus sprengeri 139
  repotting 62–4
Aspidistra:
  repotting 62–4
  sponging 290
Aster: sowing 71
Astilbe:
  forcing 36
  as pot plant 255
  starting 21
Aubergines:
  hardening off 134
  planting 159
  potting 103, 134
  sowing 70, 103
Aubrieta:
  cutting back 165
  planting 252
  sowing 156
  transplanting 84
Aucuba:
  cuttings 228
  layering 85–6
Auricula:
  dividing 161
  pests 161
  repotting 161
Azalea:
  Indian: forcing 21, 36, 273,
    277

293

303